HUMAN COMMUNICATION AS NARRATION

STUDIES IN RHETORIC/COMMUNICATION
Carroll C. Arnold, *Series Editor*

Richard B. Gregg
*Symbolic Inducement and Knowing: A Study in the
Foundations of Rhetoric*

Richard A. Cherwitz and James W. Hikins
*Communication and Knowledge: An Investigation in
Rhetorical Epistemology*

Herbert W. Simons and Aram A. Aghazarian, Editors
Form, Genre, and the Study of Political Discourse

Walter R. Fisher
*Human Communication as Narration: Toward a Philosophy of Reason,
Value, and Action*

David Payne
*Coping with Failure:
The Therapeutic Uses of Rhetoric*

Human Communication as Narration: Toward a Philosophy of Reason, Value, and Action

by Walter R. Fisher

University of South Carolina Press

Published in Columbia, South Carolina, by the
University of South Carolina Press

Manufactured in the United States of America

First Paperback Edition

Library of Congress Cataloging-in-Publication Data

Fisher, Walter R.
   Human communication as narration.

   (Studies in rhetoric/communication)
   Includes indexes.
   1. Communication—Philosophy.   2. Rhetoric.
3. Narration (Rhetoric)   4. Logic.   5. Reasoning.
I. Title.   II. Series.
P91.F52   1987   001.51'01   86-30830
ISBN 0-87249-500-0
ISBN 0-87249-624-4

To
Beverly, Roxanne, Thomas, Martin,
and
their children

CONTENTS

Foreword   ix
Afterword   xi
Preface   xiii

Part I   The Historical Exigence

  1. *In the Beginning*   5
     From Philosophy to Technical Discourse
     Voices on Behalf of Poetic
     Voices on Behalf of Rhetoric
     Conclusion

  2. *The Connection with Logic*   24
     Dialogue, Dialectic, and Logic
     Aristotle: The Beginnings of Technical and
         Rhetorical Logic
     Technical Logic: Handmaiden of Learned Discourse
     Rhetorical Logic: Handmaiden of Public Discourse
     From Geometry and Mathematics to Language and
         Jurisprudence
     Narrative Rationality as a Rhetorical Logic
     Conclusion

Part II   The Narrative Paradigm and Related Theories

  3. *Narration as a Paradigm of Human Communication*   57
     The Rational-World Paradigm
     The Narrative Paradigm
     A Case: Public Moral Argument
     Conclusion

  4. *An Elaboration*   85
     Relationships to Other Theories
     Social-Scientific Theories and the Narrative Paradigm
     Humanistic Theories and the Narrative Paradigm
     Conclusion

Part III Narrative Rationality, Good Reasons, and
          Audiences

  5. *Assessing Narrative Fidelity: The Logic of Good
     Reasons*   105

The Meaning of "Logic"
Good Reasons
The Logic of Good Reasons
Criterial Analysis
Hierarchies of Values
Rationality and Rhetorical Competence
Conclusion

6. *Narrative Rationality and Qualities of Audiences*   124
Philosophical, Political, and Personal Characteristics
   of Audiences
Justice: The Motivational Characteristic
Critical Rationalism: The Competence Characteristic
Concepts of Audiences Reconsidered
Conclusion

Part IV   Applications

7. *Narrativity and Politics: The Case of Ronald Reagan*   143
Reagan's Rhetoric
Reagan's Story
Reagan's Character
Reagan's Implied Audience
Conclusion

8. *Argument in Drama and Literature*   158
Rhetoric, Poetic, and Aesthetic Proof
Argument in *Death of a Salesman*
Argument in *The Great Gatsby*
Conclusion

9. *Choosing between Socrates and Callicles: An
Assessment of Philosophical Discourse*   180
Socrates' Story
Callicles' Story
Choosing between Socrates and Callicles
Conclusion

10. *In Retrospect*   192

Author Index   195
Subject Index   199

FOREWORD

Beginning with the assumption that humans are essentially storytellers, Walter R. Fisher proposes that all forms of human communication are most usefully interpreted and assessed from a narrational perspective. He believes that beneath the *learned* and *imposed* structures by means of which we give discourse such forms as "argument," "exposition," "drama," and "fiction," the human species is always pursuing a *narrative logic.* From infancy, Fisher argues, we interpret and evaluate new stories against older stories acquired through experience. We search new accounts for their faithfulness to what we know, or think we know, and for their internal and external coherence. Later we *learn* more sophisticated criteria and standards for assessing a story's fidelity and coherence, but constructing, interpreting, and evaluating discourse as "story" remains our primary, innate, species-specific "logic."

That principles of formal logic inadequately explain informal rationality and human valuing has been well established in recent years, especially through studies in argumentation by such writers as Stephen Toulmin, Chaïm Perelman, Douglas Ehninger, and Wayne Brockriede. Building on their work, as well as on that of other distinguished writers, especially Kenneth Burke and Alasdair MacIntyre, Fisher details a new logic, one appropriate to his basic conception of human communication as narration. He proposes a conception of logical processes that is broader than theory of argument has acknowledged to date. Fisher contends that "narrative rationality" underlies understanding and evaluation of any form of human communication that is viewed rhetorically, as an inducement to attitude, belief, or action.

During the past decade, Fisher has presented and argued for several features and applications of his general position. That work has received plaudits from both rhetoricians and philosophers interested in intentional communication. In *Human Communication as Narration,* Fisher now draws together into a single "argument" or "story" the results of his extensive reading and analyses. Here, he presents his theoretical claims in comprehensive form, places them in their context vis à vis the history of rhetorical and logical theory in the West, and illustrates the critical usefulness of his formulations by applying them in analyzing several different "forms" or "genres" of discourse.

Human Communication as Narration supplements and challenges major contributions made by other students of rhetoric in the last several decades. By providing a logic, his work moves beyond Burke's dramatism; by grounding this logic in narration, he broadens and deepens Perelman's approach to practical reasoning. Rhetorical and philosophical research on "informal logic" and "argumentation" is incorporated within Fisher's philosophical/critical system with the simple caveat that *argumentative* forms only occur *together with* and *in addition to* a ubiquitous narrative logic. Contemporary attempts to identify "generic forms" of discourse— the subject of *Form, Genre, and the Study of Political Discourse,* published by the University of South Carolina Press in its Rhetoric/Communi- In like ways, Fisher's analysis of communication accepts and incorporates principles of *narrative logic* are recognized as operating within *all* genres. In like ways. Fisher's analysis of communciation accepts and incorporates contemporary research on stylistics, on the assumption of roles in communications, on the influences of mythic conditioning, and on the nature of symbolic inducement. Fisher's claim is that all such communicative features and functions *arise from* and *evolve out of* human beings' innate impulses to explore the *coherence* of any account and its *fidelity* to the known.

Walter Fisher's highly original book merits close attention from all persons concerned with the theory and criticism of practical communication.

Carroll C. Arnold
Editor, *Rhetoric/Communication*
University of South Carolina Press

AFTERWORD

Conversation about the narrative paradigm grows apace. The most constructive contribution I can make to the dialogue at this moment, I think, is to supplement what I said in the clothbound edition of *Human Communication as Narration*, which concerned what the narrative paradigm *is*. Here I would like to indicate what it *is not*.

First, it is not a rhetoric. As I say in the conclusion, "The narrative paradigm is the foundation on which a complete rhetoric needs to be built." This structure would provide "a comprehensive explanation of the creation, composition, adaptation, presentation, and reception of symbolic messages."

Second, the book is not about rhetorical criticism, or at least the way I would deal with the topic. While it is true that the narrative paradigm concerns the interpretation and assessment of rhetorical messages, the book does not explore the ways in which the rhetorical critic thinks or writes. A book on rhetorical criticism would do this by examining the concepts and practices (actual examples) that mark the explication or evaluation of texts read from different perspectives: What can we reveal about a text by knowing its genre? What can we say of interest about a text by knowing its author? What can we disclose in a text by knowing the audience(s) for whom it is intended or meaningful? And what can we expose in a text by reconstructing or deconstructing it in terms of itself? Whatever theory a critic may adopt is but a means to answering one or more of these questions. It is the case, of course, that good answers can produce or modify theory. The interest of the critic, however, is to communicate what is remarkable about the text.

Third, the narrative paradigm is not a celebration of narration as an individuated form—as anecdote, depiction, characterization, and so on—or as a genre in and of itself. If the narrative paradigm celebrates anything, it celebrates human beings, and it does this by reaffirming their nature as storytellers. It affirms that narration as individuated form and as genre—like other individuated forms (such as argument) and genre (such as argumentation)—are expressive of good reasons, if viewed rhetorically. And when they are so experienced, they are constitutive of people, community, and the world.

Fourth, as just suggested, the narrative paradigm does not deny the utility of traditional genres—in poetic, rhetoric, philosophy, sciences, and so on. It does insist, however, that regardless of genre, discourse will always tell a story and insofar as it invites an audience to believe it or to act on it, the narrative paradigm and its attendant logic, narrative rationality, are available for interpretation and assessment. (A brief account of my approach to genre appears in chapter seven.)

Fifth, the narrative paradigm does not assert that some communication cannot be seen as serving other than rhetorical functions. For example, some communications can be described aptly as phatic or consummatory, and all human communication is recognized as reflecting unconscious motives and achieving unintended results. It is only when communication is considered seriously in regard to its advice or fostering of belief, attitude, or action that the narrative paradigm becomes relevant: to ascertain the meaning and merit of the communication as a ground for decision and performance.

Sixth, the narrative paradigm is not a rejection of the tradition of argumentation, as I hoped chapter two would clearly show. What is rejected is the specific notion that reason only appears in discourse when it takes the individuated forms of inference or implication, or the genre of argumentation. Also rejected is any conception of human communication that denies or ignores values. The "logic of good reasons," I want to stress, combines tests of reasoning and tests of values. It adds to them, considerations of coherence—structural (argumentative), material, and characteriological—to comprise the construct of narrative rationality.

Seventh, the narrative paradigm does not deny that power, ideology, distortion, or totalitarian forces are or can be significant features of communicative practices. Regardless of their presence, however, decision and action are inevitable, and their appearance is always in the context of ongoing stories. If they were the only features of communicative practices, decision and action would only and always be: whose domination shall we submit to and live by? I continue to believe that some stories are more truthful and humane than others.

In short, the narrative paradigm is a philosophical statement that is meant to offer an approach to interpretation and assessment of human communication—assuming that all forms of human communication can be seen fundamentally as stories, as interpretations of aspects of the world occurring in time and shaped by history, culture, and character.

Several books have appeared since *Human Communication as Narration* went to press, which enrich the conversation about narration as paradigm. I recommend each of them: Richard Harvey Brown, *Society as Text: Essays on Rhetoric, Reason, and Reality* (Chicago: University of Chicago Press, 1987); Jerome Bruner, *Actual Minds, Possible Worlds* (Cambridge: Harvard University Press, 1986); David Carr, *Time, Narrative, and History* (Bloomington: Indiana University Press, 1986); Wallace Martin, *Recent Theories of Narrative* (Ithaca: Cornell University Press, 1986); and the third Volume of Paul Ricouer's *Time and Narrative* (Chicago: University of Chicago Press, 1988). I should also mention three other books that significantly bear on the theme of narration and human communication: M. M. Bakhtin, *The Dialogic Imagination,* trans. Caryl Emerson and Michael Holquist (Austin: University of Texas Press, 1981); Frederic Jameson, *The Political Unconscious: Narrative as a Socially Symbolic Act* (Ithaca: Cornell University Press, 1981); and, Jean-François Lyotard, *The Post-Modern Condition: A Report on Knowledge,* trans. Geoff Bennington and Brian Massumi (Minneapolis: University of Minnesota Press, 1984).

The foregoing is offered with the hope that it may forestall unnecessary misunderstanding. There is no anticipation that it will do this completely, as human communication is too imbued with the shortcomings that people are heir to for that. Nor is there any expectation that it will eliminate disagreements. It is not meant to do this either. It is meant to keep the conversation focused on genuine disagreements rather than those caused by the fragility of the writer and readers.

W. R. F.

PREFACE

This book proposes answers to these questions: How do people come to believe and act on the basis of communicative experiences? What is the nature of reason and rationality in these experiences? What is the role of values in human decision making and action? How can reason and values be assessed? The principal historical, philosophical, and practical reasons for addressing these questions anew are discussed in the first two chapters. There I argue that prevailing theories of human communication and logic—ancient, modern, and contemporary—do not answer these questions adequately. The focal point giving rise to this inadequacy is that the role of values in the constitution of knowledge, truth, or reality has been generally denied. The result has been that in serious matters of social or political significance, technical discourse has been assigned almost unquestioned superiority over rhetorical and poetic discourse. I believe the reasons for this assignment of superiority deserve to be questioned severely and that values function in constituting all that we consider knowledge.

In accordance with these views, I propose (1) a reconceptualization of humankind as *Homo narrans*; (2) that all forms of human communication need to be seen fundamentally as stories—symbolic interpretations of aspects of the world occurring in time and shaped by history, culture, and character; (3) that individuated forms of discourse should be considered as "good reasons"—values or value-laden warrants for believing or acting in certain ways; and (4) that a narrative logic that all humans have natural capacities to employ ought to be conceived of as the logic by which human communication is assessed. The basic principles of that narrative logic are coherence and fidelity. My arguments for these proposals are the substance of chapters 3, 5, and 6. In Chapter 4, I situate what I call the narrative paradigm in relation to leading, current social-scientific and humanistic theories of communication.

To illustrate the usefulness of the narrative paradigm in interpreting and assessing various types of human communication, I examine in chapter 7 some political rhetoric from Ronald Reagan. In Chapter 8, I apply the paradigm in interpreting and evaluating the play *Death of a Salesman* and the novel *The Great Gatsby*. In Chapter 9, I apply the same interpretive and evaluative principles of the narrative paradigm to the exchange between Socrates and Callicles in Plato's *Gorgias*. The final chapter recapitulates my general theory of human communication as narration and suggests further directions along which the study of communication as narration might be profitably pursued.

Over the years that it has taken me to write the papers from which this book has developed, I have had the privilege of wise counsel from a number of constructive critics. Chief among them have been W. Lance Bennett, Ernest G. Bormann, the late Wayne Brockriede, Kenneth Burke, John Angus Campbell, Thomas B. Farrell, Thomas S. Frentz, Bruce E. Gronbeck, Michael Calvin McGee, John S. Nelson, Calvin O. Schrag, Herbert W. Simons, and John R. Stewart. I am also grateful to my colleagues Steven R. Goldzwig, Thomas A. Hollihan, Randall A. Lake, and Dallas Willard. Finally, I want to express my deep appreciation to Carroll C. Arnold, an editor's editor, who enabled me to transform what were once discrete essays into this book.

ACKNOWLEDGMENTS

Materials from several of my previously published works have been used in the writing of this book. I am pleased to credit each of the publications in which these materials have or will appear:

An earlier version of Chapter 1 appeared as "The Narrative Paradigm: In the Beginning," in the *Journal of Communication*, vol. 35, no. 4, 1985, pp. 74–89.

Chapter 2 will appear in a shorter form in *Argumentation, 1 (1987)*, 3–21, under the title, "Technical Logic, Rhetorical Logic, and Narrative Rationality." *Copyright © 1987 by D. Reidel Publisher.*

Chapter 3 is based on "Narration as a Human Communication Paradigm: The Case of Public Moral Argument," *Communication Monographs,* 51 (1984), 1–22.

Chapter 4 relates to the first half of "The Narrative Paradigm: An Elaboration," *Communication Monographs,* 52 (1985), 347–367.

Chapter 5 combines two articles: "Toward a Logic of Good Reasons," *The Quarterly Journal of Speech,* 64 (1978), 376–384 and "Rationality and the Logic of Good Reasons," which appeared in *Philosophy and Rhetoric,* Volume 13, Number 2, Spring 1980, pp. 121–130. The publisher of *Philosophy and Rhetoric* is the Pennsylvania State University Press.

Chapter 6 is a modified version of "Judging the Quality of Audiences and Narrative Rationality," in J. L. Golden and J. J. Pilotta (eds.), *Practical Reasoning in Human Affairs,* D. Reidel Publisher, 1986, pp. 85–103.

Chapter 7 utilizes material from "Romantic Democracy, Ronald Reagan, and Presidential Heroes," *Western Journal of Speech Communication,* 46 (1982), 299–310.

Chapter 8 is a reworking of an essay written with Richard A. Filloy, "Argument in Drama and Literature: An Exploration," which originally appeared in *Argumentation Theory and Research,* edited by R. Cox and C. Willard, published by Southern Illinois University Press. Copyright ©

1982, J. Robert Cox and Charles Arthur Willard. Reprinted by permission of the publishers.

Chapter 9 is a revision of the second half of "The Narrative Paradigm: An Elaboration," *Communication Monographs*, 52 (1985), 347–367.

Figures 1 and 2, chapter 2, reprinted from Cicero, *Ad C. Herennium*, trans. Harry Caplan, Harvard University Press, 1954, reprinted by permission.

Excerpts from *Isocrates*, trans. George Norlin, reprinted by permission of Harvard University Press.

Excerpt from Stephen Toulmin, *The Uses of Argument*, © Cambridge University Press 1958; reprinted by permission of Cambridge University Press.

PART I
THE HISTORICAL EXIGENCE

IN THE BEGINNING

In the beginning was the word or, more accurately, the logos. And in the beginning, "logos" meant story, reason, rationale, conception, discourse, thought. Thus all forms of human expression and communication—from epic to architecture, from biblical narrative to statuary—came within its purview. At least this was the case until the time of the pre-Socratic philosophers and Plato and Aristotle. As a result of their thinking, logos and mythos, which had been conjoined, were dissociated; logos was transformed from a generic term into a specific one, applying only to philosophical (later technical) discourse. Poetical and rhetorical discourse were relegated to a secondary or negative status respecting their connections with truth, knowledge, and reality. Poetic was given province over mythos; rhetoric was delegated the realm where logos and mythos reign in dubious ambiguity. A historical hegemonic struggle ensued among proponents of each of the three forms of discourse and it lasts to this day.

The story of these events, which I shall sketch in this chapter, is germane to an understanding of the narrative paradigm that I shall propose in chapter 3. The essential postulates of the paradigm are:

(1) Humans are . . . storytellers. (2) The paradigmatic mode of human decision making and communication is "good reasons," which vary in form among situations, genres, and media of communication. (3) The production and practice of good reasons are ruled by matters of history, biography, culture, and character along with the kinds of forces identified in the Frentz and Farrell language-action paradigm. (4) Rationality is determined by the nature of persons as narrative beings—their inherent awareness of *narrative probability,* what constitutes a coherent story, and their constant habit of testing *narrative fidelity,* whether or not the stories they experience ring true with the stories they know to be true in their lives . . . . (5) The world as we know it is a set of stories that must be chosen among in order for us to live life in a process of continual re-creation.[1]

The story told here will provide one-half of the historical context behind the narrative paradigm; the other half concerns an evolving relationship between logic and the three forms of discourse; I shall detail that half in the next chapter. The entire argument will demonstrate that the ancient conception of logos, when informed by the narrative paradigm, has validity and value for today and tomorrow.

The story of logos and mythos parallels the story of orality and literacy, as told by Walter Ong.[2] There is however, a fundamental difference between them. The issues in the orality-and-literacy story are how the mind is constituted and what the consequences are for human consciousness. At issue in the story of the interrelations of logos and mythos is which form of discourse—philosophy (technical discourse), rhetoric, or poetic—ensures the discovery and validation of truth, knowledge, and reality, and thereby deserves to be the legislator of human decision making and action. The two stories inform one another and both are necessary to a full realization of the relationship between communication and what humans are and can become.

Another parallel story is told by Samuel Ijsseling in *Rhetoric and Philosophy in Conflict*.[3] Its issue is "What is actually happening whenever something is said or written?" I propose the narrative paradigm as a response to this question and as a factor that might be part of Ijsseling's history—if it were extended. The theme of the story on which I shall focus is the transformation of the concept of logos.

Historically, the most pertinent struggle is the one among proponents of the major forms of discourse over who "owns" logos. I offer the narrative paradigm as a move beyond that struggle. Acceptance of the narrative paradigm shifts the controversy from a focus on who "owns" logos to a focus on what specific instances of discourse, regardless of form, provide the most trustworthy, reliable, and desirable guides to belief and to behavior, and under what conditions.

Prior to the pre-Socratics and to Plato and Aristotle, "mythos and logos, imagination and thought," were "not yet distinct." Truth was not then the province of privileged discourse, whether called argument or dialectic. "Living myth" was still considered "truth . . . the very instrument of truth, in the original sense of the Greek word *aletheia*. For in its saying myth lays open to sight what without it would be utterly concealed; it reveals, lifts out of primordial hiddenness and brings to light a whole world; it brings all things forth and gives them form: a visible palpable presence."[4] The evolution from story to statement began with

6

the pre-Socratics. "What they proceeded to do was to take the language of the *mythos* and manipulate it, forcing its terms into fresh syntactical relationships which had the constant effect of stretching and extending their application, giving them a cosmic rather than particular reference."[5] Then came Plato.

Plato was not so much interested in the cosmos as were the pre-Socratics. Like the Sophists and rhetoricians, his interest was human existence. Unlike the Sophists and rhetoricians, however, he did not believe that argument based on probabilities was all the world had to offer or that such argument should be accepted as constituting logos. He certainly believed that probabilities were not a proper foundation or guide to personal or public life. His project, according to Eric Havelock, was to formulate "an abstract language of descriptive science to replace a concrete language of oral memory."[6] The epitome of this language was dialectic, the only form of discourse that could ensure apprehension of true ideas. His "contribution" to the transformation of logos was to technologize logos, to make it a term appropriate only to philosophical discourse. The effects of his thought were to create "experts" in truth, knowledge, and reality; to establish the rational superiority of philosophical (technical) discourse; to relegate mythos to myth (meaning fictional); and to downgrade rhetoric and poetic. Dispensations were made for rhetoric and poetic; they had a place in the life of the community, but they were not to be considered serious intellectual arts. They were to be controlled or informed by philosopher-kings.

Aristotle, Plato's pupil, reinforced the idea that some forms of discourse are superior to others by drawing clear distinctions among them in regard to their relationship to true knowledge.[7] Only scientific discourse was productive of true knowledge, because it was the only form of discourse in which reasoning could be apodictic, that is, necessarily valid. Dialectic discourse could lead to knowledge but only to probable knowledge, based on expert opinion. Rhetoric, founded on contingent reason, was appropriate for "untrained thinkers." And to Aristotle poetic discourse did not function as much by reasoning as by "imitation" and cathartic participation. Thus, while Aristotle recognized the value of different forms of human communication in different domains of learning and life, he established a configuration that enabled later, and often lesser, thinkers to insist that their mode of discourse was superior to others and to call on him for support.

7

FROM PHILOSOPHY TO TECHNICAL DISCOURSE

After the pre-Socratics and Plato and Aristotle, the next most influential statement of the view that philosophical discourse reigns supreme over other forms of discourse is that of Francis Bacon. Actually, the effect of Bacon's thought was to elevate scientific (technical expository) discourse over all forms of discourse, including philosophy. Philosophy retained a high status, but only as it focused on science. The "demotion" of philosophy was a concomitant of the new theory of knowledge—that knowledge concerns the physical world and is strictly empirical. This was a reversal in logic from an emphasis on deduction to emphasis on induction. The new authority on knowing was not Aristotle or the church but *method,* the procedures for proper empirical investigation. One of the major results of Bacon's ideas was a reconception of rhetorical invention. The ancient theory had it that rhetoricians *discover probabilities* by considering, topically, what is known or can be believed about a given subject. Bacon's conception of rhetorical invention was that it is simply processing or finding communicative *adaptations* of knowledge originally discovered by nonrhetorical processes. The effect of his thought was to reduce rhetoric to a "managerial art"; that is, its function was to facilitate transmission of knowledge acquired through investigations regulated by other disciplines. The earliest full exposition of rhetoric so conceived was George Campbell's *The Philosophy of Rhetoric.*[8] The rhetorical writings of Hugh Blair[9] and Richard Whately[10] helped to popularize this view. In still narrower form the managerial conception of rhetoric was popularized in Great Britain by Alexander Bain, whose manual, *English Composition and Rhetoric,*[11] was very widely used, and in the United States by Adams Sherman Hill of Harvard, whose *Principles of Rhetoric*[12] became a standard textbook in America. Both men insisted that rhetoric was the study of the *forms* of prose composition and had nothing at all to do with content.

Bacon cleared the field for the new science, but Descartes determined how it was to be plowed. Descartes's contribution was to perfect the method of empirical investigation by grounding it on mathematical demonstration. He esteemed "eloquence highly, and loved poetry," yet he felt that "they were gifts of nature rather than fruits of study."[13] Other studies were rejected because they were based on traditional philosophy, which allowed a diversity of opinions, where "no more than one of them can ever be right."[14] The eventual result of Descartes's views was the doctrine of the logical positivists, who held that no statement could claim expression of knowledge unless it was empirically verifiable—at least in principle or it

8

involved a logical entailment. The doctrine also entailed the notion that values were "non-sense." The discourse of technical experts was thereby designated as the only serious form of human communication; rhetoric and poetic were considered irrational, if sometimes amusing, forms of human transaction.

Aiding and abetting the general influence of Bacon and Descartes was John Locke, whose aim was to establish that knowledge is "real only so far as there is a *conformity* between ideas and the reality of things."[15] Like his predecessors, Locke attacked the value of the syllogism, the topics (guides to rhetorical invention), and all forms of ornamental speech. In *An Essay concerning Human Understanding,* he wrote: ". . . if we would speak of things as they are, we must allow, that all the Art of Rhetorick besides Order and Clearness, all the artificial figurative application of Words Eloquence hath invented, are for nothing else, but to insinuate wrong *Ideas,* move the Passions, and thereby mislead Judgment; and so indeed are perfect cheat."[16] Thus the only form of discourse for learned study and communication was exposition.

There is, perhaps, no more instructive statement of the ideal form of scientific communication than that of Thomas Sprat. After dismissing rhetoric and poetic, he declared that the "new" form of communication would return "to the primitive purity, and shortness, when men deliver'd so many *things,* almost in an equal number of words." The style was to be a "close, naked, natural way of speaking; positive expressions; clear sense; a native easiness: bringing all things as near Mathematical plainness, as they can."[17] It is not difficult to see in this statement an impetus to twentieth-century general semantics.

Today there is much ferment about the consequences of these views: the concept of knowledge that denies a role for values, the separation of logic from everyday discourse, and the privileging of "experts" and their discourse. The narrative paradigm, as an affirmative proposal against these moves, is a case in point. These postivistic views have also been attacked by a host of philosophers, including Richard Bernstein,[18] George-Hans Gadamer,[19] Jürgen Habermas,[20] Richard Rorty,[21] and Calvin Schrag.[22] Indeed, it is not humanists alone who have been and are questioning these ideas. Following the challenges by Kurt Gödel and Werner Heisenberg to scientific certainty, scientists and philosophers of science have joined the discussion. The direction of this rethinking is illustrated by Stephen Toulmin's *Return to Cosmology*[23] and Fritjof Capra's *Turning Point.*[24] One cannot predict the outcome of the arguments, but one can hope for a concept of logos that approximates that of the ancients. Theirs was a concept that regarded all humans and their communication as not irrational and as deserving respect.

VOICES ON BEHALF OF POETIC

It is not to be supposed that proponents of poetic and rhetoric were silent in the audience of those who extolled philosophy and technical discourse. Nor is it to be assumed that those ancients who most eloquently asserted the significance of poetic argued only from poetic's permanence and beauty, its powers of providing aesthetic pleasure. During the times of the pre-Socratics, Plato, and the Sophists, Aristophanes was insisting that the standard of excellence in poetry was not only "skill in the art," but also "wise counsel for the state." In *The Clouds* he caricatured Socrates as a Sophist, a teacher of false, irresponsible logic. That Socrates was not a Sophist is beside the point that Aristophanes was making: the teachings of drama were germane to life here, now, and for eternity.

Like those who spoke for rhetoric, to be considered below, those who spoke for poetic were divided between those who claimed the primacy of their art over other forms of discourse and those who claimed supremacy only in a particular domain of life. Proponents of poetic tended to claim as their special domain personal knowledge or consciousness; rhetoricians tended to claim as their domain public knowledge oriented toward decision making and civic action.

One of the most eloquent voices on behalf of eloquence was Longinus. Significantly, his *On the Sublime* did not extol one form of discourse over another; it celebrated qualities of communication that can appear in any genre of discourse. I refer to Longinus specifically because the attributes of eloquence he identified are not strictly rhetorical. There is no mention of argument, for instance. The qualities on which he focused are also qualities that are in sharp contrast to those prescribed by Thomas Sprat for expository discourse. "The effect of elevated language," Longinus wrote, "is not persuasion but transport. At every time and in every way imposing speech, with the spell it throws over us, prevails over that which aims at persuasion and gratification."[25] To prove his point, he cited passages from drama, poetry, epic, history, philosophy, and oratory. The sources of sublimity, he said, were five: the "power of forming great conceptions"; "vehement and inspired passion"; "formation of figures"; "noble diction"; and "dignified and elevated composition."[26] Any form of discourse might display these qualities, but "mere rhetoric" and technical discourse would not. True eloquence would find its natural home in great literature.

Much clearer in asserting the primacy of poetic was Boccaccio. Writing in the fourteenth century, when the dominant mode of discourse was theological, he aligned poetry with the church's doctrine that truth could be allegorical: poetry "veils truth in a fair and fitting garment of fiction."[27] He acknowledged that poetry was informed by rhetoric (and grammar), but he declared that "among the disguises of fiction rhetoric has no part, for whatever is composed as under a veil, and thus exquisitely wrought, is poetry and poetry alone."[28] At the same time, however, Boccaccio insisted that poetry could serve rhetorically. If necessary, he wrote, poetry "can arm kings, marshal them for war, launch whole fleets from their docks, nay, counterfeit sky, land, sea, adorn young maidens with flowery garlands, portray human character in its various phases, awake the idle, stimulate the dull, retain the rash, subdue the criminal, and distinguish excellent men with their proper meed of praise."[29] Not only did Boccaccio claim truth for his art, he also held that it "is a practical art, springing from God's bosom," and is therefore moral as well.[30]

Sir Philip Sidney, writing in the sixteenth century during the rise of science, claimed that poetry is the supreme form of discourse, that its function is to foster virtue, and that its appeal is universal. Poetry, said Sidney, offers tales "which holdeth children from play, and old men from the chimney corner."[31] He attacked learned (historical and philosophical) discourse but did not directly discuss scientific discourse. He wrote that "no learning is so good as that which teacheth and mooveth to virtue; and that none can both teach and move thereto so much as Poetry."[32]

By the end of the eighteenth century, the challenge of science was sorely felt by those who spoke for aesthetic communication. Friedrich von Schiller summarized the situation in this way:

> Once the increase of empirical knowledge, and more exact modes of thought, made sharper divisions between the sciences inevitable, and once the increasingly complex machinery of the state necessitated a more rigorous separation of ranks and occupations, then the inner unity of human nature was severed too, and a disastrous conflict set its harmonious powers at variance. The intuitive and the speculative understanding now withdrew in hostility. . . . While in the one a riotous imagination ravages the hard-won fruits of the intellect, in

11

another the spirit of abstraction stifles the fire at which the heart should have warmed itself and the imagination been kindled.[33]

The effects of this severance were to fragment society and the conceptions of the individual, to create a struggle between sense and intellect, between the "sensuous drive," which "proceeds from the physical existence of man," and the "formal drive," which "proceeds from the absolute existence of man, or from his rational nature."[34] To restore balance, full humanity, Schiller held that society and individuals should celebrate "play," the ludic impulse, which is the subject of John Huizinga's classic *Homo Ludens: A Study of the Play-Element in Culture*.[35] (It is also a major theme in Gadamer's *Truth and Method*.) Schiller wrote: "Man only plays when he is in the fullest sense of the word a human being, and he is only fully a human being when he plays." Aesthetic expression, he maintained, is "the most fruitful of all in respect of knowledge and morality."[36]

By the end of the nineteenth century, proponents of poetic could not, or did not, challenge science's claim on the domain of the physical sphere of life. Instead, they reconceptualized knowledge, declaring that knowledge was of more than one kind. Benedetto Croce, for instance, held that "knowledge was two forms: it is either intuitive knowledge or logical knowledge; knowledge obtained through the imagination or knowledge obtained through the intellect; knowledge of the individual or knowledge of the universal; of individual things or of the relations between them: it is, in fact, productive either of images or of concepts."[37] It is clear that the distinction is between art as expression and science as literal impression.

In 1926 I. A. Richards took exception to the idea of "regarding Poetic Truth as figurative, symbolic; or as more immediate as truth of Intuition, not of reason, or as a higher form of the truth as reason yields."[38] In his "Science and Poetry," he held that "it is *not* the poet's business to make true statements."[39] Poetry is composed of "pseudo-statements" whose function it is to give order to attitudes and experience. Scientific discourse is composed of referential statements that produce "genuine knowledge," which, however, are limited to increasing "our practical control over Nature."[40] Rhetorical discourse, said Richards, is composed of "mixed statements" that appear in pragmatic communication. While each of the major arts of discourse was given its place in this scheme of things, Richards insisted that "Poetry is the completest mode of utterance."[41]

Allen Tate rejected not only Matthew Arnold's attempt to put science and poetry on an equal footing, Charles Morris's semiotic interpretation of

12

poetry, but also the early Richards of "Science and Poetry," which he considered too much influenced by positivism. However, Allen Tate endorsed Richards's view that poetry is the most complete utterance among those that could be made by any of the arts of discourse. He claimed in "Literature as Knowledge" that the result of poetic statements is "complete knowledge." But he insisted: "The order of completeness that it achieves in the great works of the imagination is not the order of experimental completeness aimed at by the positivist sciences, whose responsibilities are directed towards the verification of limited techniques. . . . No one can have an experience of science, or of a single science."[42] The completeness of Hamlet, Tate averred, "is not of the experimental order, but of the experienced order." His final claim was that the " 'interest' value" of poetry is a "cognitive one."[43]

There is ferment today regarding how to conceptualize and to relate science, knowledge, and praxis; there is also controversy about how to conceptualize and to relate science, knowledge, and aesthetic experience. The sharpest divisions are among representatives of poststructuralism and deconstructionism, and representatives of the literary tradition, like Gerald Graff in *Literature against Itself*,[44] and hermeneuticians, like Gadamer in *Truth and Method*, who think that poetry has cognitive significance, not, of course, the kind of cognitive significance insisted upon by logical positivists or cognitive scientists. The cognitive significance of aesthetic communication lies in its capacity to *manifest* knowledge, truth or reality, to enrich understanding of self, other, or the world.

VOICES ON BEHALF OF RHETORIC

Of the proponents of rhetoric as the central form of discourse, the most articulate in the ancient world was Isocrates, who was opposed but admired by Plato. It has been conjectured that Aristotle chose to lecture on rhetoric, not only to complete his treatment of all subjects, but also to contrast his philosophical view of rhetoric with the views of the rhetoricians, as represented by the teaching of Isocrates. According to G. Norlin, for Isocrates "logos" was consubstantial with discourse, because discourse reflected "both the outward and the inward thought; it is not merely the form of expression, but reason, feeling, and imagination as well."[45] Isocrates' defense of his art in the *Antidosis* includes a statement that declares his "philosophy," and at the same time reflects the major thrust of the West's rhetorical tradition at least to the sixteenth century:

13

We are in no respect superior to other living creatures; nay, we are inferior to many in swiftness and in strength and in other resources; but, because there has been implanted in us the power to persuade each other and to make clear to each other whatever we desire, not only have we escaped the life of wild beasts, but we have come together and founded cities and made laws and invented arts; and, generally speaking, there is no institution devised by man which the power of speech has not helped us to establish. For this it is which has laid down laws concerning things just and unjust, and things honourable and base; and if it were not for these ordinances we should not be able to live with one another. It is by this also that we confute the bad and extol the good. Through this we educate the ignorant and appraise the wise; for the power to speak well is taken as the surest index of sound understanding, and discourse which is true and lawful and just is the outward image of a good and faithful soul. With this faculty we both contend against others on matters which are open to dispute and seek light for ourselves on things which are unknown; for the same arguments which we use in persuading others when we speak in public, we employ also when we deliberate in our own thoughts; and, while we call eloquent those who are able to speak before a crowd, we regard as sage those who most skillfully debate their problems in their own minds. . . . none of the things which are done with intelligence takes place without the help of speech, . . . in all our actions as well as in all our thoughts speech is our guide, and is most employed by those who have the most wisdom.[56]

This statement is not only central to the rhetorical tradition, it is also an inspiration for the humanistic tradition "fathered" by Cicero. The Ciceronian and humanistic traditions were, in fact, virtually synonymous through the Renaissance and at the rise of scientifically oriented thinking.

Echoing Isocrates' thought, Cicero wrote in *De oratore,* "For the one point in which we have our very greatest advantage over the brute creation is that we hold converse one with another, and can reproduce our thought in word."[47] He conceded jurisdiction over "the mysteries of nature" and the "subtleties of dialectic" to the philosopher, but Cicero insisted that rhetoric was supreme in the sphere of "human life and conduct."[48] Even so, the only reason he conceded the two domains to the philosopher was the "indolence" of rhetoricians in regard to them. Perhaps the clearest statement of his view of the scope of rhetoric was this: "But in an orator we must demand the subtlety of the logician, the thought of the philosopher, a diction almost poetic, a lawyer's memory, a tragedian's voice, and the bearing almost of the consummate actor. Accordingly, no rarer

14

thing than a finished orator can be discovered among the sons of men."[49] Thus, to Cicero, the orator was foremost a statesman, a person of near universal knowledge and extraordinary gifts whose mission was to elevate civic life through action. Cicero's orator was, in a sense, the obverse of Ralph Waldo Emerson's scholar—Man thinking. Said Emerson: "Action is with the scholar subordinate, but it is essential. Without it he is not yet man. Without it thought can never ripen into truth."[50] The practicing rhetorician is the person acting on knowledge to further truth.

After Bacon, Descartes, and scientific thinking began to dominate the intellectual arts, Giambattista Vico rose to defend the rhetorical-humanistic tradition that I have just sketched. Writing in 1709, he held that "young men should be taught the totality of science and arts, and their intellectual powers should be developed to the full." This meant that they should not only know the procedures of science, but also "the art of argument."[51] This position put him in opposition to the prevailing monistic concept of knowledge and the Cartesian method. It put him firmly in the camp of Cicero. Vico believed that one needed *common* as well as *technical sense*. He characterized scientific education as generating speculative criticism, about which he wrote:

> Now, such speculative criticism, the main purpose of which is to cleanse its fundamental truths not only of all falsity, but also of the mere suspicion of error, places upon the same plane of falsity not only false thinking, but also secondary verities and ideas which are based on probability alone, and commands us to clear our minds of them. Such an approach is distinctly harmful, since training in common sense is essential to the education of adolescents, so that that faculty should be developed as early as possible; else they break into odd or arrogant behavior when adulthood is reached.

Common sense, Vico held, is the "criterion of practical judgment" and is the "guiding standard of eloquence."[52]

Vico's twentieth-century counterpart, Ernesto Grassi, carries the argument of rhetoric's supremacy further and deeper. A philosopher, Grassi delves into history and the nature of human thought and asserts "the primacy of 'topical' philosophy ('topics' as the theory of the finding of arguments) over 'rational' philosophy and . . . the primacy of rhetoric— imagistic speech and thereby dialogue—over rational speech and thereby monologue."[53] He assigns to rhetoric *ingenium*, "the sphere of wit and acuteness," the main task of which "is to 'decipher' the world without which reality would remain unknown and mute; *ingenium* is hence an activity that lets the divine shine."[54] Like Vico, Grassi ultimately retains a distinction between philosophy—technical discourse, which he calls "rational speech" or "that which strictly, 'mathematically' explains or infers what is implied in premises"—and rhetorical speech, which is "dialogue" rather than monologue and is imbued most importantly with metaphor.[55] The realm of rhetoric, for Grassi, is, then logos, a combination of religious experience, pathos, and ontological perception of human existence.

This view differs from the one I shall propose. I do not agree that what Grassi calls rational speech is purely monologue. Philosophical-technical discourse is a form of communication. It is not expressed to stand by itself; it is addressed to others and has its own modes of strategic appeal. Part of that appeal arises from metaphor and other forms of mythos. Furthermore, *ingenium* as insight is not peculiar to any particular subject matter; it is a necessary act of mind for any creative thought, whether in science, philosophy, art, religion, rhetoric, or any other. At the same time, I think Grassi's consideration of rhetoric as philosophy is a significant statement. It overcomes the notion that real logos occurs only in the privileged discourse of scientists and certain philosophers.

Paralleling the attempt by proponents of poetic to advance their art by aligning it with knowledge has been a move by rhetoricians in recent years to treat rhetoric as epistemic. Since Robert L. Scott's "On Viewing Rhetoric as Epistemic" in 1967,[56] there has been a stream of books and articles exploring the nature of rhetoric and its relationship to knowledge.[57] Theorists have argued that rhetoric is uniquely associated with the discovery and development of public or social knowledge. Bitzer has posited an idea of "public knowledge." This knowledge is "a fund of truths, principles, and values which could only characterize a public." By rhetoric he means "a method of inquiry and communication which seeks to establish correct judgments primarily in the areas of practical and humane affairs, for the speaker or writer and for the audience addressed." He holds that "rhetoric generates truth and values," "gives voice to interests and principles," and serves as an instrument with which to test public truths."[58] Bitzer explicitly distinguishes personal and public knowledge, and implicitly distinguishes technical and public knowledge.

Farrell concentrates on a concept of "social knowledge": *"conceptions of symbolic relationships among problems, persons, interests, and actions, which imply (when accepted) certain notions of preferable public behavior."* Social knowledge is to be clearly distinguished from "technical or specialized knowledge." The kinds of knowledge differ in that social

16

knowledge concerns human decisions and actions by audiences, while technical knowledge is "actualized through its perceived correspondence to the external world."[59] Thus, in both Bitzer's and Farrell's conceptions, rhetoric retains its traditional jurisdiction—civic conduct.

Each of the above conceptions has its critics. Michael Calvin McGee and Martha Ann Martin contrast Bitzer's "idealistic" view with a "materialist's" perspective. Walter M. Carlton attacks Farrell's distinction between social and technical knowledge, arguing that all knowledge is rhetorically generated and sustained. It is not my purpose to adjudicate these and similar disputes, but I want to point out that all the scholars I have mentioned—and others—reaffirm the historic, integral relations of rhetoric to *creation* of logos. I do not believe, however, that the arguments so far made concerning the epistemic dimensions of rhetoric go far enough.

I join Karlyn Campbell in believing that rhetorical experience is more usefully viewed ontologically than epistemologically.[60] Put another way: rhetorical experience is most fundamentally a symbolic transaction in and about social reality. In this experience "knowledge" may or may not loom large. For instance, one of the decisive dimensions of rhetorical experience when persons interact symbolically is their perceptions of the others' perceptions of them. These perceptions they read from what and how the other persons communicate. Unless a respondent perceives an accurate and appropriate perception of herself or himself in the message, there will be little or no communication. In its extreme, negative form, this condition is alienation. Its opposite, positive form, is charisma, which exists when there is a communicative transaction in which one person perceives the other as loving and honoring the best in them.[61] I do not mean to say that knowledge is unimportant in communication. I do mean, on the other hand, that it is ultimately configured narratively, as a component in a larger story implying the being of a certain kind of person, a person with a particular worldview, with a specific self-concept, and with characteristic ways of relating to others.

To date, the fullest, most systematically developed statement about the relationship of rhetoric to knowledge is that of the late Chaïm Perelman. He advanced the thesis that rhetoric should be "the study of the discursive techniques allowing us *to induce or to increase the mind's adherence to the thesis presented for its assent.*"[62] In Perelman's theory, rhetoric, as a study, has jurisdiction over all practical reasoning, that is, all informal logic and argumentation. Perelman acknowledged that "in a great many areas of knowledge the ideal of truth must prevail over other considera-

17

tions," but, as a student of law, he insisted that in the domain of justice—where issues of right and wrong are decided—rhetoric as argumentative reason occurs but demonstrative reason seldom if ever does.[63] Like other rhetoricians I have just cited, Perelman denied that any special privilege can be assigned to assertions about absolute standards for truth, knowledge, and reality because those matters have to be *argued* before and assented to by audiences, else they have no public significance. Another feature of Perelman's work was his implication that values are ineradicable constituents of knowledge, of practical wisdom. Accordingly, he held that the worth of arguments must be measured by the quality of the audience(s) that would adhere to them.

The most revolutionary move in the twentieth century regarding rhetoric is that of Kenneth Burke. Viewing rhetoric as the symbolic function of inducement, rather than as a form of discourse, Burke sees rhetoric as an attribute of *all* symbolic expression and action.[64] "Wherever there is persuasion, there is rhetoric and wherever there is meaning, there is persuasion."[65] He admits that one can make distinctions among forms of discourse, but they cannot be absolute distinctions, for there is no genre without appeal. The "arousing and fulfillment of desires," the anticipation and gratification created by "the sequential unfolding of the discourse" occur in all forms of discourse.[66] Experiencing rhetoric, for Burke, is not purely epistemological; it is more fundamentally an ontological experience. Rhetorical experience works by identification rather than by demonstration. As he recognizes reason as well as aesthetic qualities in all forms of human communication, Burke's theory recaptures and reinforms the original sense of logos.

The narrative paradigm, as I shall present it, is fully in accord with these views, but it differs from Burke's dramatism in two ways. The first difference is subtle but important. It concerns the precise part played by people in the interpretation and assessment of meanings in the world and in their choices of behaviors in given situations. Burke's dramatism *implies* that people function according to prescribed roles; they are actors performing roles constrained or determined by scripts provided by existing institutions. The narrative paradigm sees people as storytellers, as authors and co-authors who creatively read and evaluate the texts of life and literature. A narrative perspective focuses on existing institutions as providing "plots" that are always in the process of re-creation rather than existing as settled scripts. Viewing human communication narratively stresses that people are full participants in the making of messages, whether they are agents (authors) or audience members (co-authors).

18

The second difference derives from the first. The notion that people are actors leads to the supposition that human behavior is to be assessed by a presentational standard. The question becomes how well one performs one's various roles. This is not, of course, Burke's personal view. He seems to hold that good communication not only surmounts division, but also engenders humane, reasonable action. The norm of humane, reasonable action, however, is not intrinsic to dramatism; it is Burke's own commitment and appears to be the motivating force behind his theory. Not all successful identification results in humane, reasonable action. No theory can ensure such an end, but the narrative paradigm is designed to further it by incorporating the concept of identification to account for how people come to adopt stories and, by adding the concept of narrative rationality, a "logic" intrinsic to the very idea of narrativity. That people's symbolic actions take the form of stories and that they assess them by the principles of coherence and fidelity are the essential points of difference between dramatism and the narrative paradigm.

CONCLUSION

The historical sketch I have given here reveals that, since the time of the pre-Socratics and Plato and Aristotle, there has been a great contest that might be epitomized in "Logos, logos, who's got the logos?" One cannot blame all the ills of the intellectual world on this historic struggle for professional hegemony, but the conflicts have contributed to contemporary confusion by repressing realization of a holistic sense of self, by subverting formulation of a humane concept of rationality and sane praxis, by rendering personal and public decision making and action subservient to "experts" on knowledge, truth, and reality, and by elevating some classes of persons and discourse over others. The moral I would draw is this: some discourse is more veracious, reliable, and trustworthy in respect to knowledge, truth, and reality than some other discourse, but no *form* or *genre* has final claim to these virtues. Some persons know more than others, are wiser, and are more to be heeded than others. But no one knows all there is to know even about his or her own area of specialization. I contend further that human communication in all of its forms is imbued with mythos—ideas that cannot be verified or proved in any absolute way. Such ideas arise in metaphor, values, gestures, and so on. On occasion, they also arise through clear-cut inferential or implicative structures. I take it as fact, also, that mythos has cognitive as well as aesthetic significance.

In the beginning was the logos as a concept that incorporated all of the facts above and more. The concept should be similarly inclusive today, and it can be if the narrative paradigm or some similar construct commands the adherence of those who study and practice the arts of human communication.

I have been exploring the exigence that gives rise to the basic construct of the narrative paradigm. In the next chapter, I shall consider the exigence that calls for its logic—narrative rationality. My central contention is that *narrative* is a concept that can enhance understanding of human communication and action wherever those phenomena occur. To view discourse and action as occurring within "the human story" will allow us to account for human behavior in ways that are not possible using the theories and methods of the social sciences, especially those social sciences that attempt to approximate the paradigm of the natural sciences. The historical exigence that makes a fresh viewpoint necessary has been, as I have just shown, the tendencies of modern Western philosophies to treat truth, knowledge, and reality as the business of "experts" only, and to deny the intellectual, the cognitive content of rhetorical and poetic discourse. The difficulty has been that these tendencies place that which is not *formally* logical or which is not characterized by *expertise* within a somehow subhuman framework of behavior. I contend that we are not *irrational* in all of our nonformal, lay functions, and I turn now to the topic of what I shall call "narrative rationality." This notion implies that all instances of human communication are imbued with logos and mythos, are constitutive of truth and knowledge, and are rational.

NOTES

1. See chapter 3. For Thomas S. Frentz and Thomas B. Farrell reference, see *Quarterly Journal of Speech* 62 (1976): 333–49.
2. Walter Ong, *Orality and Literacy: The Technologizing of the Word* (London: Methuen, 1982).
3. Samuel Ijsseling, *Rhetoric and Philosophy in Conflict: An Historical Survey* (The Hague: Martinus Nijhoff, 1976).
4. Laszlo Versenyi, *Man's Measure: A Study of the Greek Image of Man from Homer to Sophocles* (Albany: State University of New York Press, 1982), p. 2. Cf. Martin Heidegger, "Logos (Heraclitus, Fragment B50)," in *Early Greek Thinking*, trans. David Farrell Krell and Frank A. Capuzzi (New York: Harper and Row, 1975).
5. Eric Havelock, "The Linguistic Task of the PreSocratics," in Kevin Robb, ed., *Language and Thought in Early Greek Philosophy* (La Salle, Ill.: Monist Library on Philosophy, 1983), p. 21.

6. Eric Havelock, *Preface to Plato* (Cambridge, Mass.: Belknap Press of Harvard University, 1963), p. 236.

7. Robert Price, "Some Antistrophes to the *Rhetoric*," *Philosophy and Rhetoric* 1 (1968): 147ff. Robert Price argues convincingly that the impression that Aristotle did not see the *Analytics* and the *Rhetoric* as parallel was created and maintained by the way his works have been arranged and treated in collections of his corpus.

8. George Campbell, *The Philosophy of Rhetoric,* ed. Lloyd F. Bitzer (Carbondale: Southern Illinois University Press, 1963).

9. Hugh Blair, *Lectures on Rhetoric and Belle Lettres,* ed. Harold F. Harding (2 vols.; Carbondale: Southern Illinois University Press, 1965).

10. Richard Whately, *Elements of Rhetoric,* ed. Douglas Ehninger (Carbondale: Southern Illinois University Press, 1963).

11. Alexander Bain, *English Composition and Rhetoric: A Manual* (London: Longmans, 1866).

12. Adams Sherman Hill, *Principles of Rhetoric* (New York: American Book Co., 1895).

13. René Descartes, *Discourse on Method,* trans. L. J. Lafeur (New York: Bobbs-Merrill, 1956), p. 5.

14. Ibid., p. 6.

15. John Locke, *An Essay concerning Human Understanding,* ed. A. C. Fraser (2 vols.; New York: Dover Books, 1959), vol. 2, p. 228.

16. Ibid., p. 146.

17. Thomas Sprat, *The History of the Royal-Society of London,* eds. Jackson I. Cope and N. W. Jones (St. Louis, Mo.: Washington University Studies, 1959), p. 114.

18. Richard Bernstein, *Beyond Objectivism and Relativism: Science, Hermeneutics, and Praxis* (Philadelphia: University of Pennsylvania Press, 1983).

19. Hans-George Gadamer, *Truth and Method* (New York: Crossroad Publishing Co., 1982).

20. Jürgen Habermas, *The Theory of Communicative Action: Reason and Rationalization of Society,* trans. Thomas A. McCarthy (Boston: Beacon Press, 1983).

21. Richard Rorty, *Philosophy and the Mirror of Nature* (Princeton, N.J.: Princeton University Press, 1979).

22. Calvin O. Schrag, *Radical Reflection and the Origins of the Human Sciences* (West Lafayette, Inc.: Purdue University Press, 1980); and *Communicative Praxis and the Space of Subjectivity* (Bloomington: Indiana University Press, 1986).

23. Stephen Toulmin, *The Return to Cosmology: Postmodern Science and the Theory of Nature* (Berkeley: University of California Press, 1982).

24. Fritjof Capra, *The Turning Point: Science, Society, and the Rising Culture* (Toronto: Bantam Books, 1983).

25. Longinus, *On the Sublime,* trans. W. R. Roberts (Cambridge, England: University Press, 1907), p. 43.

26. Ibid., pp. 57–58.

27. Giovanni Boccaccio, *Genealogy of the Gentile Gods,* in *Boccaccio on*

Poetry, trans. C. G. Osgood (Princeton, N.J.: Princeton University Press, 1930), p. 39.

28. Ibid., p. 42.

29. Ibid., pp. 39–40.

30. Ibid., p. 42.

31. Sir Philip Sidney, "An Apologie for Poetrie," in Mark Shorer, J. Miles, and G. McKensie, eds., *Criticism: The Foundation of Modern Literary Judgments* (New York: Harcourt, Brace & World, 1958), p. 416.

32. Ibid., p. 421.

33. Friedrich Wilhelm von Schiller, *On the Relation of the Plastic Arts to Nature,* trans. J. E. Cabot, in Hazard Adams, ed., *Critical Theory since Plato* (New York: Harcourt Brace Jovanovich, 1971), p. 419.

34. Ibid., pp. 419–20.

35. John Huizinga, *Homo Ludens: A Study of the Play-Element in Culture,* trans. R. F. C. Hull (London: Routledge & Kegan Paul, 1950).

36. Schiller, *Plastic Arts,* p. 426.

37. Benedetto Croce, *Aesthetic as Science Expression and General Linguistics,* trans. D. Ainslie, in Adams, *Critical Theory,* p. 727.

38. I. A. Richards, "Science and Poetry," in Shorer et al., *Criticism,* p. 519.

39. Ibid., p. 517.

40. Ibid., p. 518.

41. I. A. Richards, *Coleridge on Imagination* (Bloomington: Indiana University Press, 1965), p. 163.

42. Allen Tate, "Literature as Knowledge," in his *Essays of Four Decades* (Chicago: Swallow Press, 1968), p. 104.

43. Ibid., p. 105.

44. Gerald Graff, *Literature against Itself: Literary Ideas in Society* (Chicago: University of Chicago Press, 1979).

45. *Isocrates,* trans. G. Norlin (3 vols.; New York: G. P. Putnam, 1928), Introduction, vol. 1, p. xxiii.

46. *Isocrates,* vol. 2, pp. 327–29.

47. Cicero, *De oratore,* trans. E. W. Sutton and N. Rackman, (2 vols.; Cambridge, Mass.: Harvard University Press, 1959), vol. 1, p. 25.

48. Ibid., p. 51.

49. Ibid., pp. 89–90.

50. Ralph Waldo Emerson, "The American Scholar," in A. Craig Baird, ed., *American Public Addresses, 1740–1952* (New York: McGraw-Hill, 1956), p. 128.

51. Giambattista Vico, *On the Study of Methods of Our Time,* trans. E. Gianturco (New York: Bobbs-Merrill, 1965), p. 19.

52. Ibid., p. 13.

53. Ernesto Grassi, *Rhetoric as Philosophy: The Humanist Tradition* (University Park: Pennsylvania State University Press, 1979), p. 8.

54. Ibid., p. 16.

55. Ibid., p. 113.

56. Robert L. Scott, "On Viewing Rhetoric as Epistemic," *Central States Speech Journal* 18 (1967): 9–17; and "On Viewing Rhetoric as Epistemic: Ten Years Later," *Central States Speech Journal* 28 (1976): 258–66.

57. See Lloyd F. Bitzer, "Rhetoric and Knowledge," in Don Burks, ed., *Rhetoric, Philosophy, and Literature: An Exploration* (West Lafayette, Ind.: Purdue University Press, 1978), pp. 67–93; Alan Brinton, "William James and the Epistemic View of Rhetoric," *Quarterly Journal of Speech* 68 (1982): 158–69; Walter M. Carlton, "What Is Rhetorical Knowledge? A Reply to Farrell—and More," *Quarterly Journal of Speech* 64 (1978): 313–28, and "On Rhetorical Knowing," *Quarterly Journal of Speech* 71 (1985): 227–37; Richard A. Cheriwitz and James W. Hikins, *Communication and Knowledge: An Investigation in Rhetorical Epistemology* (Columbia: University of South Carolina Press, 1986); Douglas Ehninger, "Science, Philosophy—and Rhetoric: A Look toward the Future," in James L. Golden, G. F. Berquist, and W. E. Coleman, eds., *The Rhetoric of Western Thought* (3rd ed.; Dubuque, Iowa: Kendall/Hunt, 1983), pp. 454–64; Thomas B. Farrell, "Knowledge, Consensus, and Rhetorical Theory," *Quarterly Journal of Speech* 62 (1976): 1–14, and "Social Knowledge II," *Quarterly Journal of Speech* 64 (1978): 329–34; Richard B. Gregg, *Symbolic Inducement and Knowing: A Study in the Foundation of Rhetoric* (Columbia: University of South Carolina Press, 1984); Michael Calvin McGee and Martha Ann Martin, "Public Knowledge and Ideological Argumentation," *Communication Monographs* 50 (1983): 47–65.

58. Bitzer, "Rhetoric and Knowledge," p. 68.

59. Farrell, "Knowledge," p. 4.

60. Karlyn K. Campbell, "The Ontological Foundations of Rhetorical Theory," *Philosophy and Rhetoric* 3 (1970): 97–108.

61. Walter R. Fisher, "Rhetorical Fiction and the Presidency," *Quarterly Journal of Speech* 66 (1980): 119–26.

62. Chaïm Perelman and L. Olbrechts-Tyteca, *The New Rhetoric: A Treatise on Argumentation,* trans. J. Wilkinson and P. Weaver (Notre Dame, Ind.: University of Notre Dame Press, 1969), p. 14.

63. Chaïm Perelman, "Authority, Ideology, and Violence," in *The New Rhetoric and the Humanities: Essays on Rhetoric and Its Explications* (Dordrecht, Holland: D. Reidel, 1979), p. 142.

64. Kenneth Burke, *A Rhetoric of Motives* (New York: George Braziller, 1955), pp. 19–46.

65. Ibid., p. 172.

66. Kenneth Burke, *Counter-Statement* (Berkeley: University of California Press, 1968 reprint), p. 124.

2

THE CONNECTION
WITH LOGIC

For reasons I have sketched in chapter 1, logos in the sense of genuinely serious, rational discourse had by the twentieth century come to be thought of as occurring primarily in philosophical and technical discourse. Rhetoric and poetic were widely thought of as vacuous or irrational modes of communication. The response to this situation that I am proposing is to view human communication narratively. The narrative paradigm proposes that human beings are inherently storytellers who have a natural capacity to recognize the coherence and fidelity of stories they tell and experience. I suggest that we experience and comprehend life as a series of ongoing narratives, as conflicts, characters, beginnings, middles, and ends. The various modes of communication—all forms of symbolic action—then may be seen as stories, interpretations of things in sequences. Viewed this way, all kinds of discourse are reflective of logos in one degree or another. Not only do philosophical and technical discourses exhibit logos, so do rhetoric and poetic. By adopting this perspective, we return to the original conception of logos. In that conception all communicative behavior was presumed to be rational, although not necessarily in the same way.

In this chapter I shall explore the meanings of dialogue, dialectic, and logic, and trace key moments in the evolving relationships of "logics" to philosophical and technical discourse, and to rhetoric. The first thing to note is that there is no history of the relationship of logic to poetic, since no one has maintained that poetic is related to logic conceived as a technical discipline that provides concepts, procedures, and criteria by which to ascertain rational knowledge. However, if one views logic broadly enough to encompass metaphysics, as did Giambattista Vico, one can conceptualize "poetic logic." Vico wrote:

That which is metaphysics insofar as it contemplates things in all the forms of their being, is logic insofar as it considers things in all the forms by which they may be signified. Accordingly, as poetry has

24

been considered by us . . . as a poetic metaphysics in which the theological poets imagined bodies to be for the most part divine substances, so now that same poetry is considered as poetic logic, by which it signifies them.[1]

As I have said, there have been those who have insisted that poetic generates knowledge, but no one, including Vico, has maintained that poetry itself is produced by logic or can be assessed by it usefully.[2] I do not yet see how the narrative paradigm I am urging explains the "invention" of aesthetic forms of communication, but I shall argue in what follows that this paradigm does open up a logic for assessing such communicative forms. I shall call this logic "narrative rationality."

DIALOGUE, DIALECTIC, AND LOGIC

No unequivocal meanings can be assigned to dialogue, dialectic, and logic, but it is essential for appreciation of the story that follows to differentiate among them. Despite the frequent overlapping and confusion of them, particularly in the Middle Ages, I shall maintain with modern classical scholars that the terms and the practices to which they refer are not the same.[3] Dialogue and dialectic are not synonymous; nor are dialectic and logic. Dialogue and dialectic exhibit rationality in form and at times in content, but this is not unique; other forms of intellection, method, and communication also exhibit rationality in form and content.

Dialogue has two primary meanings. First, it names a literary form—a dramatized conversation among proponents of rival ideas. Second, it refers to a form of communication in which persons mutually engage in and constitute a transaction and the message that emerges from it. Dialogic communication contrasts with monologue, which is a transaction in which one person addresses the self or one or more others who attend. The essence of dialogic communication is implied in Martin Buber's conception of the transactions between "I" and "Thou." He writes: "There is a genuine dialogue—no matter whether spoken or silent— where each of the participants really has in mind the other or others in their present and particular being and turns to them with the intention of establishing a living mutual relationship between himself and them."[4] Truth or sound reasoning may occur in such encounters, but they are not necessary features of them.

Dialectic has several meanings, but in all of them a constant method of thinking is posited: oppositional juxtaposition of ideas or forces moving toward truth or a perfected state of knowledge or being. The earliest

25

record of dialectic is Zeno's use of *reductio ad absurdum* to refute the Pythagoreans.[5] In Plato's philosophy, dialectic was the "science of correctly dividing the structure of reality according to those Forms or Kinds which are the meanings referred to in philosophic discourse."[6] Neither Zeno's nor Plato's concept of dialectic requires dialogue or the presence of logic *as a formalized system for the assessment of reasoning.* For Zeno, dialectic was a method of argument, of revealing contradictions; for Plato, dialectic was a way of arriving at definitions, of winnowing out attributes of conceptions that did not belong so that the result was a true apprehension of things.

It is relevant to note that logic, as we know it, was not "invented" until Aristotle formulated the *Analytics.* Indeed, "The name *logic* is unknown to Aristotle, and cannot be traced further back than the time of Cicero. Even then *logica* means not so much logic as dialectic, and Alexander is the first writer to use λογική in the sense of logic."[7] Foundational to Aristotle's *Analytics* were "propositions ascribing a predicate to all the individuals in a class." As I have said, foundational to Plato's dialectic (in a sense, his logic) was "the definition of an indivisible species—a Form—by genus and specific differences." What is defined is "not 'all men' but the unique Form 'man.' "[8]

For Aristotle, dialectic was the counterpart of rhetoric. The two were alike in being concerned with argument and the contingent world.[9] However, dialectic's realm was theoretical knowledge and rhetoric's province was practical reasoning leading to civic judgments and actions. "Dialectic," Aristotle held, "is a process of criticism wherein lies the path to the principles of all inquiries."[10] Dialectic, therefore, was the modus operandi of the philosopher as he or she rationally constitutes knowledge, whether in the presence of others or only in his or her mind.

It is not surprising that dialectic is a recurrent concept throughout the history of philosophy. Following Zeno, Plato, and Aristotle, the most important variations in the idea of dialectic have been those of Kant, Hegel, Marx, and Kenneth Burke. Kant critiques dialectic in order to remove what he saw as a tendency in it to move thought away from a sound grasp of reality. Where the ancient Greeks conceived dialectic as a mode of thought, Hegel and Marx saw it not only as a way of thinking, but also as a movement in reality itself. For Hegel, dialectic at bottom was an ideational/spiritual process; for Marx, it was a dynamic materialistic movement. Marx saw this movement in the evolution of history, specifically in the struggle between workers and owners, which would eventuate in a classless society. Dialectic retains its oppositional nature in Burke's dramatism, but he uses the term to refer to "the employment of the possibilities of linguistic transformation." Its constituents include merger and division; resolution of such dualisms as action-passion, mind-body, and being-nothing; and particularity and transcendence.[11] Historically, dialectic has almost always been treated as mode of intellection, and from such thinking logic was born.

More than seventy years ago, Robert Adamson wrote a major article on logic for the *Encyclopaedia Britannica,* and it later appeared as a book, *A Short History of Logic.* In considering the "Province and Method of Logic," Adamson concluded: "Looking at the chaotic state of logical textbooks at the present time, one would be inclined to say there does not exist anywhere a recognized, currently received body of speculations to which the title logic can be unambiguously assigned."[12] The intervening years did not alter this situation. In 1958 Toulmin asserted that "The question, 'What sort of a science is logic?', leads us to an impasse."[13]

Fortunately, it is unnecessary for our purposes to resolve the problems of ambiguity and definition. It is enough to specify what I shall mean when I use the term "logic." Logic will mean a systematic set of concepts, procedures, and criteria for determining the degree of truthfulness or certainty in human discourse. The logics relevant to my inquiry are those that have been most influential in the history of rhetoric: the deductive logic of Aristotle, the inductive logics of Bacon and Mill, and the mathematical, positivistic logics of such writers as Descartes, Auguste Comte, Bertrand Russell and A. N. Whitehead, and A. J. Ayer. These are logics in the classical mode. They are what I shall call technical logics. I shall contrast them with the informal logics of Toulmin and Perelman, which have come to dominate contemporary theories and textbooks on rhetoric and argumentation. These informal logics are related to what I shall call *rhetorical logic,* and in what follows I shall juxtapose rhetorical logic to *technical logic.*

ARISTOTLE: THE BEGINNINGS OF TECHNICAL AND RHETORICAL LOGIC

As "inventor" of logic, Aristotle is "father" to both technical and rhetorical logic. The foundation of technical logic is presented in his *Categories, On Interpretation,* and the *Prior* and *Posterior Analytics.* The ideas that inform rhetorical logic are contained in his *Topics, On Sophistical Refutations,* and the *Rhetoric.* Central to both logics is argument, which Aristotle conceives as a demonstration based on the model of geometry. The classical form of argument for Aristotle is the syllogism: ". . . discourse in which, certain things being stated, something other than what is stated follows of necessity from their being so."[14] The basic form of this discourse is: all men are animals, all animals are mortal, all men are mortal. The geometric expression would be: $A = B$; $B = C$; $A = C$. What is most significant to a consideration of the relationship of logic and rhetoric is that the rules by which analytic syllogisms are judged to be *valid*, that is, the conclusions follow necessarily from their premises, are *formal*. Validity is tested without regard to the characteristics of the entities referred to in the premises. The tests concern the distribution of terms, whether the premises are general or particular, and whether the premises are affirmative or negative. For analytic syllogisms to yield true as well as valid conclusions, their premises must be true. In Aristotle's theory of knowledge only science was invested with such premises and could produce what he called apodictic proof.

The differences between technical and rhetorical logics are suggested by the foregoing. Technical logic aims at true knowledge; its procedures and criteria are formal and removed from context; and its conclusions are pan-historical, true always and everywhere. Rhetorical logic deals in probable knowledge; its procedures and criteria are analogs to those of technical logic or are distinct in content and function; and its conclusions are time-bound, contingent, civic, and cultural. Technical logic concerns argument as inference or implicature; rhetorical logic concerns arguing—reasoning with an audience, which, in Aristotle's philosophy, has a natural capacity for "practical wisdom."

To further clarify this relationship between technical and rhetorical logics, it is useful to consider Aristotle's concept of the enthymeme, a deductive argument in natural language. He promotes the enthymeme in the *Rhetoric* as the very substance of persuasion. When an arguer suppresses one or more parts of a rhetorical syllogism, the arguer invites an audience to complete it, thereby contributing to its own persuasion and exhibiting its rationality in the process. The constituents of enthymemes are signs and probabilities, contingent matters; therefore, enthymemes cannot, except in rare instances, produce true as well as valid conclusions. Furthermore, this sort of rhetorical proof, while a logical form of demonstration, cannot be an instrument of true knowledge; it is, in a sense, a shadow of reason addressed to and exercised by "untrained thinkers."

The elements of rhetorical logic can be enumerated as follows. (1) Rhetorical logic is a logic of conceptions and classifications of reasoned modes of discourse. Most often, it is a logic of argumentation—of maintaining and countering theses about what is contingent. (2) Rhetorical logic provides canons by which reason in discourse can be assessed. Usually these canons are variants of the standards of technical logic. (3) Rhetorical logic diverges from technical logic especially in the fact that it offers principles of *topical* analysis of subject matters. Rhetorical theory identifies questions *(topoi)* that can be reasonably asked about a subject that is controverted in one or another traditional way or is argued in a classifiable kind of rhetorical situation. These questions identify *possible* "lines of argument" that can then be evaluated for their appropriateness as argumentative strategies in the anticipated rhetorical situation. (4) Rhetorical logic posits *stases* or types of argumentative clash that are dictated by the "logic" of different forms of controversy such as forensic and deliberative controversies. In historic disputes about the relative merits of technical and rhetorical logics, the central questions have been whether argument that follows technical logic is appropriate and useful in making and assessing everyday argument and whether there is need or value in *topical* analysis and in the theory of *stasis*.

Aristotle made contributions to rhetorical logic beyond those I have mentioned. First, he distinguished several kinds of argument that rhetoric (and dialectic) employ; the argumentative forms are general and have no specific subject matter. They "apply equally to questions of right conduct, natural science, politics, and many other things that have nothing to do with one another."[15] Typical of general lines of argument are those that concern the possible and the impossible, more or less, and greatness and smallness. Arguments intrinsic to "particular groups or classes of things," Aristotle designated as "special Lines of Argument."[16] The more one moves into a given discipline or art, the more one moves away from rhetoric per se and requires criteria and content peculiar to some other art or science. Aristotle did not say so, but the last observation seems to imply that there can be a number of special rhetorics—of science, of fine arts, and so on.

Second, Aristotle provided, in the *Rhetoric,* twenty-eight lines of positive proof and nine examples of enthymemes that "look genuine but are not."[17] On both matters his discussion was unsystematic and ranges from possible lines of reasoning to the strategies and tactics an arguer may use in overcoming an adversary. His *Topics* is similar in treatment. It elaborates lines of dialectical reasoning and offers guides to dialectical disputation. William and Martha Kneale observe that the *Topics* influenced "students of philosophy until the seventeenth century, but we cannot in retrospect say that it has contributed much to the development of logic."[18]

29

One should note that these authors had in mind technical, not rhetorical, logic. Aristotle's *Topics* was followed by Cicero's *Topics,* which shifted in focus from largely dialectical concerns to rhetorical concerns.

Aristotle's third major contribution to rhetorical logic was his delineation of some of the genres of persuasive discourse and their characterizing themes. "The political orator," he thought, "aims at establishing the expediency or the harmfulness of a proposed course of action." The politician's concern is the future. The forensic orator is concerned with the past, with justice and injustice. And the ceremonial orator is involved in the present, whether someone or something is deserving of praise or blame.[19] His idea that forms of discourse or controversy inherently entail stock issues led to the doctrine of *stasis.*

Aristotle foreshadowed this development in his identification of the necessary considerations in forensic dispute:

> (1) If you maintain that the act *was not committed,* your main task in court is to prove this. (2) If you maintain that the act *did no harm,* prove this. If you maintain that (3) the act was *less* than is alleged, or (4) *justified,* prove these facts, just as you would prove the act not to have been committed if you were maintaining that.[20]

Later, another forensic issue was added by the Romans; it was the question of procedure. The essential issues of forensic debate are today the same as Aristotle and the Romans proposed.

Artistotle's contributions to rhetorical logic cannot be overestimated. Only his insistence on the syllogism, the geometric model of demonstration, and its formal rules of assessment limit the usefulness of his rhetorical logic. Kenneth Burke is a somewhat dubious witness to the significance of Aristotle's contribution to rhetorical logic, since he does not himself privilege argument or provide a "logic," but he writes that "those who talk of 'ethical relativity' must be impressed by the 'permanence' of 'places' or topics, when stated at Aristotle's level of abstraction." A contemporary speaker, he observes, "might often have to individuate them in a different *image* than the Greeks," but they are no less compelling than they ever were.[21]

TECHNICAL LOGIC: HANDMAIDEN OF LEARNED DISCOURSE

In using the expression "the relationship of technical and rhetorical logic," I have suggested that there has been reciprocity between the disciplines. The truth is, however, that technical logicians have never borrowed from or much countenanced the work of the rhetoricians concerned with reason and rationality in human discourse. The relationship has been basically one way: technical logicians pronounce; rhetoricians approve, renounce, or modify. This was especially the case after Aristotle's *Organon* was challenged in the sixteenth century by Francis Bacon's *Novum Organum* and technical logic became more and more the hand-maiden of the empirical science. In the process, technical logic became more and more technical, more and more removed from application to the "popular" arts of discourse and more and more divorced from the contingencies of everyday life. Technical logic shifted from an emphasis on deductive logic, to inductive methods of investigation, to mathematical models of inference, to purely symbolic forms. These shifts were accompanied by a strong tendency to identify technical logic with "learned discourse" and to distance logic and learning from such conceptions as wisdom, metaphysics, and even the "mind." This tendency, coupled with the tendency of rhetoricians in the nineteenth century to identify rhetoric with verbal form but not with content, all but expunged interest in the rationality of everyday discourse.

For those interested in the details of the history of technical logic, there are several excellent studies: *A Short History of Logic*, by Robert Adamson;[22] *The Historic Development of Logic: The Principles and Structure of Science in the Conception of Mathematical Thinkers*, by Federigo Enriques;[23] *The Development of Logic*, by William and Martha Kneale;[24] and *A History of Formal Logic*, by I. M. Bochenski.[25] For my purposes, it is sufficient to notice and emphasize that direct attacks were made on the chief components of Aristotle's conceptions of technical and rhetorical logic, specifically (1) his privileging of syllogistic (deductive) argument, and (2) his observations regarding the invention of argument for dialectical and rhetorical advocacy, using mechanisms of the topics and stasis.

Bacon's new logic was a frontal assault on both conceptions. (This attack, like that of Descartes, was not directed toward Aristotle's conceptions as he wrote them, but as they were represented in the "corrupt" textbooks of the day.[26]) First, Bacon proposed that the proper concern of logic should be "The art of interpreting Nature. . . ." Its purpose would be "to find, not arguments, but arts; not what agrees with principles, but principles themselves: not probable reasons, but plans and designs of works." Logic must be the rationale of empirical investigation. Of the syllogism, Bacon wrote that "we reject the syllogistic method as being too confused . . ." for scientific investigation.[27] He would leave it for "popular and speculative arts; while for everything relating to the nature of things, we make use of induction. . . ."[28] This inversion of deduction and induction was necessary because "Those who determine not to conjecture and guess, but to find out and know; not to invent fables and romances of worlds, but to look into, and dissect the nature of this real world, must consult only things themselves."[29] Thus, where Aristotle had seen knowledge as a product of a dialectical mind contemplating human existence, in Bacon's theory knowledge was a product of empirical investigation of physical nature. Rhetoric became for Bacon the art of transmitting the results of scientific investigations. For Aristotle, knowledge entailed understanding the manifold forms of life and matter, including communicative experiences. Bacon was interested in achieving power over things, and gave little attention to communicative experience.

A second consequence of Bacon's new logic was to diminish the value of topics. Just as he had inverted deduction and induction, so he inverted the traditional concept of invention. "The invention of arguments," he wrote, "is not properly an invention; for to invent, is to discover things unknown before, and not to recollect or admit such as already known."[30] He held that an arguer who knew little or nothing about a subject would have "no use of topics" and an arguer who did know a subject could "find and produce an argument, without the help of art." Invention through the use of topics, he insisted, is "a bare calling to memory, or a suggestion with application," rather "than a real invention."[31] In short, real invention involves *discovery*, rhetorical (dialectical) invention is a process of *recovery*.

While the move to empiricism was given substance by practicing scientists, such as Galileo Galilei (1564–1630), Johannes Kepler (1571–1630), and later Isaac Newton (1642–1727), it received its most important justification in the philosophy of John Locke (1632–1704). Like Bacon, Locke thought that traditional logic did not advance true knowledge. Indeed, this was his chief complaint against the syllogism: "This way of reasoning discovers no new proofs but is the art of marshalling and ranging the old ones we have already."[32] The textbook syllogism about Socrates' mortality illustrates Locke's meaning. It begins by asserting a truth—all men are mortal; then applies a particular instance—Socrates is a man; and concludes with what is obvious from the outset—Socrates is a mortal. The premise that all men are mortal is actually more doubtful than its conclusion. Locke held that syllogism cannot exhaust the possibilities of reasoning and that, in proper form, syllogisms will yield only consistent statements. Put another way: the syllogism is a verbal maneuver the terms of which have no necessary connection with real things. Given this view, it is no wonder that Locke dismissed Scholastic disputation, which relied on syllogistic argument. The "admired Art of Disputing," he wrote, "hath added much to the natural imperfection of languages, whilst it has been made use of and fitted to perplex the significance of words, more than to discover the knowledge and truth of things."[33] For Locke, understanding was obtained when one had clear and distinct ideas that corresponded accurately with the data of the real world. Perhaps it is needless to say that Locke gave no attention to the topics as a part of rhetorical theory.

A number of philosophers followed Bacon and Locke in advancing the new empiricism and in repudiating or minimizing the usefulness of syllogisms and the topics. Principal among these philosophers in England were Isaac Watts, William Duncan, David Hume, Thomas Reid, and John Stuart Mill who was regarded for some decades as perfecting inductive logic. Most important on the continent was René Descartes (1596–1659), who differed from the English writers in insisting on mathematics (analytic geometry) as the ideal of cognition. He was, strictly speaking, a rationalist rather than an empiricist. His central contribution to the new science was a method, which included the apperception of indubitable principles, analysis of their elementary components, and synthesis. Descartes's view of traditional logic was the same as that of Bacon and Locke. Along with the other methods of the old logic (that was cluttered with mistaken notions, including notions about the functions of the topics), syllogisms serve "to explain to another what one already knows . . ., to speak without judgment of what one does not know" rather than "to learn new things."[34]

Descartes's attitude was reflected in the *Port-Royal Logic* (1662), which in its turn influenced Locke's thinking. Its author, Antoine Arnauld, noted in his introduction to "Reasoning" that "If any man is unable to detect by the light of reason alone the invalidity of an argument, then he is probably incapable of understanding the rules by which we judge an argument valid—and still less to apply these rules." Arnauld could only have had syllogism in mind as he wrote these lines. He went on to say, however, that "these rules provide good material for mental discipline."[35] He was much less kind in talking abut the topics:

True, all arguments can be classified under the headings or general terms called Topics; but arguments are not discovered by means of

33

this classification. Common sense, a careful consideration of a subject, the knowledge of many truths—these enable us to find arguments; and then skill allows us to classify these arguments under certain headings; the Topics.[36]

Again, however, because "it may be good to know about the Topics," he discussed them—as he found them in grammar, logic, and metaphysics. In short, the elements of Aristotle's technical and rhetorical logics were alive after Bacon, but they definitely were not well. This fact was to have a profound effect on conceptions of rhetoric, which I shall demonstrate when the story turns to an explicit review of rhetorical logic.

As I have already mentioned, technical logic became more and more technical through the nineteenth and early twentieth centuries. How this came about is detailed in William Barrett's fine book, *The Illusion of Technique*.[37] It is sufficient here to note two developments that cinched the separation of logic from rhetorical concerns: positivism and mathematical (symbolic) logic. With their ascendance, metaphysics was relegated to idle speculation, values were conceived as emotive "non-sense," and even "mind" was said to be irrelevant to logical processes.

Before Nietzsche declared that God was dead, Auguste Comte, the founder of positivism, pronounced the demise of metaphysics. He held that metaphysics was but a stage in intellectual history, a stage followed by theology and then positivism. In this final stage, he wrote, "the mind has given over the vain search after Absolute notions, the origin and destination of the universe, and the causes of phenomena, and applies itself to the study of their laws—that is, the invariable relations of succession and resemblance."[38] One may read this interpretation as a pronouncement not only about the past and the present, but also about the future—henceforth serious thought will concern only verifiable laws. If Comte's pronouncement did but slow metaphysical investigation, the work of logical positivists who followed him rendered it moribund.

Writing in 1959, Rudolf Carnap serenely declared: "Metaphysics are neither true nor false, because they assert nothing, they contain neither knowledge nor error, they lie completely outside the field of knowledge."[39] One can make such a statement only if one believes in the fundamental tenet of logical positivism, which is that a statement is meaningful if, and only if, it is directly or indirectly verifiable or certifiable by the rules of logic.[40] Since rhetorical discourse is replete with what Chaïm Perelman called "confused notions," such as wisdom, justice, honor, the true and good, it obviously cannot be taken as a serious intellectual activity within a positivist framework.[41]

Adherence to the verifiability principle led to an emotive theory of values. Advanced by philosophers including G. E. Moore, C. L. Stevenson, and A. J. Ayer, this theory of values was the basis of C. K. Ogden and I. A. Richards's delineation of statements as referential (the language of science), emotive (the language of poetry and religion—pseudo-statements), and rhetorical (the language of practical life—mixed statements).[42] Thus the "end" of metaphysics was confirmed and logic was made irrelevant to any use of language that was not scientific.

While positivism was denying metaphysics, a legitimate mathematical (symbolic) logic was moving toward a negation of "mind." Following a line of thought stretching from Aristotle through the works of Gottfried Leibniz, George Boole, and Gottlob Frege, Bertrand Russell asserted in 1905:

> Throughout logic and mathematics, the existence of the human mind or any mind is totally irrelevant; mental processes are studied by means of logic, but the subject-matter of logic does not presuppose mental processes and would be equally true if there were no mental processes. It is true that in that case we should not know logic; but our knowledge must not be confounded with the truths which we know.[43]

Once this position is taken, it is extremely difficult to contemplate any meaningful or illuminating relationship of logic to philosophy, rhetoric, or any other of the disciplines concerned with human affairs. Logic is now the province of formalized systems. This turn means that logic stands apart from issues such as those addressed by the narrative paradigm: How do people come to believe and act on the basis of communicative experiences? What is the nature of reason and rationality in these experiences? What is the role of values in human decision making and action? How can reason and values be assessed?

Various forces arose to counter the formalization of logic. The investigations of Kurt Gödel[44] and Werner Heisenberg[45] made it clear that even scientific thinking is not carried out entirely within the confines of formal systems. Formal logic was found by an early true believer, Ludwig Wittgenstein, in his later writings, to be irreducibly limited in providing an account of what actually goes on in ordinary discourse and action. It was superseded by the jurisprudentially grounded informal logics proposed by Stephen Toulmin[46] and Perelman.[47] And it was opposed by existentialism and hermeneutics.

The principal consequences of these responses to the development of technical logic are: (1) a "crisis" in philosophy—how can philosophy fulfill its traditional role of systematic wonder and statement about existence if its instrument for ascertaining knowledge rules out soul, heart, and mind? and (2) a new beginning for rhetoric as a theory and practice of reason and rationality in human communication.[48] Particularly important here are the paradigm shifts effected by Wittgenstein—from formal language to ordinary language; and by Toulmin and Perelman—from formal logic to informal logic. The nature of these shifts will be summarized later. I turn now to the high and low points in the story of rhetorical logic.

RHETORICAL LOGIC: HANDMAIDEN OF PUBLIC DISCOURSE

In reviewing the development of technical logic from Aristotle to Bacon and Descartes, Adamson observed: "The long history of philosophical thought from Aristotle to the beginning of the modern period furnishes no new conception of logic so complete and methodical as to require detailed treatment."[49] The same is not true of rhetorical logic. Its high points were during the Roman era and into the Renaissance. The Romans formalized and elaborated Aristotle's concepts of argument, types of argument, standards of assessment, topics, and *stasis*. They laid the foundation for systems of invention and evaluation that sporadically informed rhetorical thought from the time of Cicero to this moment. The influence of their ideas is particularly evident in argumentation textbooks from the late nineteenth century on—in the classification of arguments, the tests of reasoning, and treatment of "stock issues," a contemporary expression for *stasis*.

The first element in Aristotle's rhetorical logic to be formalized and elaborated was the enthymeme. Rather than three parts, Cicero and other Romans held that it should have five components: major premise, proof, minor premise, proof, and conclusion.[50] Proof, in this formulation, consists of one or more statements that express a premise in alternative, imaginative ways. This "new" form of argument was called epicheireme. (Aristotle had considered an epicheireme a type of dialectical reasoning.[51]) The justification for this innovation was that philosophical conceptions of deduction were "quite unfit for oratorical practice."[52] Another reason was that the epicheireme was a mode of discourse in which an orator could display his art through amplification of proofs in support of the premises; he could thereby distinguish himself from philosophers. The epicheireme was viewed as combining reason and eloquence. Significantly, neither the enthymeme nor the epicheireme have been central constructs in philosophies of rhetoric since the Greek and Roman eras. There are decisive epistemological reasons to account for this fact, but it is also the case that many rhetoricians over time have agreed with this statement from Cicero's *De Oratore:* "For men decide far more problems by hate, or love, or lust, or rage, or sorrow, or joy, or hope, or fear, or illusion, or some other inward emotion, than by reality, or authority, or any legal standard, or judicial precedent, or statute."[53]

The second element to be extended by the Romans was the classification of arguments. Their delineation of types of argument had a profound influence on later theory and teaching. Most responsible for this effect were the writings of Cicero, in particular his *Topica* and *De inventione.* While he believed that Aristotle was the "founder" of both branches of argumentation—"one concerned with invention of arguments and the other with judgment of their validity"—his treatment was different.[54] First, it did not privilege the syllogism, the model of geometric demonstration. Second, the standard of assessment for most arguments was not formal validity but how firmly an argument "establishes a matter about which there is some doubt."[55] Third, Aristotle's interest in his *Topics* was dialectical reasoning and argument; Cicero's concern in his *Topica* was rhetorical reasoning and argument, especially forensic dispute.

Throughout his delineation of types of argument in the *Topica,* Cicero first defined and then exemplified each type. At the outset, he distinguished arguments inherent in the nature of a subject from those brought in from outside the subject. In the first category, he included not only antecedents and consequents, which can be formal arguments, but also cause, effect, and analogy. In most instances, he did not indicate criteria for assessment. His treatment of analogy was an important exception, as it pointed the way to the development of appropriate considerations for evaluating nonformal arguments. Such considerations are the core of "place Logic." Cicero wrote: "All arguments from comparison are valid if they are of the following character: What is valid in the greater should be valid in the less, as for example since there is no action for regulating boundaries in the city, there should be no action excluding water in the city."[56] We should note that "valid" here does not have the same meaning as it has when applied to formal syllogisms. It does not mean in agreement with formal rules of inference. It means true, or solid, or firm—warrantable, in contemporary language. Cicero's "validity" is topical or "place logic" validity. Implicit in this kind of logic is the assumption that knowing how an argument is constructed carries with it knowledge of what inadequacies or strengths it can have. If we know the construction, we understand deconstruction too.

In treating extrinsic arguments, Cicero reviewed all sorts of reasoning from authority. (He also included "inartistic proof"—documents, wills, oaths, etc.—in this category.) His primary concerns here were with argument from testimony, the qualities that identify a competent, reliable witness, and the conditions that favorably or unfavorably influence the credibility of different sources of proof. Once again, such argument is nonformal and is a staple of rhetorical advocacy.

The topics received their fullest and most influential treatment in Ciceros' *De inventione* and in the anonymous *Rhetorica ad Herennium*. It is unnecessary to identify all the rhetorical topics covered in these works. An overview will indicate their complexity and completeness. Cicero's work was largely devoted to forensic topics. He treated such matters as the four basic issues, whether a case is simple or complex, the nature of the case arising out of documents, and lines of reasoning especially appropriate to each part of an oration (exordium, narrative, partition, confirmation, refutation, digression, and peroration). Cicero also detailed potential arguments respecting issues of fact, definition, competence, and quality; he explored problems associated with the interpretation of documents, such as ambiguity, letter and intent, conflict of laws, reasoning by analogy, and definition; and he made a relatively short excursion into deliberative and epideictic topics. In general, there is virtually no question that might be raised about how to prepare or present forensic arguments that is not anticipated and answered by Cicero's work.

The same may be said of the *Rhetorica ad Herennium*. It traverses the ground covered in *De inventione* and more. The book is concerned with all five arts comprising the broad art of rhetoric—invention, arrangement, style, delivery, and memory. It is a more or less complete prescriptive manual of the rhetor's art. The definitive manner in which *Ad Herennium* treats topics may be seen from the schematics for deliberative and epideictic addresses (Fig. 1).

It could be argued that the Latin rhetoricians multiplied and divided the topics that could suggest useful lines of argument to such a degree as to render their use in practical argument unduly difficult. On the other hand, what their exhaustive canvasses show are at least (1) that any culture has a *finite* number of ways of developing ideas, and the person who knows most of these ways is the better equipped to discover what to say

Deliberative Topics[57]

Advantage			
1. Security		**2. Honour**	
Might	Craft (Strategy)	The Right	The Praise-worthy, in the opinion of
(a) Armies	(a) Money	(a) Wisdom	(a) The proper authorities
(b) Fleets	(b) Promises	(b) Justice	(b) Our allies
(c) Arms	(c) Dissimulation	(c) Courage	(c) All our fellow-citizens
(d) Engines of war	(d) Accelerated speed	(d) Temperance	(d) Our descendants
(e) Manpower	(e) Deception		

Epideictic Topics[58]

1. External Circumstances	2. Physical Attributes	3. Qualities of Character
(a) Descent	(a) Agility	(a) Wisdom
(b) Education	(b) Strength	(b) Justice
(c) Wealth	(c) Beauty	(c) Courage
(d) Kinds of power	(d) Health	(d) Temperance
(e) Titles to fame		
(f) Citizenship		
(g) Friendships		

Figure 1. Deliberative and epideictic topics.

about any subject; (2) rhetorical situations narrow the number of options for creating relevant argumentation; and (3) there *is* a discovery, an inventional process in the making of rhetoric, and a measure of rhetorical effectiveness is whether or not a rhetor knows how to discover his or her practical options.

I do not wish to imply that the Romans were always clear about rhetorically inventive processes or that their ways of locating, presenting, and teaching the theory and practice of topical invention was ideal. What they achieved was to prove that rhetorical invention ought to be *systematic*. The terms *topos* and *topica* have always been somewhat ambiguous in rhetorical theory, but the idea that superior rhetorical discovery needs to be systematic is clear and useful. Much the same is true of the related concept of *stasis*. Otto Dieter provided this excellent summary of the development of the theory of *stasis:*

> In Pre-Aristotelian Greek thought, in Aristotle's physical philosophy and in the metaphysical rhetoric of Post-Aristotelian Peripatetics of the Third Century before Christ, it was the rest, pause, halt, or standing still, which inevitably occurs between opposite as well as between contrary "moves," or motions. In rhetorical Noesis, it was frequently identified with the thing sought in the zetesis, i.e., the *zetema, quaestio,* or the Question. To the *Auctor ad Herennium,* it was the *constitution,* i.e., the organ of rhetorical action, the instrument or implement of controversy, the body, or functional system of argument. To Cicero it was likewise a constitution, i.e., a natural start, or physical beginning, an original form, the originative and archemorphic conflict out of which individually modified controversies arise, an archetype of dispute, or argument. To Theodorus stasis was the originative head, or primary source, to which everything moved in the debate must be related. To Quintilian and to Pseudo-Augustine it was the main question in debate.[59]

As Dieter's account shows, the notion that arguments "stop" or "stand" at identifiable "points of clash" or *stases* existed in the ancient world from very early times. The question "What will be the main point(s) of debate?" is a crucial question to answer whenever one is preparing for or is engaged in argument.

The two ancient writers who most thoroughly studied and wrote on how to answer this question were Hermagoras (late second century B.C.) and Hermogenes (second century A.D.), and some of their ideas are entirely pertinent today.[60] Although the two authors had different detailed views about *stases,* they agreed that in legal arguments the following points of clash were always possible, although not all would be likely to arise in a single argument or case: *conjectural issues* (e.g., What happened, if anything?), *definitional issues* (e.g., Was it really theft?), *qualitative issues* (e.g., How serious was it?), and issues of *objection* (e.g., This is the wrong place to decide, or That argument is irrelevant.) Hermogenes went beyond his predecessor to identify "points of clash" likely to arise in deliberative rhetoric. These he identified as clashes about the lawfulness, justice, expediency, possibility, honorableness, and anticipated effects of policies.

Both writers enumerated a number of subissues that arguers might clash on, but these details are not germane to the point I wish to stress, namely,

40

that it has been recognized for centuries that the points at which arguments are likely to clash are not infinite, and they are to a considerable degree predictable if one knows the kind of situation in which an argument will occur. Such knowledge and analysis are parts of rhetorical invention. Part of "inventing" rhetoric is deciding what can and ought to be said. The decision entails making an inventory of what the clashes are likely to be, and thereby discovering what is best to say in order to carry one's side "over" the points of stoppage or *stasis*. These decisions are not matters of impulse—if they are wise. They are decisions made through *reasoning* about subject matter, the situation, and the people involved. Wise decisions of these sorts are products of *rhetorical logic*.

Before moving on with the story of rhetorical logic, it is important to know that the rhetorical constructs *topics* and *stasis* are normative. They imply not only how one may enter a controversy, but they direct thought about an analysis of possible issues. They tell one what it will be reasonable and appropriate to say in a given situation. To summarize, rhetorical logic specifies (as formal logic does not) (1) concepts of what is rhetorically reasonable, (2) ways of constructing and deconstructing arguments, (3) means of discovering what is sayable, (4) alternative ways of presenting arguments, and (5) ways of deciding when and why an argument is relevant. Rhetorical logic isolates and addresses the questions on which a given matter does or will logically turn, and it identifies what arguments are relevant to the issues in dispute.

Rhetorical logic retained a prominent place in theories of communication through the Middle Ages and into the Renaissance. Principal among the champions of the topics were Quintilian, Fortunatianus, Victorinus, Julius Victor, Martianus Capella, and Boethius.[61] The highest point in the history of topics probably occurred in the thirteenth century. Walter Ong notes that "when the goddess of reason makes her most definitive appearance in scholastic philosophy in the most distinctive and influential of all scholastic manuals [Peter of Spain's treatise, 'On Places'], she is supported not on the pillars of science, but on the topics or arguments of merely probable dialectic or rhetoric."[62] The most valiant contemporary effort to revive the topics to this level of significance has been that of Richard P. McKeon in, for example, "The Uses of Rhetoric in a Technological Age: Architectonic Productive Arts," published in 1971.[63]

After the rise of the "new" logics of Bacon, Descartes, and Locke, the most consequential attempts to save rhetorical logic was made by Giambattista Vico. His first response was to affirm the value of (geometric) deductive methods; they "are excellent ways and means of demonstrating mathematical truths." His second move was to subvert the idea that such methods are applicable to all matters of human interest. Whenever the subject matter "is unsuited to deductive treatment," he asserted, "the geometric procedure may be a faulty and captious way of reasoning."[64] Like Cicero, he insisted that geometric methods may enable one to express apodictic proof, but such expression will be "devoid of aesthetic charm."[65] "What is eloquence," he asked, "but wisdom, ornately and copiously delivered in words appropriate to the common opinion of mankind?"[66]

Vico's third reaction, and the most important one, was to reaffirm the concept of "natural reason." "This is the only reason of which the multitude are capable, for, when they are themselves involved, they attend to the smallest considerations of the justice which is called for by cases when the facts are fully specified."[67] And the key to natural reason is a capacity for *ingenium* (ingenuity) and familarity with the topics. "In Vico's account," Donald Phillip Verene observes, "the human world is itself invented through the art of topics."[68] In direct contradiction to the teachings of Descartes and Arnauld, Vico concluded:

> . . . whosoever intends to devote his efforts, not to physics or mechanics, but to a political career, whether as a civil servant or as a member of the legal profession or of the judiciary, a political speaker or a pulpit orator, should not waste too much time, in his adolescence, on those subjects, which are taught by abstract geometry. Let him, instead, cultivate his mind with an ingenious method; let him study topics, and defend both sides of a controversy, be it on nature, man, or politics, in a freer and brighter style of expression. Let him not spurn reasons that wear a semblance of probability and verisimilitude.[69]

Unfortunately, Vico's voice was unheard by those most responsible for the direction that rhetorical theory was to take from the eighteenth to the twentieth centuries: George Campbell, Hugh Blair, and Richard Whately. It is only in the late twentieth century that Vico's conceptions have been given the serious consideration they deserve.

One will search in vain to find an approval or development of topics or *stasis* in Campbell's *Philosophy of Rhetoric*, Blair's *Lectures on Rhetoric and Belles Lettres*, or Whately's *Elements of Rhetoric*. These are, as I have indicated, "managerial rhetorics" concerned with the composition and presentation of material gained in ways with which rhetoric is presumed to be unconcerned. Campbell specifically asserted that a rhetor need not be "adept" in syllogistic reasoning. He considered syllogistic disputation "the art of fighting with words, and about words."[70] Blair held that while inventional devices, such as commonplaces, "might produce very showy academical declamations," they "could never produce useful discourse on real business."[71] All one had to do to prepare to communicate was to study one's subject matter. Unlike his immediate predecessors, Whately stressed deduction rather than induction, but he agreed that rhetoric did not guide investigation; this was the province of logic. A rhetor had only to know his material in order to be ready to compose it, and composition was the province of rhetoric.[72]

Whately did, however, make an influential contribution to rhetorical logic with his concepts of presumption and burden of proof. He indicated the responsibilities of those who would argue for or against a proposition. Presumption and burden of proof are concepts that clarify the "logic" of advocacy by identifying how arguers can discover how much they have to do to seem reasonable. Whately defined presumption as "a *pre-occupation* of the ground [such] as implies that it may stand good till some sufficient reason is adduced against it." By this he meant that some positions are presumed sound until directly attacked. Burden of proof, he said, "lies on the side of him who would dispute it [a presumption]."[73] This principle, by which the relative obligations of arguers can be worked out, is analogous to the principle of law that asserts that one is presumed innocent until proven guilty. In Whately's view, one who affirms change has the burden of proof and whoever opposes change has the advantage of a presumption in favor of what already exists. It may not be universally true that change is invariably looked on with favor, but Whately valuably pointed to the fact that in *all* argumentation there are *presumptions* and *burdens* and these have to be *reasoned out* if one is to know what he or she must do and say.

The history of rhetorical logic remained largely uneventful until the late nineteenth and early twentieth centuries when textbooks on argumentation, influenced by the tradition of Aristotle, Cicero, Quintilian, and their successors, began to appear. Leading the new movement were such writers as George Pierce Baker, *Principles of Argumentation* (1895), Craven Laycock and Robert L. Scales, *Argumentation and Debate* (1905), and A. Craig Baird, *Argumentation, Discussion,* and *Debate* (1950).[74] What is most interesting about these later textbooks is that they attempted to accommodate *both* technical and rhetorical logic. It was not until after the appearance of Stephen Toulmin's *The Uses of Argument* in 1958 that this pattern changed. The nature of this change and a concomitant shift in philosophy from an emphasis on formal language to an emphasis on informal language are my next considerations.

43

FROM GEOMETRY AND MATHEMATICS TO LANGUAGE
AND JURISPRUDENCE

The paradigm shift in philosophy that followed Wittgenstein's *Philosophical Investigations* was twofold: (1) a move from attempts to regiment logic into mathematics to efforts to dissolve philosophic problems through the analysis of ordinary language.[75] In line with this was the development of speech-act theory, perhaps best represented by the work of J. L. Austin *(How to Do Things with Words)*[76] and John R. Searle *(Speech Acts.)*[77] And (2), a move to reform philosophy, perhaps best illustrated by the writings of Alasdair MacIntyre *(After Virtue)*[78] and Richard Rorty *(Philosophy and the Mirror of Nature)*.[79] The principal effects of these developments respecting logic and rhetoric were to reopen questions about the nature of reason and rationality and to encourage a rapprochement among interdisciplinary scholars seeking answers to these questions.

Particularly important in the move in this direction are two books, Toulmin's *The Uses of Argument* (1958) and Perelman and L. Olbrechts-Tyteca's *The New Rhetoric: A Treatise of Argumentation* (1969).[80] In both works, the geometric model of reasoning was replaced by a jurisprudential model. Toulmin wrote: "Logic (we may say) is generalised jurisprudence. Arguments can be compared with law-suits, and the claims we can make and argue for in extra-legal contexts with claims made in the courts, while the cases we present in making good each kind of claim can be compared with each other."[81] And Perelman wrote: *"law plays a role in regard to argumentation analogous to that of mathematics in regard to formal logic."*[82] Through various writings, Toulmin and Perelman have provided new foundations for rhetorical logic. Without mentioning them in an examination of the current status of philosophy, Rorty made this statement: "In the course of the transition to postpositivistic analytic philosophy, the image of the scientist has been replaced, though it is not clear by what. Perhaps the most appropriate model for the analytic philosopher is now the lawyer, rather than the scholar or the scientist."[83] Another way to think about this transition is in terms of a new "turn"— from linguistics to rhetoric.

Toulmin's and Perelman's conceptions of argument, the range of application for their conceptions, and the standards by which arguments may be assessed have special importance. Toulmin conceives argument as a movement from data, to warrant, backing for the warrant, to reservations, and to conclusion. The anatomy of argument is illustrated in Figure 2.

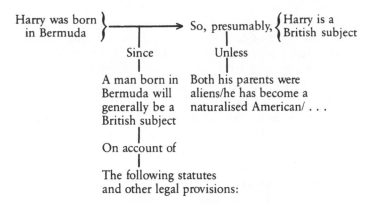

Figure 2. Anatomy of argument.[84]

In a later book, *An Introduction to Reasoning*, Toulmin and his colleagues, Richard Rieke and Allan Janik, use this model to examine reasoning in legal, scientific, artistic, management, and ethical disputes.[85] Their standard of assessment is "soundness," a standard very like Cicero's "firmness." Soundness is determined by an inspection of an argument's anatomy, the assumption being that the same act of intellection that would tell one what is a major premise, minor premise, and conclusion will serve as well as to indicate the merits of any given argument. These authors see rationality as field-dependent—differing from, say, science to art, but they also hold that rationality is certified by the way one participates in an argument, "by the manner in which he handles and responds to the offering of reasons for or against claims." *Openness to argument* is the major characteristic of "rational arguers."[86]

Perelman's approach to argument was much different from that of Toulmin and his co-authors. The key difference was that Perelman made address to an audience the foundation of his work, rather than argument per se. His concern was argumentation, the actual process of arguing. Since I analyze his theory in chapter 6, I shall note here only that he conceived argument in terms of structures of practical reasoning— quasi-logical arguments, and arguments by association and dissociation.[87] He was concerned to show that such structures appear in all sorts of discourse designed to gain the adherence of audiences. Perelman's standard of assessment was the quality of the audience that would adhere to an argument; the ultimate test would be adherence by a *universal audience*, that is, the most critically rational audience that one can conceive.[88]

The impact of the jurisprudential model on theory of argumentation is perhaps best seen from this episode in the career of Douglas Ehninger, one of the foremost rhetorical scholars in the study of speech communication. Wittgenstein's move from ideal language to ordinary language was a watershed point in the contemporary history of philosophy, and Ehninger's move from "applied logic" to the jurisprudential model signaled a parallel shift in rhetorical theory. In 1954 Ehninger wrote a chapter titled "The Logic of Argument." In it he defined argumentation as "logic applied in attempts to induce other persons to accept or reject the alleged 'truth claims' of disputed or doubtful propositions."[89] While he included a discussion of types of argument compatible with rhetorical (place) logic, his treatment featured John Stuart Mill's tests of inductive reasoning, Venn diagrams, and the rules of syllogistic inference. This exposition was in marked contrast to the handling of argument in the most influential argumentation textbook written in this century. Ehninger and Wayne Brockriede based their *Decision by Debate*[90] on Toulmin's *Uses of Argument*. Their book appeared in 1963, three years after their article "Toulmin on Argument: An Interpretation and Application."[91]

Argumentation was conceived by Ehninger and Brockriede not as "applied logic," but as a method for testing ideas through discussion and debate. Their emphasis was on debate, which they defined as *"a mode of critical decision-making in which the contending parties appeal to an adjudicating agency acting in the role of arbitrator, and agree to abide by the decision that agency hands down."*[92] A student of debate must, therefore, know not only logic, but also psychology and rhetoric. When the authors explained syllogistic reasoning, they eschewed Venn diagrams and the rules of syllogistic inference. Instead, syllogistic reasoning, like other forms of reasoning—cause, sign, generalization, parallel case, analogy, and statistics—were schematized according to the Toulmin model. In addition to these forms of "substantive proof," the authors also treated authoritative and motivational proofs, making their work applicable to the actual process of arguing and going far beyond Toulmin's *Uses of Argument*. A sound argument, they appeared to hold with Toulmin, is one that can withstand appropriate criticism. Such criticism, it is clear from the second edition of *Decision by Debate,* includes evaluation of argument as product, as process, as method, and as communicative transaction. A debate "will be a good one," the authors maintained, "if debaters and judges do the best they can in the process of clashing proofs and competing cases to recognize that arguments are developed by and for people."[93] This book, I believe, is the best representative available of what I call the "rational-world paradigm." Ehninger and Brockriede's work was essentially a rhetorical logic, based on the primacy of argument. The logic I shall propose is also a rhetorical logic, but it is based on the concept of narration. It remains for me to indicate why the concept of "narrative rationality" is needed—given all that has been recounted here.

NARRATIVE RATIONALITY AS A RHETORICAL LOGIC

I propose the narrative paradigm as a philosophy of reason, value, and action. Narrative rationality is its logic. The essential components of this logic are the following. Human communication is tested against the principles of probability (coherence) and fidelity (truthfulness and re-liability). Probability, whether a story "hangs together," is assessed in three ways: by its *argumentative* or *structural coherence;* by its *material coherence,* that is, by comparing and contrasting stories told in other discourses (a story may be internally consistent, but important facts may be omitted, counterarguments ignored, and relevant issues overlooked); and by *characterological coherence.* Concern for this third type of co-herence is one of the key differences between the concept of narrative rationality and traditional logics, and this requires some explanation.

Central to all stories is character. Whether a story is believable depends on the reliability of characters, both as narrators and as actors. Determina-tion of one's character is made by interpretations of the person's decisions and actions that reflect values. In other words, character may be consid-ered an organized set of actional tendencies. If these tendencies contradict one another, change significantly, or alter in "strange" ways, the result is a questioning of character. Coherence in life and in literature requires that characters behave characteristically. Without this kind of predictability, there is no trust, no community, no rational human order. Applying this consideration of coherence is an inquiry into motivation. Its importance in deciding whether to accept a message cannot be overestimated. Determin-ing a character's motives is prerequisite to trust, and trust is the foundation of belief. (How characterological coherence relates to ethos and other considerations of source credibility will be discussed in chapter 7.)

Fidelity, the truthfulness of a story, is assessed by applying what I call "the logic of good reasons." The "logic of good reasons," as I shall show in chapter 5, is a logic formed by combining the means of analyzing and evaluating arguments offered by such writers as Toulmin, Perelman, and

Ehninger and Brockriede with critical questions that can locate and weigh values. These are questions about *fact, relevance, consequence, consistency,* and *transcendental issues.* In other words, narrative rationality does not deny that discourse often contains structures of reason that can be identified as specific forms of argument and assessed as such. Narrative rationality incorporates this fact but goes beyond it to claim that reason occurs in human communication in other than traditional argumentative structures.

Moreover, narrative rationality does not deny the limited but necessary use of technical logic in assessing inferences or implicative forms that occur in human communication. I would observe, however, that such assessments become useful only insofar as the discourse is considered as a whole, as part of a storied context in which other features of the discourse are taken into account, including mythic and metaphoric elements. Support for this view—that technical procedures and data should be interpreted in a storied context—is provided by Alexander Marshack. Numbering, he observes, "may perhaps be thought of as 'pure' and unrelated to storied meaning, but psychologically it is, nonetheless, a symbolizing and cognitive process. As such, it is always a "time-factored" and "time-factoring" *sequential* skill. . . ."[94] Obviously, such skill is to be valued. So is the information it may produce. However, the values of technical precision are not as important as the values of coherence, truthfulness, wisdom, and humane action, which are necessary for transforming technical logic and empirical knowledge into a force for civilized existence.

Narrative rationality differs from prior logics in several other fundamental ways. It implies that reason, the movement of thought that occurs in communicative transactions, is not restricted to clear-cut argumentative forms. The concept of narrative rationality asserts that it is not the *individual form* of argument that is ultimately persuasive in discourse. That is important, but *values* are more persuasive, and they may be expressed in a variety of modes, of which argument is only one. Hence narrative rationality focuses on "good reasons"—*elements that provide warrants for accepting or adhering to the advice fostered by any form of communication that can be considered rhetorical.* The perspective of narrative rationality does not exclude the long tradition of rhetorical logic; it is a rhetorical logic itself. Other rhetorical logics, however, have dwelt on argument, argumentative genres, and specific standards of *argumentative* assessment. The perspective of narrative rationality focuses on all forms of human communication as carriers of good reasons and on a system of evaluation that incorporates the available standards of argumentative assessment but offers additional considerations.

The most fundamental difference between narrative rationality and other rhetorical logics is the presumption that no form of discourse is privileged over others because its form is predominantly argumentative. No matter how strictly a case is argued—scientifically, philosophically, or legally—it will always be a story, an interpretation of some aspect of the world that is historically and culturally grounded and shaped by human personality. Even the most well-argued case will be informed by other individuated forms besides argument, especially by metaphor. In taking this position, I propose not only a different conception of reason—as logos/mythos—but also a much broader conception of rationality.

CONCLUSION

As I have shown in this chapter, technical and rhetorical logics have had a tenuous, sometimes tortured relationship. By the twentieth century, technical logic had reified reason to mathematical symbolic forms, and rhetorical logic had continued its tradition of conceiving of reason as a form of *argumentative* proof. I propose a concept of narrative rationality as a response to these developments, insisting that reason in human communication is more diverse in its forms than these views hold and that reason is a pervasive feature of symbolic action. The concept of narrative rationality offers systematic principles, procedures, and criteria for assessing elements of discourse that provide warrants for believing or acting in particular ways. Having indicated the context out of which the narrative paradigm and its logic emerge, I shall, in the next chapter, explain the proposal in further detail.

NOTES

1. Giambattista Vico, *The New Science,* ed. and trans. Thomas Goddard Bergin and Max Harold Fish (Ithaca, N.Y.: Cornell University Press, 1984), p. 127.
2. Vico's view of poetry foreshadows what is called "aestheticism." For a criticial study of the theme in the writings of Nietzsche, Heidegger, Foucault, and Derrida, see Allan Megill, *Prophets of Extremity* (Berkeley: University of California Press, 1985).
3. Richard McKeon, "Rhetoric in the Middle Ages," *Speculum* 17 (1942): 1–32.

4. Martin Buber, *Between Man and Man,* trans. Ronald Gregor Smith (New York: Macmillan Co., 1967), p. 19. See also John Stewart, "Foundations of Dialogic Communication," *Quarterly Journal of Speech* 64 (1978): 182–201; Richard L. Johannesen, "The Emerging Concept of Communication in Dialogue, *Quarterly Journal of Speech* 57 (1971): 373–82; and Floyd W. Matson and Ashley Montague, eds., *The Human Dialogue: Perspectives on Communication* New York: Free Press, 1967).

5. Wilhelm Windelband, *A History of Philosophy: Greek, Roman, and Medieval* (New York: Harper & Row, 1958), vol. 1, p. 28; see also Frederick Copleston, S.J., *A History of Philosophy: Greece and Rome* (Garden City, N.Y.: Image Books, 1962), vol. 1, pt. 1, 71–76.

6. Francis M. Cornford, *Plato's Theory of Knowledge: The "Theaetetus" and the "Sophist" of Plato* (Indianapolis, Ind.: Bobbs-Merrill, 1957), p. 262.

7. W. D. Ross, Aristotle: *A Complete Exposition of His Works and Thought* (Cleveland, Ohio: Meridian Books, 1963), p. 25.

8. Cornford, *Plato's Theory,* p. 269.

9. Aristotle, *Rhetoric,* trans. W. Rhys Roberts (New York: Modern Library, 1954), 135a, 1–10, and passim. Robert Price argues that there are other antistrophes in Aristotle's thought besides rhetoric and dialectic, including demonstration, deliberation, evaluation, and recollection. See his essay, "Some Antistrophes to the Rhetoric," *Philosophy and Rhetoric* 1 (1968): 145–64.

10. Aristotle, *Topics,* trans. W. A. Pickard-Cambridge, in *The Complete Works of Aristotle,* ed. Jonathan Barnes, vol. 1 (Princeton: Bollingen Series LXXI–2 vols., Princeton University Press, 1984), 101b, 4.

11. Kenneth Burke, *A Grammar of Motives and a Rhetoric of Motives* (Cleveland, Ohio: Meridian Books, 1962), pp. 402–3.

12. Robert Adamson, *A Short History of Logic,* ed. W. R. Sorley (Edinburgh: William Blackwood & Sons, 1911), p. 20.

13. Stephen Toulmin, *The Uses of Argument* (London: Cambridge University Press, 1958), p. 6. Toulmin offers a study of the history of logic parallel to the one in this chapter in his account of how he came to write *The Uses of Argument.* See "Logic and the Criticism of Arguments," in J. L. Golden, G. F. Berquist, and W. E. Coleman, eds., *The Rhetoric of Western Thought* (3rd ed; Dubuque, Iowa: Kendall/Hunt, 1984), pp. 391–401. He does not trace the history of rhetorical logic.

14. Aristotle, *Prior Analytics,* trans. A. J. Jenkins, in Barnest, 24b, 18–20.

15. Aristotle, *Rhetoric,* 1358a, 12–15.

16. Ibid., 1358a, 16–18.

17. Ibid., 1400b, 35-38.

18. William Kneale and Martha Kneale, *The Development of Logic* (Oxford: Clarendon Press, 1978), p. 44.

19. Aristotle, *Rhetoric,* 1358b, 8–20.

20. Ibid., 1417b, 20–28.

21. Burke, *Motives,* p. 580.

22. See n. 12, above, for Adamson reference.

23. Federigo Enriques, *The Historic Development of Logic,* trans. Jerome Rosenthal (New York: Henry Holt, 1929).

24. See n. 18, above for reference.

25. I. M. Bochenski, *A History of Formal Logic,* trans. I. Thomas (Notre Dame, Ind.: Notre Dame University Press, 1961).

26. Lisa Jardine, *Francis Bacon: Discovery and the Art of Discourse* (Cambridge, England: Cambridge University Press, 1975).

27. Francis, Lord Bacon, *Advancement of Learning,* ed. Joseph Devey (New York: P. F. Collier & Sons, 1902), p. 22. See also Wilbur Samuel Howell, "The Plough and the Flail: The Ordeal of Eighteenth-Century Logic," *Huntington Library Quarterly* 28 (1964): 63–78.

28. Ibid., p. 22.

29. Ibid., p. 26.

30. Ibid., p. 227.

31. Ibid., p. 228. It is the case, of course, that Bacon does provide elaborate discussions of aids to rhetorical invention—the Colours of Good and Evil, Antitheses, Apothegms, etc. In addition to Bk. 3 of the *Advancement,* see also *De Augmentis,* Bk. 4.

32. John Locke, *An Essay concerning Human Understanding,* ed. Alexander Campbell Fraser (New York: Dover Books, 1959), vol. 2, p. 401.

33. Ibid., p. 126.

34. René Descartes, *Discourse on Method,* trans. Lawrence J. Lafleur (Indianapolis, Ind.: Bobbs-Merrill, 1956), p. 11.

35. Antoine Arnauld, *The Art of Thinking* (Port-Royal Logic), trans. James Dickoff and Patricia James (Indianapolis, Ind.: Bobbs-Merrill, 1964), p. 175.

36. Ibid., p. 237.

37. William Barrett, *The Illusion of Technique: A Search for Meaning in a Technological Age* (Garden City, N.Y.: Doubleday Anchor Books, 1979).

38. Cited in Franklin L. Baumer, *Modern European Thought: Continuity and Change in Ideas, 1600–1950* (New York: Macmillan Co., 1977), p. 307.

39. Rudolf Carnap, "The Rejection of Metaphysics," in A. Smullya, P. Dietrichson, D. Keyt, and L. Miller *Introduction to Philosophy: Readings in Epistemology, Metaphysics, Ethics, and Philosophy of Religion* (Belmont, Calif.: Wadsworth Publishing Co., 1962), p. 22.

40. A. J. Ayer, *Language, Truth, and Logic* (New York: Dover Books, 1946), p. 13.

41. Chaïm Perelman and L. Olbrechts-Tyteca, *The New Rhetoric: A Treatise on Argumentation,* trans. John Wilkinson and Purcell Weaver (Notre Dame, Ind.: University of Notre Dame Press, 1969), pp. 132ff.

42. C. K. Ogden and I. A. Richards, *The Meaning of Meaning: A Study of the Influence of Language upon Thought and of the Science of Symbolism* (New York: Harcourt, Brace & World, 1923), pp. 266ff.

43. Cited in Enriques, *Development of Logic,* pp. 170–71, from an article appearing in the *Hibbert Journal,* July 1904, p. 812.

44. See Kurt Gödel, *On Formally Undecidable Propositions of Principia Mathematica and Related Systems,* trans. B. Meltzer (New York: Basic Books, 1962).

45. See Werner Heisenberg, *Physics and Philosophy* (New York: Harper & Row, 1958).

46. Toulmin, *The Uses of Argument* (1958).

47. Perelman and Olbrechts-Tyteca, *The New Rhetoric* (1969).

48. Calvin O. Schrag, "Rhetoric Resituated at the End of Philosophy," *Quarterly Journal of Speech* 71 (1985):164–74.

49. Adamson, *Short History of Logic*, p. 80.

50. Cicero, *De inventione*, trans. H. M. Hubbell (Cambridge, Mass.: Harvard University Press, 1949), 1. 37. 67–68ff.

51. Prentice Meador, "Muncian, *On Epicheiremes:* An Introduction and Translation," *Speech Monographs* 31 (1964):54.

52. Cicero, *De inventione*, 1. 41. 77.

53. Cicero, *De oratore*, trans. E. W. Sutton (Cambridge, Mass.: Harvard University Press, 1949), 2. 41. 178.

54. Cicero, *Topica*, trans. N. M. Hubbell (Cambridge, Mass.: Harvard University Press, 1949), 1. 6.

55. Cicero, *Topica*, 1. 8.

56. Cicero, *Topica*, 4. 23.

57. [Cicero], *Ad C. Herennium*, trans. Harry Caplan (Cambridge, Mass.: Harvard University Press, 1954), p. li.

58. Ibid., p. lii.

59. Otto Alvin Loeb Dieter, "Stasis," *Speech Monographs* 17 (1959):369. See also Lee S. Hultzén, "Status in Deliberative Analysis," in Donald C.Bryant, ed., *The Rhetorical Idiom: Essays in Rhetoric, Oratory, Language and Drama* (Ithaca, N.Y.: Cornell University Press, 1958), pp. 97–123.

60. See Ray Nadeau, "Hermogenes on Stases: A Translation with an Introduction and Notes," *Speech Monographs* 31 (1964):373. See also Ray Nadeau, "Hermogenes on 'Stock Issues' in Deliberative Speaking," *Speech Monographs* 25 (1958):59–66; Ray Nadeau, "Some Aristotelian and Stoic Influences on the Theory of Stases," *Speech Monographs* 26 (1959):248–54.

61. Michael C. Leff, "The Topics of Argumentative Invention in Latin Rhetorical Theory from Cicero to Boethius," *Rhetorica* 1 (1983):23. See also Otto Bird, "The Tradition of Logical Topics: Aristotle to Ockham," *Journal of the History of Ideas* 23 (1961):307–23.

62. Walter J. Ong, S. J., *Ramus: Method, and the Decay of Dialogue* (Cambridge, Mass.: Harvard University Press, 1983), p. 65.

63. Richard McKeon, "The Uses of Rhetoric in a Technological Age: Architectonic Productive Arts," in Lloyd F. Bitzer and Edwin Black, eds.,*The Prospect of Rhetoric* (Englewood Cliffs, N.J.: Prentice-Hall, 1971), pp. 44–63.

64. Giambattista Vico, *On the Study Methods of Our Times,* trans. Elio Gianturco (Indianapolis, Ind.: Bobbs-Merrill, 1965), p. 22.

65. Ibid., p. 24.

66. Ibid., p. 78.

67. Ibid., p. 349.

68. Donald Phillip Verene, *Vico's Science of Imagination* (Ithaca, N.Y.: Cornell University Press, 1981), p. 169.

69. Vico, *Study Methods*, p. 41. Rather than to Vico, many rhetoricians turned to the work inspired by Ramus. For the nature and influence of Ramus's thinking, see Ong and Wilbur Samuel Howell, *Logic and Rhetoric in England, 1500–1700* (New York: Russell & Russell, 1961), pp. 146–281.

70. George Campbell, *The Philosophy of Rhetoric,* ed. Lloyd F. Bitzer (Carbondale: Southern Illinois University Press, 1963), p. 69.

71. Hugh Blair, *Lectures on Rhetoric and Belles Lettres,* ed. Harold F. Harding (Carbondale: Southern Illinois University Press, 1965), vol. 2, p. 181.

72. Richard Whately, *Elements of Rhetoric,* ed. Douglas Ehninger (Carbondale: Southern Illinois University Press, 1963), p. 36.

73. Ibid., p. 112.

74. Mention should also be made of John Henry Cardinal Newman's *An Essay in and of a Grammar of Assent* (Notre Dame, Ind.: University of Notre Dame Press, 1979). See especially his exploration of "Informal Inference," pp. 230–60. This is a work deserving more attention than it has received from scholars concerned with logic and rhetoric.

75. Ludwig Wittgenstein, *Philosophical Investigations* trans. G. E. M. Anscombe (Oxford: Basil Blackwell, 1953).

76. J. L. Austin, *How to Do Things with Words* (Oxford: Oxford University Press, 1972).

77. John R. Searle, *Speech Acts: An Essay in the Philosophy of Language* (Cambridge, England: Cambridge University Press, 1969).

73. Alasdair MacIntyre, *After Virtue: A Study in Moral Theory* (Notre Dame, Ind.: University of Notre Dame Press, 1981).

79. Richard Rorty, *Philosophy and the Mirror of Nature* (Princeton, N.J.: Princeton University Press, 1979).

80. For an alternative approach to formal logic, see J. Anthony Blair and Ralph H. Johnson, eds., *Informal Logic: The First International Symposium* (Inverness, Calif.: Edgepress, 1980).

81. Toulmin, *The Uses of Argument,* p. 7. See also Gidon Gottlieb, *The Logic of Choice: An Investigation of the Concepts of Rules and Rationality* (New York: Macmillan Co., 1968).

82. Chaïm Perelman, "The New Rhetoric and the Rhetoricians: Remembrances and Comments," *Quarterly Journal of Speech* 70 (1984): 195.

83. Richard Rorty, "Philosophy in America Today," *American Scholar* 51 (1982): 192.

84. Toulmin, *The Uses of Argument,* p. 105.

85. Stephen Toulmin, Richard Rieke, and Allan Janik, *An Introduction to Reasoning* (New York: Macmillan Co., 1979).

86. Ibid., p. 13.

87. Perelman and Olbrechts-Tyteca, *The New Rhetoric* (1969).

88. See, for instance, Perelman and Olbrechts-Tyteca, *The New Rhetoric* (1969), p. 31; Perelman, "The New Rhetoric and the Rhetoricians," p. 191; Chaïm Perelman, "The New Rhetoric: A Theory of Practical Reasoning," in *The New Rhetoric and the Humanities: Essays in Rhetoric and Its Applications* (Dordrecht, Holland: D. Reidel, 1979), p. 14. See also Chaïm Perelman, "Philosophy, Rhetoric, and Commonplaces," in *The New Rhetoric and the Humanities,* pp. 52–61.

89. Douglas Ehninger, "The Logic of Argument," in David Potter, ed., *Argumentation and Debate: Principles and Practices* (New York: Henry Holt, 1954), p. 102.

90. Douglas Ehninger and Wayne Brockriede, *Decision by Debate* (New York: Dodd, Mead, 1963).

91. Wayne Brockriede and Douglas Ehninger, "Toulmin on Argument: An

Interpretation," *Quarterly Journal of Speech* 46 (1960): 44–53.

92. Ehninger and Brockriede, p. 10.

93. Douglas Ehninger and Wayne Brockriede, *Decision by Debate* (2nd ed.; New York: Harper & Row, 1979), p. 224.

94. Alexander Marshack, *The Roots of Civilization: The Cognitive Beginnings of Man's First Art, Symbol and Notation* (New York: McGraw-Hill, 1972), p. 25.

PART II
THE NARRATIVE PARADIGM AND RELATED
THEORIES

NARRATION AS A PARADIGM
OF HUMAN COMMUNICATION

The narrative paradigm that I have discussed in introductory fashion rests on a key assumption and a particular concept of "good reasons." I assume that *humans as rhetorical beings are as much valuing as reasoning animals.* I take good reasons to be *those elements that provide warrants for accepting or adhering to advice fostered by any form of communication that can be considered rhetorical.* My assumption does not seriously disturb the customary view of rhetoric as practical reasoning, but my conception of good reasons maintains that reasoning need not be bound to argumentative prose or be expressed in clear-cut inferential or implicative structures. I contend that reasoning can be discovered in all sorts of symbolic actions—nondiscursive as well as discursive. That this is so will be apparent from studies of Ronald Reagan's rhetoric (chap. 7), argument in *Death of a Salesman* and *The Great Gatsby* (chap. 8), and the dialogue of Socrates and Callicles in Plato's *Gorgias* (chap. 9). My version of what reasoning is, is consistent with Gerald Graff's thesis that a theory or practice of literature has cognitive as well as aesthetic significance.[1] At the very least, some dramatic and literary works do, in fact, argue.

The traditional view of reason does not serve well for understanding fictive discourse or even much realistic discourse. The latter fact I shall illustrate later in this chapter by analyzing the current controversy over nuclear warfare. The cause of both interpretive difficulties is the conception of rationality as exclusively based on argument. Certainly any argumentative form purports to be rational, but many nonargumentative modes of human communication invite adherence based on reason, also. Alfred Tennyson's characterization of John Bright and his opposition to the Crimean War in *Maud* is an apt illustration. In just a few lines, Tennyson suggests warrants for rejecting Bright and his position:

This broad-brimm'd hawker of holy things,
Whose ear is cramm'd with his cotton and rings,

Even in dreams to the chink of pence,
This husker put down war! Can he tell
Whether war be cause or consequence?[2]

A conception of rationality that does not permit us to see a *reasoned* inducement here is clearly too narrow. For this and many related reasons, I am proposing a conception of rationality based on narration. This conception invites us to examine the sequence of images and the question that Tennyson gives us and to test their coherence and fidelity. From this examination, we shall be able to determine the truthfulness of the characterization and decide to believe or not to believe in it. Even if we decide that the characterization of Bright is inaccurate, it cannot be called irrational.

The view of reason and rationality that I am proposing is based, as I have said, on narration. When I use the term "narration," I do not mean a fictive composition whose propositions may be true or false and have no necessary relationship to the message of that composition. By "narration," I mean symbolic actions—words and/or deeds—that have sequence and meaning for those who live, create, or interpret them. I agree with Alasdair MacIntyre, who wrote: "Man is in his actions and practice, as well as in his fictions, essentially a storytelling animal";[3] "enacted dramatic narrative is the basic and essential genre for the characterisation of human actions."[4] So understood, narration has relevance to real as well as fictive creations, to stories of living and to stories of the imagination.

The narrative paradigm can be considered a dialectical synthesis of two traditional strands that recur in the history of rhetoric: the argumentative, persuasive theme and the literary, aesthetic theme. The narrative paradigm implies that human communication should be viewed as historical as well as situational, as stories or accounts competing with other stories or accounts purportedly constituted by good reasons, as rational when the stories satisfy the demands of narrative probability and narrative fidelity, and as inevitably moral inducements. The narrative paradigm challenges the notions that human communication—if it is to be considered rhetorical—must be argumentative in form, that reason is to be attributed only to discourse marked by clearly identifiable modes of inference and implication, and that the norms for evaluation of rhetorical communication must be rational standards taken exclusively from informal or formal logic. The paradigm I offer does not disregard the roles of reason and rationality; it expands their meanings, recognizing their potential presence in all forms of human communication.

I should clarify the sense in which I use the term "paradigm." By paradigm, I refer to a representation designed to formalize the structure of a component of experience and to direct understanding and inquiry into the nature and functions of that experience—in this instance, the experience of human communication. Margaret Masterman designates this form of paradigm "metaphysical" or as a "metapardigm."[5] As I indicated in chapter 2, the narrative paradigm is meant to be a philosophy of reason, value, and action. That is, it is a conception that recognizes the interplay of all three of these features of human communication.

This perception is in marked contrast to the view that narration is merely an element in rhetorical discourse or is a specific literary genre. A growing number of contemporary writers have hinted that entire rhetorical actions can be usefully conceived as narrative in the sense that I have defined it. These scholars include W. Lance Bennett and Marsha S. Feldman,[6] Thomas B. Farrell,[7] W. B. Gallie,[8] Leonard L. Hawes,[9] Leon O. Mink,[10] Calvin O. Schrag,[11] Robert L. Scott,[12] and Herbert W. Simons.[13] Theologians also have shown the usefulness of the idea; principal among them are Robert Alter,[14] M. Goldberg,[15] and Stanley Hauerwas.[16] And the concept is encouraged by philosophers, literary theorists and critics, anthropologists, political scientists, and historians: Arthur C. Danto,[17] Jacques Derrida,[18] Frank Kermode,[19] John S. Nelson,[20] Paul Ricoeur,[21] T. Todorov,[22] Victor Turner,[23] and Hayden White.[24]

None of these writers, however, has specifically proposed narration as a paradigm for general study of human communication. The prevailing paradigm used in theory and criticism of communication is what I call the rational-world paradigm.

THE RATIONAL–WORLD PARADIGM

This paradigm is very familiar, having been in existence since Aristotle's *Organon* became foundational to Western thought about reasoning. Regardless of its various historic forms, the rational-world paradigm presupposes: (1) humans are essentially rational beings; (2) the paradigmatic mode of human decision making and communications is argument—discourse that features clear-cut inferential or implicative structures; (3) the conduct of argument is ruled by the dictates of situations—legal, scientific, legislative, public, and so on; (4) rationality is determined by subject-matter knowledge, argumentative ability, and skill in employing the rules of advocacy in given fields; and (5) the world is a set of logical puzzles that can be solved through appropriate analysis and application of reason conceived as an argumentative construct. In short, argument as product and process is *the* means of being human, the agency of all that humans can know and realize in achieving their *telos*. The philosophical ground of the rational-world paradigm is epistemology. Its linguistic materials are self-evident propositions, demonstrations, and proofs—the verbal expressions of certain and probable knowing.

Actualization of the rational-world paradigm depends on a form of society that permits, if not requires, participation of qualified persons in public decision making. It further demands a citizenry that shares a common language, general adherence to the values of the state, information relevant to the questions that confront the community, and an understanding of argumentative issues, the various forms of reasoning, and their appropriate assessment. In other words, there must exist something that can be called public or social knowledge and there must be a "public" for argument to have the kind of force envisioned for it.[25] Because the rational-world paradigm has these requirements and because *being rational* (being competent in argument) *must be learned,* the historic mission of education in the West has been to generate a consciousness of national and institutional community and to instruct citizens in at least the rudiments of logic and rhetoric.[26]

Needless to say, the rational-world paradigm, which is by and large a heritage of the classical period, has not been untouched by "modernism." The impact of modernism has been recounted and reacted to by many writers.[27] The lines of thought that have done most to subvert the rational-world paradigm are existentialism and naturalism. One of naturalism's schools starts with physics and mathematics and makes the logical structure of scientific knowledge fundamental; another school, involving biology, psychology, and the social sciences, adapts this structure and conception of knowledge to the human sciences. According to John Herman Randall, Jr.:

> The major practical issue still left between the two types of naturalism concerns the treatment of values. The philosophies starting from physics tend to exclude questions of value from the field of science and the scope of scientific method. They either leave them to traditional non-scientific treatment, handing them over, with Russell, to the poet and mystic; or else with the logical empiricists they dismiss the whole matter as "meaningless," maintaining with Ayer, that any judgment of value is an expression of mere personal feeling. The philosophies of human experiences—all the heirs of Hegel, from dialectical materialism to Dewey—subject them to the same scientific

60

methods of criticism and testing as other beliefs; and thus offer the hope of using all we have learned of scientific procedure to erect at last a science of values comparable to the science that was the glory of Greek thought.[28]

It is clear that with the first type of naturalism, there can be neither public or social knowledge nor rational public or social argument, for both are permeated by values. As Habermas notes, "the relationship of theory to practice can now only assert itself as the purposive rational application of techniques assured by the empirical science."[29]

With the second type of naturalism, one can hope with Randall that it produces the work he sees possible in it. But the fact is that no science of values has appeared or seems likely to do so. Further, Dewey himself noted the eclipse of the "public" and doubted its reemergence.[30] His hope was the development of "communities." Interestingly, sixty years later, MacIntyre concluded *After Virtue* with the observation: "What matters at this state is the construction of local forms of community within which civility and the intellectual and moral life can be sustained."[31]

The effects of naturalism have been to restrict the rational-world paradigm to specialized studies and to treat everyday argument as irrational exercise. The reaction to this state of affairs has been a historic effort to recover the rational-world paradigm for human decision making and communication by: (1) reconstructing the conception of knowledge;[32] (2) reconceptualizing the public—in terms of rational enterprises, fields, and communities;[33] (3) formulating a logic appropriate for practical reasoning;[34] and (4) reconceiving the conceptions of validity, reason, and rationality.[35] Many of those who have tackled these problems intimate, if they do not specifically state, proposals for reconstructing the concept of argument itself. Writers explicitly working on this task include Wayne Brockriede,[36] Brant Burleson,[37] Scott Jacobs and Sally Jackson,[38] Ray McKerrow,[39] Daniel O'Keefe,[40] Joseph Wenzel,[41] and Charles Willard.[42]

The motive underlying these various studies, and the movement of which they are an energizing force, is, as I have suggested, to repair the rational-world paradigm so that it once again will apply to everyday argument. One may applaud the motive and the movement and yet ask two questions: (1) Has the reformation been successful? (2) Is there a more beneficial way to conceive and to articulate the structures of everyday argument? It is too early to answer the first question with finality but one cannot deny that much useful work has been done, especially in establishing at least the semblance of rationality for specific fields of argument. I maintain, however, that similar progress has not been made in the area where argument is most general and is most obviously concerned with values, namely, public moral argument.

This failure suggests to me that the problem in discovering the rationality of everyday argument may be in the assumption that reaffirmation of the rational-world paradigm is the only available solution. I believe that the narrative paradigm may offer a better solution, one that will provide substance not only for public moral argument, but also all other forms of argument, for human communication in general. My answer to the second question, then, is, "Yes, I think so." Adoption of the narrative paradigm, I hasten to repeat, does not mean rejection of all the good work that has been done. It does mean a rethinking of it and an investigation of new moves that can be made to enrich our understanding of communicative interaction.

THE NARRATIVE PARADIGM

Many different root metaphors have been put forth to represent the essential nature of human beings: *Homo faber, Homo economicus, Homo politicus, Homo sociologicus,* "psychological man," "ecclesiastical man," *Homo sapiens,* and, of course, "rational man." I propose that *Homo narrans* be added to the list.

Before proceeding further I should indicate how the *Homo narrans* metaphor relates to those that have preceded it. Each of the root metaphors may be held to be a master metaphor that can stand as the ground, while the other metaphors are manifest as figures. In the terminology of the narrative perspective, a master metaphor sets the plot of human experience and the others the subplots. When any of the other metaphors is asserted as the master metaphor, narration is figure: a type of human interaction—an activity, an art, a genre, or a mode of expression.

When narration is taken as the master metaphor, it subsumes the others. The other metaphors become conceptions that inform various ways of *recounting* or *accounting for* human choice and action. Recounting takes such forms as history, biography, or autobiography. Accounting for takes such forms as theoretical explanation or argument. Recounting and accounting for can be also expressed in poetic forms: drama, poetry, novel, and so on. Recounting and accounting for are, in addition, the bases for all advisory discourse. Regardless of the form they are given, recounting and accounting for constitute stories we tell ourselves and each other to establish a meaningful life-world. The character of narrator(s), the conflicts, the resolutions, and the styles will vary, but each mode of recounting and accounting for is but a way of relating a "truth" about the human condition.

The *Homo narrans* metaphor is thus an incorporation and extension of Burke's definition of "man" as the "symbol-using (symbol-making, symbol-misusing) animal."[43] The idea of human beings as storytellers posits the generic form of all symbol composition. It holds that symbols are created and communicated ultimately as stories meant to give order to human experience and to induce others to dwell in them in order to establish ways of living in common, in intellectual and spiritual communities in which there is confirmation for the story that constitutes one's life. One's life is, as suggested by Burke, a story that participates in the stories of those who have lived, who live now, and who will live in the future. He asks: "Where does the drama get its materials?" I would modify the question to read: "Where do our narratives get their materials?" And I would accept his answer:

> From the "unending conversation" that is going on in history when we are born. Imagine that you enter a parlor. You come late. When you arrive, others have long preceded you, and they are engaged in a heated discussion, a discussion too heated for them to pause and tell you exactly what it is about. In fact, the discussion had already begun long before any of them got there, so that no one present is qualified to retrace for you all the steps that had gone before. You listen for awhile, until you decide that you have caught the tenor of the argument; then you put in your oar. Someone answers; you answer him; another comes to your defense; another aligns himself against you, to either the embarrassment or gratification of your opponent, depending upon the quality of your ally's assistance. However, the discussion is interminable. The hour grows late, you must depart. And you do depart, with the discussion still vigorously in progress.[44]

As Heidegger observed, "We are a conversation . . . conversation and its unity support our existence."[45] Viewing all discourse in terms of the narrative paradigm accommodates this insight.

To clarify the narrative paradigm further, I should specify how it is related to Bormann's concepts of "fantasy themes" and "rhetorical visions,"[46] and to the Frentz and Farrell language-action paradigm.[47] Fantasy, Bormann holds, is a technical term, meaning "the creative and imaginative interpretation of events that fulfills a psychological or rhetorical need."[48] Fantasy themes arise "in group interaction out of a recollection of something that happened to the group in the *past* or a dream of what a group might do in the *future*."[49] When woven together, they become composite dramas, which Bormann calls "rhetorical visions."[50] From the narrative view, each of these concepts translates into dramatic stories constituting the fabric of social reality for those who compose them. They are, thus, "rhetorical fictions," constructions of fact and faith having persuasive force, rather than fantasies.[51] Nevertheless, without getting into the problem of how group-generated stories become public stories, I would note that Bormann[52] and others have demonstrated that "rhetorical visions" do exist.[53] I take this demonstration as partial evidence for the validity of the narrative paradigm.

With minor adaptation, I find no incompatibility between the narrative paradigm and the language-action paradigm. Indeed, language action is meaningful only in terms of narrative form,[54] like that proposed by Frentz and Farrell. What they designate as "form of life" and "encounters"— implicit matters of knowledge, aesthetic expectations, institutional constraints, and propriety rules—can be considered the forces that determine the structure of narratives in given interpersonal environments. What they call an "episode," a "rule-conforming sequence of symbolic acts generated by two or more actors who are collectively oriented toward emergent goals," can be thought of as the process by which one or more authors generate a short story or chapter—deciding on plot, the nature of characters, resolutions, and their meaning and import for themselves and others.[55]

I do not want to leave the impression that the narrative paradigm merely accommodates the constructs of Bormann and of Frentz and Farrell. Their work enriches the narrative paradigm. I shall rely specifically on the language-action paradigm in what follows.

The presuppositions that undergird the narrative paradigm are the following: (1) Humans are essentially storytellers. (2) The paradigmatic mode of human decision making and communication is "good reasons," which vary in form among situations, genres, and media of communication. (3) The production and practice of good reasons are ruled by matters of history, biography, culture, and character along with the kinds of forces identified in the Frentz and Farrell language-action paradigm. (4) Rationality is determined by the nature of persons as narrative beings—their inherent awareness of *narrative probability*, what constitutes a coherent story, and their constant habit of testing *narrative fidelity*, whether or not the stories they experience ring true with the stories they know to be true in their lives. (Narrative probability and narrative fidelity are analogous to the concepts of dramatic probability and verisimilitude; and as MacIntyre observes, "The difference between imaginary characters and real ones is not in the narrative form of what they do; it is in the degree of their authorship of that form and of their own deeds."[56]) (5) The world as we know it is a set of stories that must be chosen among in order for us to live life in a process of continual re-creation. In short, good reasons are the stuff of stories, the means by which humans realize their nature as reasoning-valuing animals. The philosophical ground of the narrative paradigm is ontology. The materials of the narrative paradigm are symbols, signs of consubstantiation, and good reasons, the communicative expressions of social reality.

Actualization of narrative does not require a given form of society. Where the rational-world paradigm is an ever-present part of our consciousness because we have been educated into it, the narrative impulse is part of our very being because we acquire narrativity in the natural process of socialization.[57] That narrative, whether written or oral, is a feature of human nature and that it crosses time and culture is attested by White: "Far from being one code among many that a culture may utilize for endowing experience with meaning, narrative is a metacode, a human universal on the basis of which trans-cultural messages about the shared reality can be transmitted. . . . the absence of narrative capacity or a refusal of narrative indicates an absence or refusal of meaning itself."[58] Turner agrees: "If we regard narrative ethically, as the supreme instrument for building 'values' and 'goals,' in Dilthey's sense of these terms, which motivate human conduct into situational structures of 'meaning,' then we must concede it to be a universal cultural activity, embedded in the very center of the social drama, itself another cross-cultural and transtemporal unit in social process."[59] Dell Hymes concurs: "The narrative use of language is not a property of subordinate cultures, whether folk, or working class, or the like, but a universal function."[60] Gregory Bateson goes so far as to claim, "If I am at all fundamentally right in what I am saying, then *thinking in terms of stories* must be shared by all mind or minds, whether ours or those of redwood forests and sea anemones."[61] And Burke observes, "We assume a time when our primal ancestors became able to go from SENSATIONS to WORDS. (When they could duplicate the experience of tasting an orange by saying 'the taste of an orange,' that was WHEN STORY CAME INTO THE WORLD)."[62]

In theme, if not in every detail, narrative is meaningful for persons in particular and in general, across communities as well as cultures, across time and place. Narratives enable us to understand the actions of others "because we all live out narratives in our lives and because we understand our own lives in terms of narratives."[63]

Rationality within this perspective invokes principles of narrative probability and narrative fidelity. These principles contrast with but do not contradict the traditional concepts or constituents of rationality. They are, in fact, subsumed within the narrative paradigm. The rational-world paradigm implies that rationality is a matter of argumentative competence: knowledge of issues, modes of reasoning, appropriate tests, and rules of advocacy in given fields. These are essential constituents of traditional "rhetorical rationality," as I have shown through surveying that tradition in chapter 2. This rationality is something to be learned, and being rational in these ways involves a high degree of self-consciousness. Narrative rationality makes these demands only to the degree that it incorporates the aspects of rationality that tradition has focused on. Behind this, however, narrative rationality presupposes the logic of narrative capacities that we all share. It depends on our minds' being as Booth represents them in *Modern Dogma and the Rhetoric of Assent*, a key point of which is: "Not only do human beings successfully infer other beings' states of mind from symbolic clues; we know that they characteristically, in all societies, build each other's minds. This is obvious knowledge—all the more genuine for being obvious."[64] The operative principle of narrative rationality is *identification* rather than deliberation.

Narrative rationality differs from traditional rationality in another significant way. Narrative rationality is not simply an account of the "laws of thought," nor is it normative in the sense that one *must* reason according to prescribed rules of calculation or inference making. Traditional rationality prescribes the ways people should think when they reason truly or toward certainty. MacIntyre notes, "To call an argument fallacious is always at once to describe and to evaluate it."[65] Traditional rationality is, therefore, a normative construct. Narrative rationality is, on the other hand, descriptive; it offers an account, an understanding, of any instance of human choice and action, including science.[66] At the same time, narrative rationality (although not necessarily the paradigm itself) provides a basis of critique. Where freedom and democracy are ideals, narrative rationality will imply a praxis constant with an ideal egalitarian society. Traditional rationality implies some sort of hierarchical system, a community in which some persons are qualified to judge and to lead and some other persons are to follow.

For the sake of clarity, I should note that, while the narrative paradigm can provide a radical democratic ground for social-political critique, it does not deny the legitimacy (the inevitability) of hierarchy. History records no community, uncivilized or civilized, without key storymakers/ storytellers, whether sanctioned by God, a "gift," heritage, power, intelligence, or election. Narration implies, however, that the "people" judge the stories that are told for and about them and that they have a rational capacity to make such judgments. To apply a narrative paradigm to communication is to hold, along with Aristotle, that "people" have a natural tendency to prefer what they perceive as the true and the just.[67] However, the narrative paradigm does not deny that the "people" can be wrong. But, then, so can elites, especially when a decision is social or political. Nor does the theory behind the narrative paradigm deny the existence and desirability of genius in individuals or the capacity of "people" to formulate and adopt new stories that better account for their lives or the mystery of life itself. The sort of hierarchy to which the narrative paradigm is inimical is hierarchy based on the assumption that some people are qualified to be rational and others are not. The conception of narrative rationality for which I am contending assigns basic rationality to *all* persons not mentally disabled.

Denials of fundamental rationality have appeared repeatedly—in slave states, in monarchic states, in fascist states, in communist states, and even in democratic states. One reason is that the traditional conception of rationality has no necessary egalitarian bias. The traditional conception of rationality implies that rationality is learned, is formal, is not innate. Within this tradition it tends to be claimed that rationality is the exclusive possession of those who (1) know most about the issue in question, (2) are cognizant of argumentative procedures and forms and functions, and (3) weigh in systematic and deliberative fashion all arguments heard or seen. This is the prevalent notion of who is and who is not rational, and it informs American political thinking today with consequences I shall shortly discuss in connection with contemporary controversy over nuclear power and weapons. First, however, in behalf of the contrary assumptions of narrative rationality, I want to cite V. O. Key's classic study of presidential voting between 1936 and 1960. He concluded that "voters are not fools." But this is what they must have been if measured by the standards of traditional rationality that I have just cited. The voters were not expertly informed, familiar with principles of argumentation, or systematic pursuers of all available arguments. Nonetheless, Key's data led him to insist that the American electorate was not "straightjacketed by social determinants or moved by unconscious urges triggered by devilishly skillful propagandists." They were moved by their perceptions and appraisals of "central and relevant questions of public policy, of governmental performance, and of executive personality."[68] In short, they were rational. Their perceptions and appraisals of political discourse and action became stories, narratives that must stand tests of probability and fidelity. These stories, I insist, were no less valuable than the stories constructed by persons who were rational in the traditional way. There is no evidence to support the claim that "experts" know better than anyone else who should be elected president.

Obviously some stories are better stories than others, more coherent, more "true" to the way people and the world are—in perceived fact and value. In other words, some stories better satisfy the criteria of the logic of good reasons, which is attentive to reason *and* values. Persons may even choose not to participate in the making of public narratives (vote) if they feel that they are meaningless spectators rather than co-authors. But all persons are seen as having the capacity to be rational under the narrative paradigm. And, by and large, persons are that—at least in fashioning their daily lives. People do not, however, have the capacity to be equally rational under the rational-world paradigm. Under the narrative paradigm all are seen as possessing equally the logic of narration—a sense of coherence and fidelity. This is what is implied by the commonplace that everyone has "common sense," and this is what makes it reasonable to have juries of laypersons and to have popular elections, as Bennett and Feldman have well demonstrated.[69] I want to stress, however, that the concept of narrative rationality does not exclude traditional rationality. Where traditional rationality has been learned, it will be an aspect of narrative rationality and, indeed, I would emphasize that the principles of traditional rationality are especially relevant where discourse is about specialized knowledge and judgment, and those principles are also frequently relevant and operative in arenas where narrative logic is predominantely meaningful and useful.

Certain other features of the narrative paradigm should be noted. First, the paradigm is a ground for resolving the dualisms of modernism: fact-value, intellect-imagination, reason-emotion, and so on. Stories are enactments of the whole mind in concert with itself. Second, narratives are moral constructs. As White asserts: "Where, in any account of reality, narrativity is present, we can be sure that morality or a moral impulse is present too."[70] Third, the narrative paradigm is consonant with the notion of reason proposed by Schrag: "Reason, as the performance of vision and insight, commemoration and foresight, occasions the recognition of a process of the meaning-formation that gathers within it the logic of technical reason and the *logos* of myth."[71] The appropriateness and validity of this view of reason is supported by Angel Medina. In a statement that reiterates several of the points I have made, he writes:

> . . . it is necessary to define our reason primarily as biographical, that is, above all narrative and then symbolic. Human reason is narrative because it extends from its inception and in every one of its acts toward the foreshadowing of its total course. It is symbolic in that the major aim in the formation of this totality is its own self-presentation within the dialogue of consciousness. The meaning of my whole life is communicative; it emerges, as such, for the benefit of another consciousness when I attempt to present myself totally to it. Reciprocally, the meaning of another life becomes a totality only when received fully within my life.[72]

And, fourth, as I shall attempt to show next, the narrative paradigm offers ways of resolving problems of public moral argument.

A CASE: PUBLIC MORAL ARGUMENT

It should be apparent that I think MacIntyre's *After Virtue* is a remarkable work. Equally remarkable, in its way, is Jonathan's Schell's *The Fate of the Earth*.[73] Schell's book is an example of contemporary moral argument intended to persuade a general audience, the "public." His concluding argument is:

> Either we will sink into the final coma and end it all or, as I trust and believe, we will awaken to the truth of our peril, a truth as great as life itself, and, like a person who has swallowed a lethal poison but shakes off his stupor at the last moment and vomits the poison up, we will break through the layers of denials, put aside our faint-hearted excuses, and rise up to cleanse the earth of nuclear weapons.[74]

The validity of Schell's argument is not the question here. My concern is with its reception, which reveals the limits, perhaps the impossibility, of persuasive moral argument in our time, given the rational-world paradigm.

Critical response to *The Fate of the Earth* has been of two sorts. The first is celebratory. Reviewers in this group are obviously in sympathy with the book's moral thrust, its depiction of the results of nuclear war and its call for action—for life instead of death. Reviewers in this group included distinguished figures from a variety of professions: journalists Walter

Cronkite, James Reston, and James Kilpatrick; historians Harrison Salisbury, John Hersey, and Henry Steele Commanger; and politicians Barry Commoner, W. Averell Harriman, and Walter Mondale. None was a current member of the federal administration or the defense establishment. Each bore witness to an attitude—opposition to nuclear annihilation—but none testified to the technical merits of Schell's representation of "deterrence theory," his inferences about its meaning in regard to strategy and tactics, or his conclusions about national sovereignty. They, like Schell, were not "experts" in the field in which the argument was made. They, like Schell, were active in the realm of rhetorical knowledge, in the sphere of social-political policy and behavior.

Reviewers in the second group, on the other hand, were purveyors of ideological, bureaucratic, or technical arguments. Such arguments may overlap and be used by the same arguer, but each is distinguished by a particular privileged position: possession of political "truth," administrative sanction, or subject-matter expertise. The thrust of the ideological argument was that Schell violated ultimate "facts," was fundamentally wrong-headed; the bureaucratic argument stressed feasibility, especially in regard to administrative approval; and the technical argument alleged ignorance of the "facts," that opponents were "unrealistic," meaning they did not have a firm grasp on reality. These are, of course, familiar lines of refutation or subversion. Their opposites would be constructive arguments of affirmation or reaffirmation.

The subversive pattern of ideological, bureaucratic, and technical arguments is evident in the following attacks on Schell's reasoning. S. McCracken labeled Schell an "alarmist" and concluded: "The danger is that Mr. Schell's followers may triumph and bring about a freeze that by making present inequities permanent will prove destabilizing in the short run and in the long run productive of both redness and deadness."[75] Focusing on the linchpin arguments of *The Fate of the Earth* (Schell's interpretation of deterrence theory and his suggested solution of abolishing national sovereignty), M. Hausknecht first cited Alexander Haig and then observed that "It is not hard to imagine Ronald Reagan saying, 'Okay, so it may be the end of the species, but we can't let the bastards get away with it.'" In regard to Schell's solution, he concluded that "Successful political action demands significant but realizable goals."[76] The same charge was leveled by A. J. Pierre, who approved the moral force of Schell's position but then charged that "Schell provides no realistic alternative to our nuclear policy based on the concept of deterrence. His

70

argument—that knowledge that nuclear weapons can extinguish mankind must be the new deterrent in a disarmed world—is very weak."[77]

The strategy of these reviews is clear: reaffirmation of the moral concern, subversion of the reasoning. The tactics are obvious: juxtapose Schell's reasoning with what is right-headed, what is approved by the administration, or what is "realistic." Insofar as there is merit in these "arguments," it lies not in the way they foreclose dialogue but in their narrative probability and narrative fidelity. Yet this is not their intended appeal or effect. The effects were to discredit Schell as an arguer and to dismiss his argument as unfounded. Public moral argument was thus overwhelmed by privileged argument. Put another way, it was submerged by ideological and bureaucratic arguments that insisted on rival moralities and technical argument, which denuded it of morality altogether, making the dispute one for "experts" alone to consider.[78]

A question that arises at this point is: What happens when "experts" argue about moral issues in public? Let me first sketch the general characteristics of "public moral argument."

Public moral argument needs to be distinguished from reasoned discourse in interpersonal interactions and from arguments occurring in specialized communities, such as theological disputes, academic debates, and arguments before the Supreme Court. The features differentiating *public* moral argument from such encounters are: (1) it is publicized, made available for wide consumption and persuasion of the polity at large; and (2) it is aimed at what Aristotle called "untrained thinkers," or, to be effective, it should be.[79] Most important *public* moral argument is a form of controversy that inherently crosses professional fields. It is not contained, in the way that legal, scientific, or theological arguments are, by their subject matter, particular conceptions of argumentative competence, and well-recognized rules of advocacy. Because this is so and because its realm is public-social knowledge, *public* moral argument naturally invites participation by field experts and tends to become dominated by the rational superiority of their arguments. *Public* moral argument, which is oriented toward what ought to be, is often undermined by the "truth" that prevails at the moment. The presence of "experts" in *public* moral arguments makes it difficult, if not impossible, for the public of "untrained thinkers" to win an argument or even to judge arguments well—given, again, the rational-world paradigm.

Public *moral* argument is moral in the sense that it is founded on ultimate questions—of life and death, of how persons should be defined

71

and treated, of preferred patterns of living. Joseph Gusfield designates such questions as "status issues." Their resolution, he writes, indicates "the group, culture, or style of life to which the government and society are publicly committed."[80] In addition to nuclear warfare, desegregation would be included in this category, as would disputes about abortion and school prayer.

Public moral *argument* refers to clear-cut inferential structures, according to the rational-world paradigm, and to "good reasons," according to the narrative paradigm. Public moral *argument* may also refer to public controversies—disputes and debates—about moral issues. The nuclear-warfare controversy is an obvious case in point, but so are others mentioned above. One could add disputes over pornography, the Equal Rights Amendment (ERA), and crime and punishment. This characterization of public moral *argument* is attentive to argument as product and as process.

The problem posed by the presence of experts in public moral argument is illustrated by the dispute between Hans Bethe and Edward Teller over the 1982 nuclear-freeze proposition in California. Their positions were published in the *Los Angeles Times,* so they were public.[81] They obviously concerned a moral issue and they were reasoned statements. Both men were credible. Which one was to be believed and followed? Who in the general public could contend with them? Teller answered the second question in unequivocal terms: "The American public is ignorant, even of the general ideas on which they [nuclear weapons] are based." Here was revealed the fate of nonexperts who would argue about nuclear warfare. Only experts can argue with experts, and their arguments—although public—cannot be rationally questioned by nonexperts. As Perelman noted, rationality of the traditional sort forecloses discussion and debate if it becomes full and final as an ideal.[82] In the presence of experts—those best qualified to argue, according to the rational-world paradigm—the public has no compelling reason to believe one expert over the other. Nonexperts cannot be judges; they become spectators whose choice becomes only a nonrational choice between actors on a stage. Within the narrative paradigm's perspective, however, the experts' stories are not at all beyond analysis by the layperson. The lay audience can test the stories for coherence and fidelity. The lay audience is not perceived as a group of observers, but as active, irrepressible participants in the meaning-formation of the stories that any and all storytellers tell in discourses about nuclear weapons or any other issue that impinges on how people are to be conceived and treated in their ordinary lives.

72

It may be asked at this point: How is it that freeze referendums were approved in eight out of nine states and in twenty-eight cities and counties in 1982? One answer is "fear," the "most intelligent feeling of our time." Another answer is "distrust," distrust of those responsible for the development, deployment, and use of nuclear weapons. The second answer is, I believe, more accurate. It does not deny the existence of fear. It insists on the "rationality" of fear *among other things,* as reasons for those who voted for and against the referendum. Those who opposed the referendum did so because of a basic distrust of Soviet leaders and a fundamental trust of our own. What I am saying is that there were good reasons for trust and distrust, that the response of voters was rational, given the narrative paradigm. A most important point is that the good reasons that are expressed in public moral argument relate to issues not accounted for in the rational-world paradigm. These issues include motivations and values of the characters involved in the ongoing narrative of nuclear warfare, the way in which they conceive and behave in respect to the conflict, and the narrative probability and narrative fidelity of the particular stories they tell, which may well take the form of "reasoned argument." When the *full* range of good reasons for responses is taken into consideration, experts and laypersons meet on the common ground of their shared, human interests. And it is fair to judge arguers on those broad terms, for, as Toulmin observed, "a scientist off duty is as much an 'ordinary' man as a tinker or a bus-conductor off duty."[83]

From the narrative perspective, the proper role of an expert in public moral argument is that of a counselor, which is, as Walter Benjamin notes, the true function of the storyteller.[84] His or her contribution to public dialogue is to impart knowledge, like a teacher, or wisdom, like a sage. It is not to pronounce a story that ends all storytelling. An expert assumes the role of public counselor whenever she or he crosses the boundary of technical knowledge into the territory of life as it ought to be lived. Once this invasion is made, the public, which then includes the expert, has its own criteria for determining whose story is most coherent and reliable as a guide to belief and action. The expert, in other words, then becomes subject to the demands of narrative rationality. Technical communities have their own conceptions and criteria for judging the rationality of communication. But, as G. Holton has demonstrated, the work even of scientists is inspired by stories; hence their discourse can be interpreted usefully from the narrative perspective. Holton writes tellingly of the "nascent movement" in science, the impulse to do science in a particular

73

or in a new way, and how science is informed by "themes"—thematic concepts, methods, and hypotheses inherited from Parmenides, Heraclitus, Pythagoras, Thales, and others.[85]

Viewed from the perspective of the rational-world paradigm, Schell's case, his argument and its reception, evokes despair. If one looks to MacIntyre's *After Virtue* for relief, one will be disappointed and disheartened further, for he provides the historical and philosophical reasons for the fate of *The Fate of the Earth* and similar such arguments. His own argument is that "we still, in spite of the efforts of three centuries of moral philosophy and one of sociology, lack any coherent, rationally defensible statement of a liberal individualist point of view."[86] He offers some hope with the idea that "the Aristotelian tradition can be restated in a way that restores intelligibility and rationality to our moral and social attitudes and commitments." He observes, however, "the new dark ages" are "already upon us." The "barbarians are not waiting beyond the frontiers; they have already been governing us for quite some time. And it is our lack of consciousness of this that constitutes part of our predicament. We are waiting not for Godot, but for another—doubtless very different—St. Benedict."[87]

The reasons for this state of affairs are: (1) the rejection of a teleological view of human nature and the classical conception of reason as embodied in Aristotelian logic and rhetoric; (2) the separation of morality from theological, legal, and aesthetic concerns; and (3) the evolution of the individualistic sense of self and the rise of emotivism. The consequence of these movements is a situation in which ethical arguments in public are rendered ineffectual because of "conceptual incommensurability."

A case in point is protest—where advocates of reform argue from a position of "rights" and those who oppose them reason from the stance of "utility." MacIntyre observes:

> . . . the facts of incommensurability ensure that protestors can never win an *argument;* the indignant self-righteousness of protestors arises because the facts of incommensurability ensure equally that the protestors can never lose an argument either. Hence, the *utterance* of protest is characteristically addressed to those who already *share* the protestors' premises. . . . This is not to say that protest cannot be effective; it is to say that protest cannot be *rationally* effective.[88]

Thus, when arguers appealing to justice and equality contend with adversaries who base their cases on success, survival, and liberty, they talk past each other.

74

From the perspective of the narrative paradigm, the dynamic of this situation is that rival stories are being told. Any story, any form of rhetorical communication, not only says something about the world, it also implies an audience, persons who conceive of themselves in very specific ways. If a story denies a person's self-conception, it does not matter what it says about the world. In the instance of protest, rival factions' stories deny each other in respect to self-conceptions and the world. The only way to bridge this gap, if it can be bridged through discourse, is by telling stories that do not negate the self-conceptions that people hold of themselves.

There is hope in the fact that narrative as *a mode of discourse* is more universal and probably more efficacious than argument for nontechnical forms of communication. There are several reasons why this should be true. First, narration comes closer to capturing the experience of the world, simultaneously appealing to the various senses, to reason and emotion, to intellect and imagination, and to fact and value. It does not presume intellectual contact only. Second, one does not have to be taught narrative probability and narrative fidelity; one culturally acquires them through a universal faculty and experience. Obviously one can, through education, become sophisticated in one's understanding and application of these principles. But, as Gadamer observes, "I am convinced of the fact that there are no people who do not 'think' sometime and somewhere. That means there is no one who does not form general views about life and death, about freedom and living together, about the good and about happiness."[89] In other words, people are reflective and from such reflection they make the stories of their lives and have the basis for judging narratives for and about them. On the other hand, appreciation of argument requires not only reflection, but also specialized knowledge of issues, reasoning, rules of rationality, and so on. Third, narration works by suggestion and identification; argument operates by inferential moves and deliberation. Both forms are modes of expressing good reasons, so the differences between them are structural rather than substantive.

CONCLUSION

In concluding this chapter, I should like to make one additional, general comment about what makes one story better than another. Two features come to mind: formal and substantive. Formal features are attributes of narrative probability: the consistency of characters and actions, the accommodation to auditors, and so on. In epistemological terms, the

75

question would be whether or not a narrative satisfied the demands of a coherence theory of truth. The most compelling, persuasive stories are mythic in form, stories reflective of "public dreams" that give meaning and significance to life.[90] Substantive features relate to narrative fidelity. While there is work to be done on the problem, I think the logic of good reasons is the most viable scheme presently available by which narratives can be tested. Its application requires an examination of reasoning and an inspection of facts, values, self and society. In epistemological terms, narrative fidelity is a matter of truth according to the doctrine of correspondence. Though the most engaging stories are mythic, the most helpful and uplifting stories are moral. As John Gardner wrote, "Moral action is action that affirms life."[91]

One may get the impression that the conception of rationality I have presented leads to a denial of logic. It does so only if logic is conceived so that persons can be considered irrational beings. With Heidegger, I would assert that "To think counter to logic does not mean to stick up for the illogical, but only means to think the *logos,* and its essence as it appeared in the early days of thought; i.e., to make an effort first of all to prepare such an act of re-flecting *(Nachdenka).*"[92]

Application of narrative rationality to specific stories may further clarify its nature and value. From the perspective of narrative rationality, Hitler's *Mein Kampf* must be judged a bad story. Although it has formal coherence in its structure, as Michael McGuire demonstrated,[93] it denies the identity of significant persons and demeans others. It also lacks fidelity to the truths that humanity shares in regard to reason, justice, veracity, and peaceful ways to resolve social-political differences. On the other hand, one may cite the cosmological myths of Lao-tse, Buddha, Zoroaster, Christ, and Muhammad, which satisfy both narrative probability and narrative fidelity for those cultures for whom they were intended—and many others across time and place. Far from denying the humanity of persons, they elevate it to the profoundest moral and metaphysical level the world has known. One could also cite such works as the *Iliad,* the *Odyssey,* the tragedies of Aeschylus, Sophocles, and Euripides, Virgil's *Aeneid,* Dante's *Commedia,* the plays of Shakespeare, and the novels of Tolstoy, Melville, Thomas Mann, and James Joyce. One could point to the lives of Jesus, Socrates, Lincoln, and Gandhi. Regarding political discourse, one could mention many of the speeches and writings of Adlai Stevenson and Winston Churchill. While these classic manifestations of religious, social, cultural, and political life have been celebrated by persons committed to traditional rationality, it has been because these persons did not restrict themselves to "logic" but recognized and responded to the values fostered, and by reaffirmations of the human spirit as the transcendent ground of existence.

For a more detailed illustration of how narrative probability and fidelity can be usefully estimated, I offer this brief analysis of *The Epic of Gilgamesh*, "the finest surviving epic poem from any period until the appearance of Homer's *Iliad:* and it is immeasurably older."[94] It is, in fact, 1,500 years older.

The story, in sum, is as follows: Gilgamesh, the king of Urak, two-thirds god and one-third man, is possessed of a perfect body, unbounded courage, and extraordinary strength. He is a hero, a tragic hero, the "first tragic hero of whom anything is known."[95] His youth is spent in pursuit of fame as the means to immortality.

He is restless, with no one to match his appetites and physical feats. His people ask the gods to create a companion for him, which they do in Enkidu. Enkidu is Gilgamesh's counterpart in strength, energy, and exuberance for life. After a wrestling match, they become inseparable, brothers in every way but birth. Gilgamesh learns what it means to love.

Because Enkidu begins to lose his physical prowess—he had been an inhabitant of the wilds and ran with animals—Gilgamesh proposes that they pursue and slay Huwawa, a terrible monster. At first Enkidu is reluctant but is chided into joining the quest. The monster is met, subdued, and, because of an insult, is slain by Enkidu.

When they return to Urak, the goddess Ishtar proposes to Gilgamesh. He not only refuses her, but he and Enkidu heap scorn upon her. She goes to her father, Anu, and asks him to have the bull of heaven kill Gilgamesh. But Gilgamesh and Enkidu kill the bull instead. It appears at this point that the "brothers" cannot be defeated by man, monsters, or the gods.

It turns out, however, that in killing Huwawa, Gilgamesh and Enkidu incurred the wrath of Enlil, guardian of the forest in which the monster lived. Enlil demands the death of Gilgamesh, but the sun god intervenes and Enkidu is doomed and dies.

With Enkidu's death, the world of Gilgamesh is shattered. He has not only lost his loving companion, he must now directly confront the fact of death. Up to this point, he has lived as a willful child, acting as though the meaning of live is a matter of dominating it.

At first Gilgamesh refuses to accept Enkidu's death as real. He becomes obsessed with death and starts a quest to learn the secret of immortality. His journey is tortured and long. He finally arrives, after incredible hardships, at the island of Utanapishtim and asks him how one gains eternal life. Utanapishtim suggests that he try not to sleep for six days and seven nights. But he soon falls alseep for seven days, a form of living death. He is awakened and realizes there is no escape from death. He resigns himself to his fate, the fate of all humankind, and returns home. On his return he learns to value the wall he has built around the city: immortality is, he apparently concludes, to be found in the monuments that one leaves behind.

The story provides good reasons to accept not only this truth, but others as well: Life is fullest when one loves and is loved; death is real; and maturity is achieved by accepting the reality of death. We learn these truths by dwelling in the characters in the story, by observing the outcomes of the several conflicts that arise throughout it, by seeing the unity of characters and their actions, and by comparing the truths to the truths we know to be true from our own lives. In other words, the story exhibits narrative probability and fidelity across time and culture.[96]

Finally, I do not mean to maintain that "knowledge" of agents is superior to "knowledge of objects." With Toulmin, I would hold that "A decent respect for each kind of knowledge is surely compatible with conceding the legitimate claims of the other."[97] With knowledge of agents, we can hope to find that which is *reliable* or *trustworthy;* with knowledge of objects, we can hope to discover that which has the quality of *veracity.* The world requires both kinds of knowledge.

Karl Wallace was right: "One could do worse than characterize rhetoric as the art of finding and effectively presenting good reasons."[98] MacIntyre is also right:

> The unity of human life is the unity of a narrative quest. Quests sometimes fail, are frustrated, abandoned or dissipated into distractions; and human lives may in all these ways also fail. But the criteria for success or failure in a human life as a whole are the criteria of success or failure in a narrated or to-be-narrated quest."[99]

And that quest is "for the good life" for all persons.

The next chapter will elaborate many of the ideas presented here. In particular, it will show how the narrative paradigm relates to contemporary thought in the social sciences and the humanities.

NOTES

1. Gerald Graff, *Literature against Itself: Literary Ideas in Society* (Chicago: University of Chicago Press, 1979).

2. Alfred Tennyson, *Maud* (New York: Dodd Mead and Co., 1905), p. 37. For

an alternative characterization of John Bright and his opposition to the Crimean War, see my essay "John Bright: 'Hawker of Holy Things,'" *Quarterly Journal of Speech* 51 (1965):157–63.

3. Alasdair MacIntyre, *After Virtue: A Study in Moral Theory,* (Notre Dame Ind.: Notre Dame University Press, 1981), p. 201.

4. Ibid., p. 194.

5. Margaret Masterman, "The Nature of a Paradigm," in I. Lakotos and A. Musgrave, eds., *Criticism and the Growth of Knowledge* (London: Cambridge University Press, 1970), p. 65. See also Thomas S. Kuhn, "Second Thoughts on Paradigms," in F. Suppe, ed., *The Structure of Scientific Theories* (Urbana: University of Illinois Press, 1974), pp. 459–82.

6. W. Lance Bennett and Marsha S. Feldman, *Reconstructing Reality in the Courtroom: Justice and Judgment in American Culture* (New Brunswick, N.J.: Rutgers University Press, 1981). See also W. Lance Bennett, "Political Scenarios and the Nature of Politics," *Philosophy and Rhetoric* 8 (1975):23–42.

7. Thomas B. Farrell, "The Tradition of Rhetoric and the Philosophy of Communication," *Communication* 7 (1983):151–80.

8. W. B. Gallie, *Philosophy and Historical Understanding* (New York: Schocken Books, 1964).

9. Leonard C. Hawes, "The Reflexivity of Communication Research," *Western Journal of Speech Communication* 42 (1978):12–20.

10. Leon O. Mink, "Narrative Form as a Cognitive Instrument," in R. H. Canary, ed., *The Writing of History* (Madison: University of Wisconsin Press, 1978), pp. 129–49.

11. Calvin O. Schrag, *Communicative Praxis and the Space of Subjectivity* (Bloomington: Indiana University Press, 1986).

12. Robert L. Scott, "Evidence in Communication: We Are Such Stuff," *Western Journal of Speech Communication* 42 (1978):29–36.

13. Herbert W. Simons, "In Praise of Muddle Headed Anecdotalism," *Western Journal of Speech Communication* 42 (1978):21–28.

14. Robert Alter, *The Art of Biblical Narrative* (New York: Basic Books, 1981).

15. M. Goldberg, *Theology and Narrative* (Nashville, Tenn.: Parthenon Press, 1982).

16. Stanley Hauerwas, *A Community of Character: Toward a Constructive Christian Ethic* (Notre Dame Ind.: University of Notre Dame Press, 1981).

17. Arthur C. Danto, *Narration and Knowledge* (New York: Columbia University Press, 1985).

18. Jacques Derrida, "The Law of Genre," *Critical Inquiry* 7 (1980):55–81.

19. Frank Kermode, "Secrets and Narrative Sequence," *Critical Inquiry* 7 (1980):83–101.

20. John S. Nelson, "Tropal and History and the Social Sciences: Reflections on Struever's Remarks," *History and Theory* 19 (1980):80–101.

21. Paul Ricoeur, *Time and Narrative,* trans. Kathleen MacLaughlin and D. Pellauer (2 vols.; Chicago: University of Chicago Press, 1984, 1985).

22. T. Todorov, *The Poetics of Prose,* trans. R. Howard (Ithaca, N.Y.: Cornell University Press, 1977).

23. Victor Turner, "Social Dramas and Stories about Them," *Critical Inquiry* 7 (1980):141–68.

24. Hayden White, *Metahistory; Tropics of History* (Baltimore, Md.: Johns Hopkins University Press, 1978). See also White, "The Value of Narrativity in the Representation of Reality," *Critical Inquiry* 7 (1980): 5–27.

25. See Lloyd F. Bitzer, "Rhetoric and Public Knowledge," in Don Burks, ed., *Rhetoric, Philosophy, and Literature: An Exploration* (West Lafayette, Ind.: Purdue University Press, 1978), pp. 67–93; and Thomas B. Farrell, "Knowledge, Consensus, and Rhetorical Theory," *Quarterly Journal of Speech* 62 (1976): 1–14.

26. M. Hollis, *Models of Man: Philosophical Thoughts on Social Action* (Cambridge, England: Cambridge University Press, 1973), pp. 165–66. See also Stephen Toulmin, "Reasons and Causes," in R. Borger and F. Cioffi, eds., *Explanation in the Social Sciences* (Cambridge, England: Cambridge University Press, 1970), pp. 1–41.

27. See William Barrett, *The Illusion of Technique: A Search for Meaning in a Technological Civilization* (Garden City, N.Y.: Anchor Press/Doubleday, 1979); Wayne C. Booth, *Modern Dogma and the Rhetoric of Assent* (Notre Dame, Ind.: University of Notre Dame Press, 1974); Hans-Georg Gadamer, *Truth and Method* (New York: Crossroad Publishing Co., 1982), and *Reason in the Age of Science* (Cambridge, Mass.: MIT Press, 1981); Bernard J. F. Lonergan, *Insight: A Study of Human Understanding* (New York: Harper & Row, 1958); Richard Rorty, *Philosophy and the Mirror of Nature* (Princeton, N.J.: Princeton University Press, 1979); Calvin O. Schrag, *Radical Reflection and the Origins of the Human Sciences* (West Lafayette, Ind.: Purdue University Press, 1980); Richard Sennett, *The Fall of Public Man: On the Social Psychology of Capitalism* (New York: Vintage Books, 1978); Stephen Toulmin, *Human Understanding* (Princeton, N.J.: Princeton University Press, 1972), and *The Return to Cosmology: Postmodern Science and Theology of Nature* (Berkeley: University of California Press, 1982); Eric Vogelin, *The New Science of Politics* (Chicago: University of Chicago Press, 1952), and *From Enlightenment to Revolution* (Durham, N.C.: Duke University Press, 1975).

28. John H. Randall, Jr., *The Making of the Modern Mind* (New York: Columbia University Press, 1976), p. 651.

29. Jürgen Habermas, *Theory and Practice: The History of a Concept* (Notre Dame, Ind.: University of Notre Dame Press, 1967), p. 254. See also Martin Heidegger, *On Time and Being*, trans. J. Stanbaugh (New York: Harper & Row, 1972), pp. 58–59.

30. John Dewey, *The Public and Its Problems* (Chicago: Swallow Press, 1927).

31. MacIntyre, *After Virtue*, p. 245.

32. See Bitzer, "Rhetoric and Public Knowledge"; Farrell, "Knowledge, Consensus and Rhetorical Theory"; Jürgen Habermas, *Knowledge and Social Interests* (Boston: Beacon Press, 1973); John Lyne, "Discourse, Knowledge, and Social Process," *Quarterly Journal of Speech* 68 (1982): 201–14; Michael Calvin McGee and Martha A. Martin, "Public Knowledge and Ideological Argumentation," *Communication Monographs* 50 (1983): 47–65; M. Polanyi, *Personal Knowledge: Towards a Postcritical Philosophy* (Chicago: University of Chicago Press, 1958); J. Ziman, *Public Knowledge* (London: Cambridge University Press, 1968).

33. Ray E. McKerrow, "On Argument Communities" and "On Fields and

Rational Enterprises: A Reply to Willard," in Jack Rhodes and S. Newell, eds., *Proceedings of the Summer Conference on Argumentation* (Falls Church, Va.: Speech Communication Association, 1980), pp. 214–27 and pp. 401–11 respectively; Stephen Toulmin, *The Uses of Argument* (Cambridge, England: Cambridge University Press, 1958), and Toulmin, Richard Rieke, and Allan Janik, *Introduction to Reasoning* (New York: Macmillan Co., 1979); Charles A. Willard, "A Reformulation of the Concept of Argument: The Constructivist/ Interactionist Foundations of a Sociology of Argument," *Journal of the American Forensic Association* 14 (1978): 121–40.

34. See chapt. 5, which is in part based on my "Toward a Logic of Good Reasons," *Quarterly Journal of Speech* 64 (1978): 376–84; Chaïm Perelman and L. Olbrechts-Tyteca, *The New Rhetoric: A Treatise on Argumentation,* trans. John Wilkinson and Purcell Weaver (Notre Dame, Ind.: University of Notre Dame Press, 1969); Toulmin, *The Uses of Argument;* Joseph W. Wenzel, "Toward a Rationale for Value-Centered Argument," *Journal of the American Forensic Association* 13 (1977): 150–58.

35. Karl-Otto Apel, "Types of Rationality Today: The Continuum of Reason between Science and Ethics," in T. F. Geraets, ed., *Rationality To-Day* (Ottawa: University of Ottawa Press, 1979), pp. 309–39; Douglas Ehninger, "Validity as Moral Obligation," *Southern Speech Journal* 33 (1968): 215–22; Thomas B. Farrell, "Validity and Rationality: The Rhetorical Constituents of Argumentative Form," *Journal of the American Forensic Association* 13 (1977): 142–49; chap. 5 of the present work, which is based in part on "Rationality and the Logic of Good Reasons," *Philosophy and Rhetoric* 13 (1980): 121–30; Gidon Gottlieb, *The Logic of Choice: An Investigation of the Concepts of Rule and Rationality* (New York: Macmillan Co., 1968); Henry W. Johnstone, Jr., *Validity and Rhetoric in Philosophical Argument* (University Park, Pa.: Dialogue Press of Man and World, 1978); Ray E. McKerrow, "Rhetorical Validity: An Analysis of Three Perspectives on the Justification of Rhetorical Argument," *Journal of the American Forensic Association* 13 (1977): 133–41, and "Rationality and Reasonableness in a Theory of Argument," in Robert R. Cox and C. A. Willard, eds., *Advances in Argumentation Theory and Research* (Carbondale: University of Southern Illinois Press, 1982), pp. 105–22.

36. Wayne Brockriede, "Where Is Argument?" *Journal of the American Forensic Association* 11 (1975): 129–32, and "Arguing about Human Understanding," *Communication Monographs* 49 (1982): 137–47.

37. Brant R. Burleson, "Characteristics of Argument," in George Ziegelmueller and Jack Rhodes, eds., *Dimensions of Argument: Proceedings of the Second Conference on Argumentation* (Annandale, Va.: Speech Communication Association, 1981), pp. 955–79.

38. Scott Jacobs and Sally Jackson, "Argument as a Natural Category: The Routine Grounds for Arguing in Conversation," *Western Journal of Speech Communication* 45 (1981): 118–32.

39. Ray E. McKerrow, "Senses of Argument: Uses and Limitations of the Concept," in Ziegelmueller and Rhodes, *Dimensions of Argument,* pp. 980–86.

40. Daniel J. O'Keefe, "Two Concepts of Argument," *Journal of the American Forensic Association* 13 (1977): 121–28, and "The Concepts of Argument and Arguing," in Cox and Willard, *Argumentation Theory,* pp. 3–23.

41. Joseph W. Wenzel, "Perspectives on Argument," in Rhodes and Newell, *Proceedings* (1980), pp. 112–33.

42. For Willard reference, see n. 33, above.

43. Kenneth Burke, "Definition of Man," in *Language as Symbolic Action: Essays on Life, Literature, and Method* (Berkeley: University of California Press, 1968), p. 16. See also Ernst Cassirer, *An Essay on Man: An Introduction to a Philosophy of Human Culture* (New Haven, Conn.: Yale University Press, 1944), p. 26; Susanne Langer, *Feeling and Form: A Theory of Art* (New York: Charles Scribner's Sons, 1953), pp. 264ff.

44. Kenneth Burke, *Philosophy of Literary Form* (rev. ed.; New York: Vintage Books, 1957), pp. 94–97.

45. Martin Heidegger, *Existence and Being* (Chicago: Henry Regnery, 1949), p. 278. See also Gadamer, *Truth and Method,* pp. 330ff.; Rorty, *Philosophy and the Mirror of Nature,* pp. 315ff.

46. Ernest G. Bormann, "Fantasy and Rhetorical Vision: The Rhetorical Criticism of Social Reality," *Quarterly Journal of Speech* 59 (1972): 396–407.

47. Thomas S. Frentz and Thomas B. Farrell, "Language-Action: A Paradigm for Communication," *Quarterly Journal of Speech* 62 (1976): 333–49.

48. Ernest G. Bormann, "Fantasy Theme Analysis," in James L. Golden, G. F. Berquist, and W. E.Coleman, eds., *The Rhetoric of Western Thought* (3rd ed.; Dubuque, Iowa: Kendall/Hunt, 1983), p. 434.

49. Bormann, "Fantasy and Rhetorical Vision," p. 397.

50. Ibid., p. 398.

51. Walter R. Fisher, "Rhetorical Fiction and the Presidency," *Quarterly Journal of Speech* 66 (1980): 120–22.

52. Ernest G. Bormann, "The Eagleton Affair: A Fantasy Theme Analysis," *Quarterly Journal of Speech* 59 (1973): 143–59.

53. See Charles R. Bantz, "Television News: Reality and Research," *Western Journal of Speech Communication* 39 (1975): 123–30; Virginia Kidd, "Happily Ever After and Other Relationship Styles: Advice on Interpersonal Relations in Popular Magazines, 1951–1973," *Quarterly Journal of Speech* 61 (1975): 31–39; David L. Rarick, M. B. Duncan, and L. W. Porter, "The Carter Persona: An Empirical Analysis of the Rhetorical Visions of Campaign '76," *Quarterly Journal of Speech* 63 (1977): 258–73.

54. Paul Ricoeur, *Interpretation Theory: Discourse and the Surplus of Meaning* (Fort Worth: Texas Christian University Press, 1976).

55. Frentz and Farrell, "Language-Action," p. 336.

56. MacIntyre, *After Virtue,* p. 200.

57. See J. Goody and I. Watt, "The Consequences of Literacy," *Comparative Studies in Society and History* 5 (1962–63), pp. 304–26, 332–45; Stephen D. Krashen, *Principles and Practice in Second Language Acquisition* Elmsford, N.Y.: Pergamon Press, 1982).

58. White, "The Value of Narrativity," p. 6.

59. Turner, "Social Dramas," p. 167.

60. Dell Hymes, "A Narrative View of the World," in *Language in Education: Ethnolinguistic Essays* (Washington, D.C.: Center for Applied Linguistics, 1980), p. 132. See also Roland Barthes, "Introduction to the Structural Analysis of Narratives," in S. Heath, ed., *Image-Music-Text* (New York: Hill and Wang,

1977), pp. 79–124; Walter Ong, *Orality and Literacy: The Technologizing of the World* (London: Methuen, 1982).

61. Gregory Bateson, *Mind and Nature: A Necessary Unity* (Toronto: Bantam Books, 1979), p. 14.

62. Kenneth Burke, lecture outline, "Logology: An Overall View," personal correspondence.

63. MacIntyre, *After Virtue*, p. 197. See also Kenneth J. Gergen and Mary M. Gergen, "Narratives of the Self," in T. R. Sarkin and K. E. Scheibe, eds., *Studies in Social Identity* (New York: Praeger, 1983), pp. 254–73.

64. Booth, *Modern Dogma*, pp. 114ff.

65. Alasdair MacIntyre, "Rationality and the Explanation of Action," in *Against the Self-Images of the Age: Essays on Ideology and Philosophy* (Notre Dame, Ind.: University of Notre Dame Press, 1978), p. 258.

66. See Gadamer, *Reason in the Age of Science;* Heidegger, *On Time and Being;* G. Holton, *Thematic Origins of Modern Science* (Cambridge, Mass.: Harvard University Press, 1973); Ian T. Ramsey, "Religion and Science: A Philosopher's Approach," in D. M. High, ed., *New Essays and Religious Language* (New York: Oxford University Press, 1969), pp. 36–53.

67. Aristotle, *Rhetoric*, trans. W. Rhys Roberts (New York: Modern Library, 1954), 1.1.1355 20.

68. V. O. Key, *The Responsible Electorate: Rationality in Voting, 1936–1960* (New York: Vintage Books, 1966), pp. 7–8.

69. Bennett and Feldman, *Reconstructing Reality in the Courtroom.*

70. White, "The Value of Narrativity," p. 26. See also Walter Benjamin, "The Storyteller," in Hannah Arendt, ed., *Illuminations* (New York: Schocken Books, 1969), pp. 83–109.

71. Schrag, *Radical Reflection*, p. 126.

72. Angel Medina, *Reflection, Time, and the Novel: Toward a Communicative Theory of Literature* (London: Routledge & Kegan Paul, 1979), p. 30.

73. Jonathan Schell, *The Fate of the Earth* (New York: Avon Books, 1982).

74. Ibid., p. 231.

75. S. McCracken, "The Peace of the Grave," *National Review,* July 23, 1982, p. 905.

76. M. Hausknecht, "Waiting for the End? Prospects for Nuclear Destruction," *Dissent* 29 (1982): 284.

77. A. J. Pierre, "Review of *The Fate of the Earth,*" *Foreign Affairs* 60 (1982): p. 1188.

78. See Thomas B. Farrell and G. Thomas Goodnight, "Accidental Rhetoric: The Root Metaphor of the Rule Island," *Communication Monographs* 48 (1981): 271–300.

79. Aristotle, *Rhetoric*, 1.2.1257 10.

80. Joseph R. Gusfield, *Symbolic Crusade: Status Politics and the American Temperance Movement* (Urbana: University of Illinois Press, 1976), p. 173.

81. *Los Angeles Times,* October 17, 1982, pt. 4, pp. 1–2.

82. Chaïm Perelman, "The Rational and the Reasonable," in *The New Rhetoric and the Humanities: Essays on Rhetoric and Its Applications* (Dordrecht Holland: D. Reidel, 1979), pp. 117–23.

83. Toulmin, *The Return to Cosmology,* p. 81.

84. Benjamin, "The Storyteller," pp. 108–9.

85. Holton, *Thematic Origins,* pp. 28–29. See also Ong, *Orality and Literacy,* p. 140.

86. MacIntyre, *After Virtue,* p. 241.

87. Ibid., p. 245.

88. Ibid., p. 69.

89. Gadamer, *Reason in the Age of Science,* p. 58. See also S. M. Ogden, "Myth and Truth," in *The Reality of God* (University Park: The Pennsyvlania State University Press, 1977), p. 114; Lonergan, *Insight,* p. xiv, xxii, xxx.

90. Joseph Campbell, *The Hero with a Thousand Faces* (New York: Bollingen Series XVII, Pantheon Books, 1949), p. 19. See also Campbell, *Myths to Live By* (New York: Bantam Books, 1973); Mircea Eliade, *Myth and Reality* (New York: Harper Colophon Books, 1963).

91. John Gardner, *On Moral Fiction* (New York: Basic Books, 1978), p. 23.

92. Martin Heidegger, "Letter on Humanism," in R. Zaner and D. Ihde, eds., *Phenomenology and Existentialism* (New York: G. P. Putnam Capricorn Books, 1973), p. 170.

93.Michael McGuire, "Mythic Rhetoric in *Mein Kampf:* A Structural Critique," *Quarterly Journal of Speech* 68 (1977):1–13.

94. N. K. Sandars, *The Epic of Gilgamesh* (New York: Penguin Books, 1982), p. 7.

95. Ibid., p. 7.

96. Thorkild Jacobsen, *The Treasures of Darkness: A History of Mesopotamian Religion* (New Haven, Conn.: Yale University Press, 1976).

97. Toulmin, *The Return to Cosmology,* p. 244.

98. Karl Wallace, "The Substance of Rhetoric: Good Reasons," *Quarterly Journal of Speech* 49 (1963):248.

99. MacIntyre, *After Virtue,* p. 203.

4

AN ELABORATION

Chapter 3 concluded with the observation that both "knowledge of agents," which the narrative paradigm specifically opens to view, and "knowledge of objects," our means of determining veracity, are important to all social thinking. Traditional theories applied in the social sciences and at least some traditional theories in the humanities address themselves to alleged verities about phenomena. For that reason, I want in this chapter to offer an answer to the question: How does the narrative paradigm relate to traditional theories used in the social sciences and the humanities? This endeavor will lead inevitably to questions about the explanatory or critical power of the narrative paradigm. I shall therefore have to touch in general terms on the paradigm as a critical construct. I shall, however, defer detailed illustrations of the paradigm's critical applications until later chapters.

Preliminary to examining the narrative paradigm in relation to specific social-scientific and humanistic theories, I need to make two general points. First, the narrative paradigm, as I conceptualize it, is not a radical or entirely new construct. It reflects a set of ideas that is shared in whole or in part by many scholars from diverse intellectual disciplines, and especially by those whose work is informed by or centers on the character and role of narrativity in human life. Much that I shall say, then, draws upon research and speculations of other scholars. I hope, however, to give some of their ideas wider applicability than they have perhaps seen heretofore. Second, I shall say little about applying the narrative paradigm to one genre or another, although I do not think it is useless to draw distinctions among macroforms of discourse such as philosophy, rhetoric, and poetic or such microforms of discourse as myths, metaphors, and arguments. (Later, in chap. 7, I shall present my own view of genre.) My position here is simply that there is no genre, including even technical discourse, that is not an episode in the story of life (a part of "conversation") and that is not constituted by both logos and mythos. Put another way, I contend that even technical discourse is imbued with myth and metaphor, and that aesthetic discourse has cognitive import for anyone who experiences it. Accordingly, in my view, what can be said about interpreting and assessing one kind of discourse, using the narrative paradigm, can in principle be said about interpreting and assessing any other kind of discourse.

RELATIONSHIPS TO OTHER THEORIES

In discussing how the narrative paradigm relates to social-scientific and humanistic theories, I risk suggesting that absolute boundaries can be drawn between the assumptions and methods of those who identify themselves in one or another of these intellectual realms. I wish therefore to emphasize at the outset that work in conversational analysis focusing on narrativity clearly crosses disciplines,[1] and that there is a "third world of inquiry."[2] Its title is "human sciences," and its practitioners include researchers who employ empirical, historical, linguistic, hermeneutical, ethnomethodological, and philosophical methods of investigation. What unites them, I believe, is their rejection of or resistance to what Richard Bernstein calls the "Cartesian Anxiety": "With a chilling clarity Descartes leads us with an apparent and ineluctable necessity to a grand and seductive Either/Or. *Either* there is some support for our being, a fixed foundation for our knowledge, *or* we cannot escape the forces of darkness that envelope us with madness, with intellectual and moral chaos."[3] The narrative paradigm provides a ground where human scientists can and do meet, however they pursue their individual projects.

SOCIAL-SCIENTIFIC THEORIES AND THE NARRATIVE PARADIGM

The theories I shall mention here are representative; they are basic to communication inquiry, and they illustrate constructs that are not controlled by Cartesianism.[4] I have in mind attribution theory,[5] balance theory,[6] constructivism,[7] social-convergence theory,[8] reinforcement theory,[9] social-exchange theory,[10] and symbolic interactionism.[11] By and large, these theories are inspired by the dream of Cartesianism: descriptive, explanatory, and predictive knowledge. In practice, however, they are, or at least can be interpreted as, various ways to account for *how* people come to adopt stories that guide behavior. In this, and in their ultimate nonpositivism, they are related to the narrative paradigm, for it, too, seeks to account for *how* people come to adopt stories that guide behavior. It, too, is productive of description, explanation, and even prediction—in the sense that if one's character can be determined and if one's story in regard to a particular issue can be ascertained, it is possible to predict a person's probable actions. That is the best prediction that social-scientific theories can offer.[12]

Where the narrative paradigm goes beyond these theories is in providing a "logic" for assessing stories, for determining whether or not one *should* adhere to the stories one is encouraged to endorse or to accept as the basis for decisions and actions. For the most part, social-scientific theories ignore the role of values or they deny the possibility of developing rational schemes for their assessment. They thereby disregard ultimate questions of good and evil—of the good life, which is the very topic of the Socrates-Callicles exchange that will be considered in chapter 9. And this applies to any other critical theory that, like Descartes's, denies room for values. This is not to say that social scientists do not have values or that they have no concern for humane relations. It is to say that their standard theories, by their nature, do not take the *assessment* of values into consideration.

On the other hand, social-scientific theories are characteristically normative, presupposing that there are such goods as appropriate meanings, psychological equilibrium, co-orientation, consensus, mutual benefit, and unity of mind and action. Balance theory and Burke's concept of identification,[13] which is central to symbolic interactionism, are cases in point. Neither balance theory nor dramatism is tied to a rational system for assessing the stories one *should* adopt to achieve psychological equilibrium or to achieve consubstantiality in order to resolve human conflicts. The norm that marks many models in scientific constructs is "efficacy," the power or capacity to control one's environment stategically.

Erving Goffman's theory of interpersonal interaction is illustrative. While Goffman took a "storytelling" approach in his studies of human relations, his focus was on the presentation of self and impression management.[14] "The goal of the Goffmanesque role player," as Alasdair MacIntyre observes, is "effectiveness and success" and success is "nothing but what passes for success."[15] The epistemology that underlies the model is inherited from Francis Bacon—knowledge is power over things—but it is implicitly extended in Goffman's social-scientific theory to: knowledge is also power over people.

The precise way in which the narrative paradigm goes beyond such traditional social-scientific theories is in introducing the concept of narrative rationality. This concept provides principles—probability and fidelity—which are considerations for judging the merits of stories, whether one's own or another's. No guarantee exists that one who uses the principles of narrative rationality will not adopt "bad" stories, rationalizations, but utilizing the principles does mitigate this tendency. Their use engenders critical self-awareness and conscious choice.

An example should clarify the distinction I am making between the domains of the narrative paradigm and of traditional social-science theories. Balance theory predicts that a person will manifest balance-restoring behavior when he or she experiences psychological disequilibrium. Someone tries out for a track team or a play, or runs for office and is not successful. To restore balance, the person searches for a story that will justify his or her effort. Such stories may be positive or negative: I wasn't chosen but I had a great experience. I made new friends, learned valuable skills, and had lots of fun. Or, I wasn't chosen because I just wasn't prepared for the contest. Besides, some of the other contestants cheated and I wasn't treated fairly. For the person involved, these stories would satisfy the need for equilibrium and the demands of narrative probability and fidelity—or at least they could be defended by using these principles. It may be, however, that another observer would think otherwise, that the involved person was rationalizing. In any event, it is precisely in this sort of situation that the notion of narrative rationality is relevant as a system for determining whether or not one *should* accept a story, whether or not a story is indeed trustworthy and reliable as a guide to belief and action. Knowing something about the character of the speaker and his or her actual experience, one can judge whether his or her story "hangs together" and "rings true."

Having made these claims, I want to develop the concept of narrative rationality in some detail. Narrative *coherence* refers to formal features of a story conceived as a discrete sequence of thought and/or action in life or literature (any recorded or written form of discourse); that is, it concerns whether the story coheres or "hangs together," whether or not a story is free of contradictions. Narrative *fidelity* concerns the "truth qualities" of a story, the degree to which it accords with the logic of good reasons: the soundness of its reasoning and the value of its values.

To test soundness, one may, *when relevant,* employ standards from formal or informal logic. Thus one must be attentive to facts, particular patterns of inference and implicature, and issues—conceived as traditional questions arising in forensic (fact, definition, justification, and procedure) or deliberative (the nature of a problem and the desirability of proposed solutions) practices. However, use of the narrative paradigm forces recognition that reasons are expressed by elements of human communication that are not always clear-cut inferential or implicative forms. Any individuated form of human communication may constitute a good reason if it is taken as a *warrant for accepting or adhering to the advice fostered* by that communication.

To weigh values, one considers questions of fact, relevance, consequence, consistency, and transcendent issue. These questions involve determination of what the values are; whether or not they are pertinent to the story or case at hand; whether or not their impact on one's concept of self, one's relationship with others, and the process of rhetorical transaction is desirable; what would follow from their confirmation or disconfirmation in one's life, the lives of those whom one admires, and the best life that one can conceive; and evaluation of their effects on the quality of life generally. Narrative rationality is an attempt to recapture Aristotle's concept of *phronesis,* "practical wisdom."

HUMANISTIC THEORIES AND THE NARRATIVE PARADIGM

Narrativity has been of primary interest to diverse scholars in the humanities for a long period of time. In what follows, I hope to give force to the idea that there is a community that sees narrativity as a legitimate and useful way to interpret and understand human relations.

The humanistic stories I shall examine include structuralism/poststructuralism, critical theory, analytic/postanalytic philosophy, and hermeneutics. Obviously, I cannot reconstruct these theories historically or in all of their permutations. Except for analytic philosophy, all of them are compatible with or constitutive of the narrative paradigm. My primary consideration in examining them will be how each orientation responds to the question: How and to what do symbols refer? I believe it is in respect to answers to this question that the various schools of thought may be differentiated.[16] Another consideration will be whether or not the theory offers a scheme for critique. If it does, I shall ask what the scheme is and how it relates to narrative rationality. Finally, I want to observe an important way that hermeneutics enriches the conception of human communication in the narrative paradigm.

One of the most significant lines of inquiry into narrativity has been made on the basis of structuralism, poststructuralism, and semiotics. These studies have made major contributions to the interpretation of texts. Whether of the classical, semiotic, or deconstructionist schools, structuralist thinkers tend to regard narrative synchronically, as a form or genre, and not as a way of understanding lived as well as imagined stories. Narratology, for instance, the "scientific" study of narrative discourse,[17] which was advanced by such writers as J. Greimas, Tzvetan Todorov, Gerard Genette, and Roland Barthes, took as given that:

> Narrative does not show, does not imitate; the passion which may excite us in reading a novel is not that of a "vision" (in actual fact, we do not "see" anything). Rather it is that of a meaning, that of a higher order or relation which also has its emotions, its hopes, its dangers, its triumphs. "What takes place" in a narrative is from the referential (reality) point of view literally *nothing;* "what happens" is language alone, the adventure of language, the unceasing celebration of its coming.[18]

In short, structuralism approaches narrative formally; whereas, the narrative paradigm approaches it, along with other genres, rhetorically, as a mode of social influence.

Second, as indicated in Barthes's observation, structuralists, at least of the classical school, deny the relevance of reference in their studies. A poststructuralist exponent of this position is Paolo Valesio, a student of Roman Jakobson who has been a pivotal figure in the structuralist movement. Valesio argues that *"every discourse in its functional aspect is based on a relatively limited set of mechanisms—whose structure remains essentially the same from text to text, from language to language, from historical period to historical period—that reduce every referential choice to formal choice."*[19] He also insists that "All facts are accessible to us only as linguistic constructions."[20] Thus, by viewing narration or any other kind of discourse only in terms of making meanings and by restricting understanding of praxis to linguistic constructions, structuralism neglects two of the most basic features implied by the narrative paradigm.

The narrative paradigm is a paradigm in the sense that it expresses and implies a philosophical view of human communication; it is not a model of discourse as such. The primary function of the paradigm is to offer a way of interpreting and assessing human communication that leads to critique, to a determination of whether or not a given instance of discourse provides a reliable, trustworthy, and desirable guide to thought and action *in the world*. It predicates that all normal human discourse is meaningful and is subject to the tests of narrative rationality. Contrary to structuralist thinking, it holds that meaning is a matter of history, culture, and character as well as of linguistic convention and interanimation.

In taking this position, I invite Derrida's now famous (or infamous) charge of "logocentrism." However, I do not privilege oral over written communication or adhere to a positivist view of the world. I agree that symbols are indeed "indeterminant" if one pushes them far enough, that an author's name (or presence) is irrelevant for understanding many mundane forms of communication, and that one of the pervasive functions of language is to foster ideology. Meaning for Derrida, however, is a matter of use rather than reference to people and things in the world. The purpose of critique, according to Derrida, is to reveal this fact in a Nietzschian fashion and to deform the basis of "Western metaphysics," which includes everyday thought and language as well as the philosophical tradition. His method is well illustrated in his essay on Plato's *Phaedrus*, "Pharmacia."[21] It is clear what Derrida seeks to subvert;[22] it is unclear what he seeks to affirm.[23] A problem is that epistemological skepticism can lead anywhere, as evidenced by the uses to which Nietzsche's thought has been put in the twentieth century.

Critical theory, however, has had a historic direction—"liberation," "emancipation," or a "rational society"; and, until now, a consistent method of critique—dialectic. There is no lack of leading philosophical critics who function in this general tradition. Departing from the Frankfurt School's early focus on "consciousness," then "instrumental reason," Jürgen Habermas has turned his attention to a theory of communicative action.[24] Like Karl-Otto Apel,[25] Habermas conceives rationality as grounded in the presuppositions of speech, specifically argumentative interactions. Rationality is determined by "whether, if necessary," persons could, "*under suitable circumstances,* provide reasons for their expressions."[26] Thus he reserves rationality for argumentation, "that type of speech in which participants thematize contested validity claims and attempt to vindicate or criticize them through arguments. An argument contains reasons or grounds that are connected in a systematic way with the *validity claim* of a problematic expression."[27]

Validity claims may concern truth in terms of the objective world; the rightness, appropriateness, or legitimacy of speech acts; or the sincerity or authenticity of intentions or feelings. The nature of validity claims relates to Habermas's conception of communicative functions: *teleological,* which is manifest in monologic communication; *normative,* which is featured in interpersonal (cultural) communication; and dramaturgical, which is evidenced in self-presentational communication.[28] Habermas maintains that his view of language encompasses all three functions and that his "communicative model of action" is in the traditions of "Mead's symbolic interactionism, Wittgenstein's concept of language games, Austin's theory of speech acts, and Gadamer's hermeneutics."[29]

The end of communication, Habermas holds, is understanding, by which he means "valid agreement."[30] In order for understanding to be achieved rationally, a communicative interaction must not only include arguers, it must also be symmetrical and noncoercive. Such communicative encounters would be exhibited in an "ideal speech situation." There would be equal opportunity to participate, to criticize, to express personal aims and attitudes, and to perform these acts without regard to power or ideology. These requirements are parallel to the conditions I presuppose as necessities of human communication. Beyond the physical requirements of communicants who share some commonality in symbol systems, human communication relies on some degree of trust, a willingness to participate in the process, a belief in the desirability of the interaction, and an interest in (or expectation of) the attainment or advancement of truth. These necessities can be formed as norms and then can serve as standards for the evaluation of communicative interaction, like the requirements of the "ideal speech situation." However, two features of these requirements/necessities should be noted. First, Habermas's requirements are "counterfactual"; the necessities are empirical. Second, neither the requirements nor the necessities speak to the soundness of the reasoning that occurs in a communicative interaction. This judgment can be accomplished only through some scheme such as that provided by narrative rationality.

Thus, while contemporary humanistic, critical theories anticipate themes that I develop in the narrative paradigm and while there are common objectives in Habermas's project and mine, there are also differences. Habermas posits persons as arguers; I see them, including arguers, as storytellers. He conceives reasons as warrants tied to claims of validity; I conceive reasons as warrants that are or entail values (good reasons). His interest is argumentation; mine is all forms of human communication. His concept of the end of communication is understanding; my concept of the end of communication is practical wisdom and humane action. In sum, our differences primarily concern the nature and functions of human communication. Ordinary discourse, in my view, is not inherently "distorted," and there are many forms of human communication beyond argumentation and the specific, individuated units we call arguments.

Except for Alasdair MacIntyre, analytic and postanalytic philosophers neglect the idea of narrative. The concept of narrative rationality is specifically denied by such analytic philosophers as A. J. Ayer, Donald Davidson, Hilary Putnam, and Gilbert Ryle. They hold strongly to an epistemological position generally referred to as "foundationalism." This is the position that insists that only certain forms of discourse can lay claim to knowledge and that there are absolute grounds or methods that can assure such claims. Postanalytic philosophers regard this position with skepticism or outright rejection. Among them, Rorty argues, are John Dewey, Ludwig Wittgenstein, Martin Heidegger, and himself. It is obviously beyond the scope of my present argument to review and characterize each camp. One can get an excellent overview of them from *The Linguistic Turn,*[31] *Philosophy and the Mirror of Nature,*[32] and *Beyond Objectivism and Relativism.*[33] My own position is indicated by my heavy reliance on MacIntyre's *After Viture;* this puts me on the side of the postanalytic philosophers. The narrative paradigm stresses ontology rather than epistemology, which is not to say that knowledge does not exist but that it does not have an absolute foundation in ordinary discourse. The subject of such discourse is symbolic action that creates social reality.

MacIntyre is explicit in supporting the narrative view of human decision making and action. He holds that the essential genre "for the characterisation of human actions"[34] is "enacted dramatic narrative."[35] Rorty does not mention narration, but he does subscribe to a view of conversation that is compatible with the narrative paradigm. He writes, "If we see knowing not as having an essence, to be described by scientists or philosophers, but as a right, by current standards, to believe, then we are well on the way to seeing *conversation* as the ultimate context within which knowledge is to be understood."[36] I concur with the substance of this statement and its implication for how persons should relate to one another, but I do not wholly accept Rorty's pragmatism. There are two problems with the position, as I see it. First, it suggests that whatever keeps the "conversation going" is good;[37] second, it ignores criteria for determining whether what is said in the conversation is worthy of belief and action. As I have already indicated, I believe that there are rational criteria for distinguishing the reliability, trustworthiness, and desirability of statements made in the conversation of life.

Bernstein, whom I would include among the postanalytic philosophers, characterizes the modern state of intellectual thought as needing to get beyond objectivism and relativism. The solution to this problem, he argues, cannot be a "typical modern response . . . the idea that we can make, engineer, impose our collective will to form" communities marked by intersubjective practices and freedom, "a willingness to talk and to listen, mutual debate, and a commitment to rational persusasion."[38] The solution, he proposes, is "to try again and again to foster and nurture those forms of communal life in which dialogue, conversation, *phronesis,* practical discourse, and judgment are concretely embodied in our everyday practices."[39] He finds ideas conducive to this effort in the visions of Gadamer, Habermas, Rorty, and Arendt.

This aim is a historic feature of classical conceptions of rhetoric. The aim is evident in Aristotle's view of *phronesis.* His view recognized contingency in the social world, the particularities of practical existence, and the possibility of wisdom. In so doing, the view also made room for an interest in the matters that transcend immediate circumstances. A parallel aim is also present in Kenneth Burke's concept of "permanence and change" and his idea of identification, which may move dialectically from the particular to the universal. It is also a significant part of Perelman's theory of rhetoric, specifically his distinction between particular and universal audiences, a distinction that is never absolute. And it is a constituent of the narrative paradigm. Good reasons express practical wisdom; they are, in their highest expression, an encompassment of what is relative and objective in situations. They function to resolve exigencies by locating and activating values that go beyond the moment, making it possible that principles of decision or action can be generalized.

Except for the narrative paradigm's dramatism, the narrative paradigm is most compatible with the themes of the later Heidegger, Gadamer, and Ricoeur, the leading contemporary figures in developing hermeneutics. Particularly helpful to me is Heidegger's view that "man is a *thinking,* that is, a *mediating* being."[40] This concept was put forth as an antithesis to the idea that "man" is, or should be always, a "calculative thinker, a person who 'computes' "—weighs, measures, and counts—possibilities, benefits, and outcomes but does not "contemplate the meaning which reigns in everything that is."[41] The idea of narrative rationality presupposes (synthesizes) both notions but lays stress on the mediative as the foundation. In another essay, Heidegger celebrates a line from a poem by Friedrich Hölderlin: "Poetically Man Dwells."[42] I would alter the line to read: "Narratively Persons Dwell."[43]

A number of themes in Gadamer's work enrich the conception of the narrative paradigm. I share his ontological perspective on human action. His view that "Language is not just one of man's possessions in the world, but on it depends the fact that man has a world at all" seems eminently sound to me.[44] I agree with his view of the constitutive nature of communication: "The process of communication is not mere action, a purposeful activity, a setting-up of signs, through which I transmit my will to others . . . it is a living process in which a community of life is lived out."[45] His conception of reason is consonant with the one that informs the narrative paradigm. He holds that "Reason exists for us only in concrete, historical terms, *i.e.,* it is not its own master, but remains constantly dependent on the given circumstances in which it operates."[46] His theory endorses Aristotle's concept of *phronesis,* as does mine. In addition, Gadamer takes a position on aesthetic and scientific forms to which I subscribe. He maintains that the object of aesthetic awareness "is part of the essential process of representation"[47] and that "all scientific research has the form of literature insofar as it is essentially bound to language. If words can be written down, then they are literature, in the widest sense."[48] And, finally, I concur in Gadamer's view of conversation as dialogue.[49]

The narrative paradigm advances the idea that good communication is good by virtue of its satisfying the requirements of narrative rationality, namely, that it offers a reliable, trustworthy, and desirable guide to belief and action. Gadamer suggests that communication is good, along with whatever truth it may advance, if it honors the dignity and worth of the participants. (This standard is also suggested by Habermas, Rorty, Arendt, and Bernstein.) This is also the thesis of Martin Buber's *I and Thou*[50] and the premise of John Stewart's approach to interpersonal communication.[51] The standard is also a primary feature of the praxis supported by narrative rationality as I have described it.

The narrative paradigm diverges from Gadamerian thought exactly at the point where hermeneutics and rhetoric diverge. Gadamer holds that "hermeneutics is a kind of inversion of rhetoric and poetic."[52] Hermeneutics seeks understanding; rhetoric and poetic seek to project understanding into the world. Put another way: hermeneutics is concerned with the recovery or an appropriation of truth in texts, and rhetoric and poetic are modes of expressing truth; they provide texts. But in my view, and traditionally, rhetoric is more than a form of discourse; it is also theory and offers the basis of critique, which is the purpose of the concept of narrative rationality. Calvin O. Schrag makes the case for hermeneutic critique in his *Communicative Praxis and the Space of Subjectivity.*[53] He specifically cites the narrative paradigm and narrative rationality as useful in moving hermeneutics to a critical stance.

Paul Ricoeur's recent writings also inform and reinforce the narrative paradigm. In his essay "The Narrative Fiction," he maintains that "the form of life to which narrative discourse belongs is our historical condition itself."[54] He asserts that "all narrative makes, in a certain sense, a referential claim,"[55] and he argues that "history is both a literary *artifact* (and in this sense a fiction) and a representation of *reality*."[56] Ricoeur contends that "all symbolic systems make and remake reality";[57] and he concludes, in part, that *"the world of fiction leads us to the heart of the real world of action."*[58] These are all ideas incorporated within the notion of the narrative paradigm, but I do not think they go quite far enough.

While Ricoeur sees the concept of "text" as relevant to the interpretation of human action, it is clear that he views narration as a distinct form.[59] I do not deny that narration is a distinct form, as argument is a form or explication is a form. And I can agree that narration as a form reveals or unfolds a world that is a "temporal world." Ricoeur's discussion of metaphor[60] and *mimesis*[61] are especially helpful in filling out the conception of the narrative paradigm. The poetic function of language, he writes in the preface to *Time and Narrative,* "is not limited to the celebration of language for its own sake, at the expense of the referential function, which is predominant in descriptive language."[62] He goes on to observe that "whereas metaphorical redescription reigns in the field of sensory, emotional, aesthetic, and axiological values, which make the world a habitable world, the mimetic function of plots takes place by preference in the field of action and its temporal values."[63] The narrative paradigm is, in a sense, a radicalization of these ideas, an extension of Ricoeur's logic to its own conclusion. It adds to them a conception of rationality and praxis. It posits, furthermore, that even scientific (technical) discourse, which is a form of literature, is informed by metaphor (and myth), contains "plots," and is time-bound.

From the narrative-paradigm perspective, there is no form of human communication that is purely descriptive. Hence works such as Charles Darwin's *Origin of the Species* and Albert Einstein's *Relativity: The Special and the General Theory* are as usefully interpreted and assessed through the narrative paradigm as the United States President's last speech or the latest popular film. The criteria for assessment of these texts would certainly vary, as the form of good reasons varies in each of the forms of communication, but the principles of coherence and fidelity apply to all. In short, I believe that the structural elements that Ricoeur attributes to narrative form are relevant and instructive in understanding nonfiction as well as fiction, the texts of life are well as learned and unlearned discourse.

Michael Foucault poses a special problem in this exploration of the relationship of the narrative paradigm to contemporary humanistic thought. He is not exactly a structuralist, a deconstructionist, a critical theorist, a professional philosopher, or a follower of hermeneutics, but there are elements of each of these orientations in his work. It has even been alleged that his work is "anti-humanist."[64] There is prima-facie evidence for this claim in a series of Foucault's studies[65] in which "subjects" are reduced to "role players" controlled by existing *epistemes*, or discourse formations. The claim is also supported by Foucault's wanting to dismiss not only subjects, but also tradition, influence, development and evolution, spirit, genre, book and oeuvre.

Equally troubling is Foucault's view of truth. By truth, he writes, "I do not mean 'the ensemble of truths which are to be discovered and accepted,' but rather 'the ensemble of rules according to which the true and false are separated and specific effects of power are attached to the true.' "[66] One may, in addition, see an antihumanistic bias in his genealogical method, "a form of history which can account for the constitution of knowledges, discourses, domains of subjects etc., without having to make reference to a subject which is either transcendental in relation to the field of events or runs in its empty sameness throughout the course of history."[67] Whether one accepts or rejects the claim depends, it seems to me, on whether or not one sees humanistic value in Foucault's aim: "to question our will to truth; to restore its character as event; to abolish the sovereignty of the signifier."[68] I suggest that the historical problem of politics is not the will to truth in and of itself, but the will to truth tied to a will to power. Accordingly I applaud the demystification of practices that oppress or repress persons, but I cannot endorse subversion without affirmation. And I am sure, where Foucault is uncertain, about narration. He writes: "I suppose, though I am not altogether sure, there is barely a society without its major narratives, told, retold and varied."[69]

The final theorist I wish to mention is Perelman, whose theory of rhetoric is to be counted with Kenneth Burke's as one of the most significant of the twentieth century. I delineate the relationship of the narrative paradigm to "the new rhetoric" in chapter 6. Suffice it to say here that our differences stem from differences in our views of human beings. Perelman sees people as arguers; I see them as storytellers. Perelman's view of rationality is that an argument is *as good as the audience that would adhere to it*. Narrative rationality, as I have described it, takes an argument to be as good as its coherence and fidelity. Nevertheless, Perelman's overall theory of rhetoric would seem to grant, as the narrative paradigm insists, that arguers tell stories and storytellers argue.

CONCLUSION

At the beginning of this chapter, I raised the question of how the narrative paradigm—with its associated concept of narrative rationality—compares and contrasts with leading contemporary social-scientific and humanistic concepts of action and discourse. The analysis I have just completed allows the following summary answer. The narrative paradigm is a fabric woven of threads of thought from both the social sciences and the humanities. It seeks, like any other theory of human action, to account for how persons come to believe and to behave. It differs from received social-scientific and humanistic theories in that it projects narration not as an art, genre, or activity, but as paradigmatic of human discourse. It goes beyond other theories in providing a "new" logic, the concept of narrative rationality. That logic is applicable to all forms of human communication, as I hope to show in later chapters. Finally, the paradigm is a response to the exigence of our time identified by Gadamer: "In the age of science, is there any way of preserving and validating the great heritage of knowledge and wisdom?"[70] I hold that the way is to formulate a theory of human communication that recognizes permanence and change, culture and character, reason and value, and the practical wisdom of *all* persons. I hope to show that the narrative paradigm fulfills this need.

NOTES

1. See Wayne A. Beach, "Background Understanding and the Situated Accomplishment of Conversational Telling-Explanations," in Robert T. Craig and K. Tracy, eds., *Conversational Coherence: Form, Structure and Strategy* (Beverly Hills, Calif.: Sage Publications, 1983), pp. 196–221; Robert E. Nofsinger, "Tactical Coherence in Courtroom Conversation," in Craig and Tracy, pp. 243–58.

2. Wayne Brockriede, "Constructs, Experience, and Argument," *Quarterly Journal of Speech* 71 (1985): 151–63.

3. Richard Bernstein, *Beyond Objectivism and Relativism: Science, Hermeneutics, and Praxis* (Philadelphia: University of Pennsylvania Press, 1983).

4. See Thomas D. Daniels and Kenneth D. Frandsen, "Conventional Social Science Inquiry in Human Communication," *Quarterly Journal of Speech* 70 (1984): 223–40.

5. See Fritz Heider, *The Psychology of Interpersonal Relations* (New York: John Wiley, 1958) See also H. Kelly, "Attribution in Social Interaction," in E. E.

Jones, et al., *Attribution: Perceiving the Causes of Behavior* (Morristown, N.J.: General Learning Press, 1971), pp. 1–26.

6. Fritz Heider, "Attitudes and Cognitive Organization," *Journal of Psychology* 27 (1946): 107–12, and T. Newcomb, "An Approach to the Study of Communicative Acts," *Psychological Review* 60 (1953): 393–404.

7. Jesse G. Delia, "Constructivism and the Study of Communication," *Quarterly Journal of Speech* 63 (1977): 66–83.

8. Ernest G. Bormann, "Fantasy Theme Analysis," in James L. Golden, G. F. Berquist, and W. E. Coleman, eds., *The Rhetoric of Western Thought* (3rd ed.; Dubuque, Iowa: Kendall/Hunt, 1983), pp. 433–49.

9. C. Hovland, I. Janis, and H. Kelly, *Communication and Persuasion* (New Haven, Conn.: Yale University Press, 1953).

10. J. W. Thibaut and H. Kelly, *The Social Psychology of Groups* (New York: John Wiley, 1959).

11. H. Blumer, *Symbolic Interactionism: Perspective and Method* (Englewood Cliffs, N.J.: Prentice-Hall, 1969). See also George H. Mead, *Mind, Self, and Society: From the Standpoint of a Social Behaviorist,* ed. C. W. Morris (Chicago: University of Chicago Press, 1934).

12. See James D. Barber, *The Presidential Character: Predicting Performance in the White House* (Englewood Cliffs, N.J.: Prentice-Hall, 1972).

13. Kenneth Burke, *A Rhetoric of Motives* (New York: George Braziller, 1955), pp. 1–49.

14. Erving Goffman, *The Presentation of Self in Everyday Life* (Garden City, N.Y.: Doubleday, 1959), *Interaction Ritual: Essays on Face-to-Face Behavior* (Garden City, N.Y.: Doubleday, 1967); *Relations in Public: Microstudies of the Public Order* (New York: Basic Books, 1971).

15. Alasdair MacIntyre, *After Virtue: A Study in Moral Theory* (2nd. ed.; Notre Dame, Ind.: University of Notre Dame Press, 1981), pp. 108–9.

16. Relevant works include: E. H. Gombrich, "Representation and Misrepresentation," *Critical Inquiry* 11 (1984): 195–218; Murray Krieger, "The Ambiguities of Representation and Illusion: An E. H. Gombrich Retrospective," *Critical Inquiry* 11 (1984): 181–94; Paul Ricoeur, *Time and Narrative,* trans. Kathleen McLaughlin and D. Pellaur (2 vols.; Chicago: University of Chicago Press, 1984, 1985); J. B. Thompson, "Problems in the Theory of Reference and Truth," in *Critical Hermeneutics: A Study in the Thought of Paul Ricoeur and Jürgen Habermas* (Cambridge, England: Cambridge University Press, 1983), pp. 182–218; Hayden White, "The Question of Narrative and Contemporary Historical Theory," *History and Theory* 23 (1984): 1–33.

17. See J. D. Andrews, "The Structuralist Study of Narrative: Its History, Use, and Limits," in Paul Hernadi, ed., *The Horizon of Literature* (Lincoln: University of Nebraska Press, 1982), pp. 99–124.

18. Roland Barthes, "Introduction to the Structural Analysis of Narratives," in S. Heath, ed., *Image-Music-Text* (New York: Hill & Wang, 1977), p. 124. See also G. Genette, *Narrative Discourse: An Essay in Method,* trans. J. E. Lewin (Ithaca, N.Y.: Cornell University Press, 1980); Tzvetan Todorov, *The Poetics of Prose,* trans. R. Howard (Ithaca, N.Y.: Cornell University Press, 1977), pp. 19–28.

19. Paolo Valesio, *Novanthiqua: Rhetorics as a Contemporary Theory* (Bloomington: Indiana University Press, 1980), p. 21.

20. Ibid., p. 113.

21. Jacques Derrida, *Dissemination,* trans. B. Johnson (Chicago: University of Chicago Press, 1981), pp. 65–171.

22. Jacques Derrida, *Margins of Philosophy,* trans. A. Bass (Chicago: University of Chicago Press, 1982), p. 67.

23. For another view of Derrida's project, see Richard Rorty, "Deconstruction and Circumvention," *Critical Inquiry* 11 (1984): 1–23.

24. Jürgen Habermas, *The Theory of Communicative Action: Reason and Rationalization in Society,* trans. Thomas A. McCarthy (Boston: Beacon Press, 1984), vol. 1. See also *Communication and the Evolution of Society,* trans. Thomas A. McCarthy (Boston: Beacon Press, 1979).

25. See Karl-Otto Apel, "The *A Priori* of Communication and the Foundations of the Humanities," in F. R. Dallmayr and T. A. McCarthy, eds., *Understanding and Social Inquiry* (Notre Dame, Ind.: University of Notre Dame Press, 1977), pp. 292–315.

26. Habermas, *The Theory,* p. 17.

27. Ibid., p. 18.

28. Habermas relies on Erving Goffman for his understanding of dramaturgy instead of on Kenneth Burke; this reliance accounts, I suspect, for some of the differences in his theory and mine.

29. Habermas, *The Theory,* p. 95.

30. Ibid., p. 392.

31. Richard Rorty, ed., *The Linguistic Turn: Recent Essays in Philosophical Method* (Chicago: University of Chicago Press, 1967). See also Calvin O. Schrag, "Rhetoric Situated at the End of Philosophy," *Quarterly Journal of Speech* 71 (1985): 164–74.

32. Richard Rorty, *Philosophy and the Mirror of Nature* (Princeton, N.J.: Princeton University Press, 1979).

33. See n. 3, above, for Bernstein reference.

34. MacIntyre, *After Virtue,* p. 194.

35. Ibid., p. 200.

36. Rorty, *Philosophy,* p. 389.

37. Ibid., p. 377.

38. Bernstein, *Beyond Objectivism,* p. 226.

39. Ibid., p. 229.

40. Martin Heidegger, *Discourse on Thinking: A Translation of Gelassenheit,* trans. J. M. Anderson and E. H. Freund (New York: Harper & Row, 1966), p. 47.

41. Ibid., p. 46.

42. Martin Heidegger, *Poetry, Language, and Thought,* trans. A. Hofstader (New York: Harper & Row, 1971), p. 42.

43. Another version of Hölderlin's title is proposed by Michael Hyde in his essay, "Rhetorically Man Dwells: On the Making Known Function of Discourse," *Communication* 7 (1983): 201–20.

44. Hans-Georg Gadamer, *Truth and Method* (New York: Crossroad Publishing Co., 1982), p. 401.

45. Ibid., p. 404.

46. Ibid., p. 245.

47. Ibid., p. 104.

48. Ibid., p. 144.
49. Ibid., p. 347.
50. Martin Buber, *I and Thou,* trans. Walter Kaufman (New York: Charles Scribner's Sons, 1970).
51. John R. Stewart, "Foundations of Dialogic Communication," *Quarterly Journal of Speech* 64 (1978): 183–201. See also John R. Stewart and G. D'Angelo, *Together: Communicating Interpersonally* (2nd. ed.; Reading, Mass.: Addison-Wesley, 1980).
52. Gadamer, *Truth and Method,* p. 166.
53. Calvin O. Schrag, *Communicative Praxis and the Space of Subjectivity* (Bloomington: Indiana University Press, 1986).
54. Paul Ricoeur, "The Narrative Function," in J. B. Thompson, ed., *Paul Ricoeur, Hermeneutics and the Human Sciences: Essays on Language, Action, and Interpretation* (Cambridge, England: Cambridge University Press, 1983), p. 288.
55. Ibid., p. 289.
56. Ibid., p. 291.
57. Ibid., p. 293.
58. Ibid., p. 296.
59. Paul Ricoeur, "The Model of the Text: Meaningful Action Considered as Text," in Dallmayr and McCarthy, eds., *Understanding,* pp. 316–34.
60. Paul Ricoeur, *The Rule of Metaphor: Multi-Disciplinary Studies in the Creation of Language,* trans. Robert Czerny with K. McLaughlin and J. Costello, S.J. (Toronto: University of Toronto Press, 1977), pp. 216–56.
61. Ricoeur, *The Rule,* p. 31ff., and *Time and Narrative,* vol. 1, p. 45ff.
62. Ricoeur, *Time and Narrative,* p. x.
63. Ibid., p. xi.
64. Charles C. Lemert and Garth Gillan, *Michael Foucault: Social Theory and Transgression* (New York: Columbia University Press, 1982).
65. See, e.g., Michel Foucault, *Madness and Civilization: A History of Sanity in an Age of Reason,* trans. R. Howard (New York: Vintage Books, 1965); *The Order of Things: An Archaeology of the Human Sciences* (New York: Pantheon Books, 1969); *The Archaeology of Knowledge and the Discourse on Language,* trans. A. M. S. Smith (New York: Pantheon Books, 1972); *The Birth of the Clinic: An Archaeology of Medical Perception* (New York: Vintage Books, 1973); *Discipline and Punish: The Birth of the Prison,* trans. A. Sheridan (New York: Pantheon Books, 1977).
66. Michel Foucault, *Power/Knowledge: Selected Interviews and Other Writings,* trans. C. Gordon, et al. (New York: Pantheon Books, 1980), p. 132.
67. Ibid., p. 117.
68. Foucault, *The Order of Things,* p. 229.
69. Foucault, *The Archaeology of Knowledge,* p. 220.
70. Gadamer, *Reason in the Age of Science,* p. 159.

101

PART III
NARRATIVE RATIONALITY, GOOD REASONS, AND AUDIENCES

5

ASSESSING NARRATIVE FIDELITY:
The Logic of Good Reasons

I introduced the concept of narrative rationality in chapter 2 and called it a rhetorical logic. I have discussed one of its principles, *probability*, or coherence, in some detail, but I have not treated the other component of narrative rationality in detail. This component is *fidelity*. The principle of coherence brings into focus the integrity of a story as a whole, but the principle of fidelity pertains to the individuated components of stories— whether they represent accurate assertions about social reality and thereby constitute good reasons for belief or action. The problem I wish to pose and discuss in this chapter is how fidelity of reasons is to be assessed.

The answer I shall develop in the pages to follow is built upon the work of Stephen Toulmin, Chaïm Perelman, Gidon Gottlieb, Karl Wallace, and Wayne Booth.[1] To amplify and defend the notion of fidelity, I shall analyze the meaning of "logic" in the frequently used expression of "logic of good reasons," offer a reconstruction of the concept "good reasons," present the design of a "logic of good reasons," and suggest ways of implementing the "logic of good reasons" using existing systems of logical assessment. The final question to be asked and answered is how, if at all, rationality or logic is related to rhetorical competence.

A number of assumptions underlie my approach to this task. First is a conviction that the most indispensable need in contemporary rhetoric is for a scheme by which values can be identified and their implications critically considered. This conviction derives from the belief that rhetorical communication is as laden with values as it is with what we call reasons. *Humans as rhetorical beings are as much valuing as they are reasoning animals.* I am also convinced that value judgments are inevitable, that they are not irrational, that consensus about them will never be fully realized, and that no analytically grounded hierarchy of values will ever claim universal adherence. Finally, I believe that rhetoricians have an obligation to inform students and to raise the consciousness of citizens about the nature and functions of values just as we have informed them

105

about the nature and functions of reasons. As Gary Cronkhite has observed: *"The best antidote for a sophistic rhetor is a sophisticated rhetoree, and we had best get at the business of providing such an antidote."*[2]

THE MEANING OF "LOGIC"

The first problem to be dealt with is the meaning of "logic" in the expression "logic of good reasons." By logic, I do not refer to the study of the principles or structures that constitute a concept or an activity, as in the "logic of the humanities" or the "logic of legal controversy." Nor do I mean a formal system, such as a deontic logic that seeks to reveal the structures of reasoning about matters of permission and obligation. The general inappropriateness of formal logic to rhetorical reasoning has been well demonstrated by Toulmin[3] and Perelman.[4] I use "logic" here to designate a systematic set of procedures that will aid in the analysis and assessment of elements of reasoning in rhetorical interactions. The procedures I shall offer consist of a series of criterial questions meant to reveal the role of values in practical reasoning and to provide a basis on which one can begin to assess them. The scheme is an adjunct to existing "logics" used in the study of rhetorical reasoning. It is an informal (noncategorical) system, coordinate with the kind of logic that dominates argumentation textbooks—the classification of types of reasoning (sign, causal, analogical, etc.) with appropriate tests.

GOOD REASONS

The second problem is defining "good reasons." The nature of this problem can be seen clearly if we examine the concepts of good reasons offered by Wallace and Booth. My complaint about the concept as these authors present it is that their conceptions are too narrowly constructed. How this is so will be demonstrated. My intent is not to contradict them, but to expand on what they say.

Evaluation inherently involves tautology. For example, if we say a good essay is logical, it follows that an essay cannot be good and not logical. Therefore, my concern is not to avoid circularity; it is to increase the diameter of the circle that contains good reasons.[5] The circle can be expanded by broadening the concept of good reasons to allow more instances of reasons and values to find their place within it. Then clear criteria will be needed for their assessment. The result should be a more useful circle.

Wallace took the position that "One could do worse than characterize rhetoric as the art of finding and effectively presenting good reasons."[6] "A good reason," he wrote, "is a statement offered in support of an *ought* proposition or of a value-judgment." And he defined "good reasons" as "a number of statements, consistent with each other, in support of an *ought* proposition or of a value-judgment."[7] In other words, a reason is good if it is tied to a value, and a value is reasonable if it is tied to a reason. Given this view, there is no way to distinguish the merits of competing good reasons, and the view ignores the possibility that values may be reasons and that reasons affirm values in and of themselves.

In *Modern Dogma and the Rhetoric of Assent,* Booth writes that he will "be pursuing . . . the art of discovering good reasons, finding what really warrants assent because any reasonable person ought to be persuaded by what has been said."[8] I think Booth's inquiry is learned and useful, but I cannot find in his book any clearer concept of good reasons than what is suggested in this statement. Booth seems to be saying that good reasons are what good people affirm and that reasonable people know what is good. This is, of course, a circular view, like that of Wallace, which makes it impossible to judge between the good reasons of conflicting good persons. An advantage of Booth's approach is that one can contemplate the possibility of finding good reasons in art and literature as well as in the usual forms of rhetorical communication. But how to assess them remains the difficulty. It is not very helpful to know that "A satisfactory account of good reasoning in any one domain of life would necessarily require a sizable book," or that "The repertory of good reasons could never be constructed by any one person, since it would include all good discourse about the grounds of valid discourse in any subject."[9]

To remedy the difficulties in the views of Wallace and Booth, I propose that good reasons be conceived as *those elements that provide warrants for accepting or adhering to the advice fostered by any form of communication that can be considered rhetorical.* By "warrant," I mean that which authorizes, sanctions, or justifies belief, attitude, or action—these being the usual forms of rhetorical advice. The term "good reasons," I should stress, does not imply that every element of rhetorical transaction that warrants a belief, attitude, or action—that any "good reason"—is as good as any other. It only signifies that whatever is taken as a basis for adopting a rhetorical message is inextricably bound to a value—to a conception of the good. Needless to say, good reasons are not necessarily effective, persuasive reasons.

Given this conception of good reasons, it seems to me that a person can isolate and begin to weigh them, to compare and contrast them. The concept requires a rethinking of argumentative forms, however, for they must now include all modes of communication, not just those that have clear-cut inferential structures. The concept can then open a way to get at the rhetorical components of literature, film, and drama. Indeed, I think that a next step in pursuing the nature and functions of good reasons is to identify the modes of warrant in diverse kinds of communication, the ways, for instance, that narration, character, action, scene, and music induce audiences to think, feel, or behave as an author intends.

THE LOGIC OF GOOD REASONS

I turn now to the third problem in this project—the design and implementation of a logic of good reasons. A logic of reasons is the heart of courses and textbooks in argumentation; it focuses on the soundness of reasoning in public or problem-solving discourse. The pattern is to explore the role of argument in society, the nature of argumentative controversy, the formulation of propositions, the analysis of cases, the responsibilities of arguers, and the definitions of such terms as argument, claim, warrant, evidence, proof, presumption, burden of proof, and fallacy. But these are the *means*, not the *end* of the instruction. The aim is to instill the arts involved in "acting rationally," to implant habits of perception and procedure that inform the preparation, presentation, and evaluation of argumentative communication.[10] My concern is with the evaluation habit, the set of criterial questions that one is supposed to internalize so that one can ascertain the weight of reason in any given message, including one's own.

There are five components in the logic of reasons. First, one considers whether the statements in a message that purport to be "facts" are indeed "facts"; that is, are confirmed by consensus or reliable, competent witnesses. Second, one tries to determine whether relevant "facts" have been omitted and whether those that have been offered are in any way distorted or taken out of context. Third, one recognizes and assesses the various patterns of reasoning, using mainly standards from informal logic. Fourth, one assesses the relevance of individual arguments to the decision the message concerns, not only are these arguments sound, but are they also all the arguments that should be considered in the case. Fifth, armed with the traditional knowledge that forensic issues are those of "fact," definition, justification, and procedure, and that deliberative decision making centers on questions of policy and problem solving (reasons for and against change and the wisdom of particular proposals), one makes a judgment as to whether or not the message directly addresses the "real" issues in the case. In other words, one asks whether or not the message deals with the questions on which the whole matter turns or should turn.

The components needed to transform the logic of reasons into a logic of *good* reasons are also fivefold. First is the question of *fact:* What are the implicit and explicit values embedded in a message? Second is the question of *relevance:* Are the values appropriate to the nature of the decision that the message bears upon? Included in this question must be concern for omitted, distorted, and misrepresented values. Third is the question of *consequence:* What would be the effects of adhering to the values—for one's concept of oneself, for one's behavior, for one's relationships with others and society, and to the process of rhetorical transaction? Inherent in this question are such concerns as Ehninger's criterion of moral obligation,[11] Eubanks and Baker's distinction between civilizing and brutalizing values,[12] and Wallace's delineation of democratic values.[13] Fourth is the question of *consistency:* Are the values confirmed or validated in one's personal experience, in the lives or statements of others whom one admires and respects, and in a conception of the best audience that one can conceive? Implied in these standards are McKerrow's notion of the self as the validating agent in argumentative interactions,[14] Booth's concept of "weighty witnesses,"[15] and Perelman's suggestion of a "universal audience."[16] Fifth is the question of *transcendent issue:* Even if a prima-facie case exists or a burden of proof has been established, are the values the message offers those that, in the estimation of the critic, constitute the ideal basis for human conduct? This is clearly the paramount issue that confronts those responsible for decisions that impinge on the nature, the quality, and the continued existence of human life, especially in such fields as biology and weapons technology and employment. Transcendent values are present even in ordinary cases, but they are rarely matters of dispute. They concern ultimate values and are generally taken for granted by the arguer, but when brought to the surface, they reveal one's most fundamental commitments. Their role in argument is shown in Figure 3.

I have said that all serious discourse expresses values. The discourse that constitutes an interpreter's or critic's exploration of the values in messages will also inevitably express values. This inevitably becomes especially evident in asking and answering the third, fourth, and fifth questions. One can be fairly "objective" about what values are in fact present in a message, but as one moves to the questions of relevance, effects, confirmation, and ideals, greater and greater degrees of "subjectivity" enter

109

into the assessment. The intrusion of such "subjectivity" is not a fault in a logic of good reasons. Instead, it is a recognition of the very nature of human communication, and of the nature of subjects amenable to rhetorical expression. By making the considerations of values a systematic and self-conscious process, the logic of good reasons fills the space left open by technical logic with its primary concern with formal relationships and certitude. It also goes beyond traditional rhetorical logics, which have not provided such a system of assessment. In other words, the logic of good reasons is important because it renders open and intelligible the grounds and valuing of interpreter-critics. And by so doing, it acknowledges and encourages awareness of the contingent character of rhetorical communication and provides information that enhances discourse on truly fundamental matters.

CRITERIAL ANALYSIS

The foregoing criterial questions can be used to implement a logic of good reasons in at least three ways. First, they can be added to the criterial questions of the logic of reasons. Second, they can be infused with the tests of different types of reasoning: example, analogy, sign, cause, definition, and authority. Insofar as each of these types of reasoning involves values, the criterial questions of fact, relevance, consequence, and consistency are pertinent; and the criterial question of transcendent issue is germane whenever a critic weighs a whole message to determine if it addresses those matters on which the decision *should* turn. Third, the criterial questions can be applied within Toulmin's model of argument. There may be other ways to implement a logic of good reasons, but these are the ones that I think are the most promising in the present state of our understanding.

However the considerations of fact, relevance, consistency, consequence, and transcendent issue are incorporated into other logical schemes, it is important that they be recognized as a system with each element depending on each other. Although essentially a descriptive system, the questions I have posed indicate norms, and the judgments that the measures call for require that one consider one's relations with others. Because norms and values are social constructs, socially derived and maintained, one cannot assess them without at least the implicit involvement of others. As John Donne reminded us, persons are not islands unto themselves.

The difference between my conception of good reasons and those of Wallace and Booth should be evident. My quarrel with them is that, given

110

their formulations, to identify a good reason is at the same time to assess it. That is, in Wallace's view the value of a value is that it is tied to a reason, and in Booth's view the value of a value resides in who expresses it. The definition I offer says that a good reason is a warrant for a belief, attitude, or action and the value of a value lies in its relevance, consistency, and consequence, and the extent to which it is grounded on the highest possible values. Put another way, a value is valuable not because it is tied to a reason or is expressed by a reasonable person per se, but because *it makes a pragmatic difference in one's life and in one's community.*

Figure 3 is an adaptation of the logic of good reasons applied within Toulmin's model of argument. It is meant to illustrate where values enter an argument and the function they perform—*to determine the argument's outcome.* With this sort of display, embedded values are revealed and the questions of relevance, consistency, consequence, and transcendent issue can be raised and answered. To determine the relevance of a value, one must know the "facts" of the matter and the nature and function of values.[17]

With such knowledge, one should be able to discern whether the values in the message are appropriate to the case. The same act of intellection that tells one if the evidence given in support of a claim authorizes that claim also tells one whether or not a value is appropriate to it. It was by this sort of knowledge and thinking that I identified the relevant issues in Figure 3. My assumption is that anyone with even modest intelligence could perform the same feat. To apply the tests of consistency, consequence, and transcendent issue, one need only know oneself and those whom one regards as expert or best qualified to know or judge in the given case. The final judgment of what to believe or do is thus made by inspection of "facts," values, self, and society; it is inevitably an intersubjective and pragmatic decision. What is more, it is a rational one.

Figure 3 is also designed to show that no hierarchy of values exists to resolve conflicts of transcendent values. Although it may be possible to find persons who are unalterably committed either to duty to country or to moral conscience (religious conviction/reverence for life) no matter the situation, I believe that individual Americans hold both values and that the context determines which will be treated as salient. It is not unreasonable that a person—not necessarily a militarist—who was convinced by national-administration arguments that national pride was at stake in Vietnam should take a position ultimately based on the duty-to-country value. Nor would it be unreasonable for a person—not necessarily a pacifist—who was persuaded by the war's opponents that America's professed

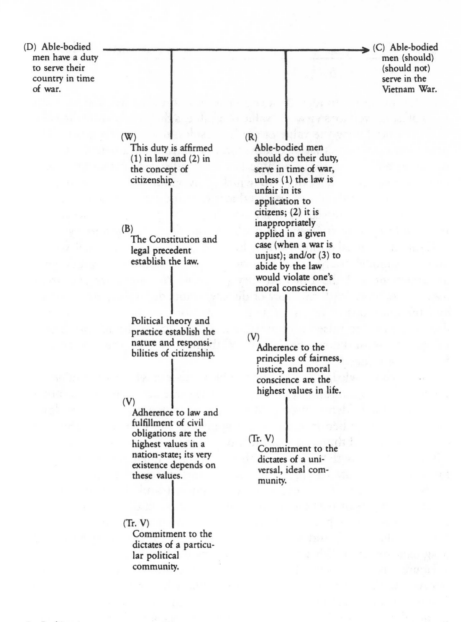

(D) Able-bodied men have a duty to serve their country in time of war.

(C) Able-bodied men (should) (should not) serve in the Vietnam War.

(W)
This duty is affirmed (1) in law and (2) in the concept of citizenship.

(B)
The Constitution and legal precedent establish the law.

Political theory and practice establish the nature and responsibilities of citizenship.

(V)
Adherence to law and fulfillment of civil obligations are the highest values in a nation-state; its very existence depends on these values.

(Tr. V)
Commitment to the dictates of a particular political community.

(R)
Able-bodied men should do their duty, serve in time of war, unless (1) the law is unfair in its application to citizens; (2) it is inappropriately applied in a given case (when a war is unjust); and/or (3) to abide by the law would violate one's moral conscience.

(V)
Adherence to the principles of fairness, justice, and moral conscience are the highest values in life.

(Tr. V)
Commitment to the dictates of a universal, ideal community.

B = Backing
C = Claim
D = Data
R = Reservations
Tr. V = Transcendent Value
V = Values
W = Warrant

Figure 3. Where values enter an argument.

112

reverence for life was at stake should take a position grounded on the moral-conscience value.

A critical point to be made here is that duty to country and duty to one's moral conscience are *context-specific* values; that is, they arise only in *particular* decisional situations. Some other values, it seems, are *general* and apply in *all* decision-making situations. In other words, some values appear to be field-dependent—appropriate to only certain subject matters; and some are field-invariant—having to do with the necessary constituents of communicative acts.[18] Beyond the physical requirements of communicants who share some commonality in symbol systems, human communication depends on some degree of trust, on a willingness to participate in the process, on a belief in the desirability of the interaction, and on an interest in (or expection of) the attainment/or the advancement of some presumed truth. Some invariance in communication values is indicated by the fact that some members of all known cultures have found it possible to communicate with some members of other cultures. In addition to these cross-cultural values, one may find other specifiable invariant values underlying communicative interactions in given cultures—for example, respect for the dignity and worth of the individual, in the United States. In the argument displayed in Figure 3, adherence to respect for the dignity and worth of the individual would make dialogue-dispute possible between those who disagreed about the argument's conclusions. It would have the additional effects of opening the way for persuasion, maintaining the participants' sense of worth, and furthering the likelihood of real community among those concerned about the argument.

HIERARCHIES OF VALUES

As I have indicated, a logic of good reasons is not a mechanism for resolving disputes over values, transcendent or otherwise. Like the logic of reasons, it provides measures for assessing elements in reasoning. The purpose of a logic of good reasons is to offer a scheme that can generate a sense of what is good as well as what is reasonable, to ensure that people are conscious of the values they adhere to and would promote in rhetorical transactions, and to inform their consciousness *without dictating what they should believe*.

On the other hand, I would want the user of a logic of good reasons not only to know the nature and functions of values generally, but also to be familiar with the hierarchies of values that are available. I am impressed by

113

the hierarchy outlined by the geneticist Hermann J. Muller. He has proposed survival and extension of humankind as the most primitive values, and promotion of intelligence, making for cooperative behavior, gratification of curiosity in the pursuit of truth for its own sake, fulfillment of love, and freedom to achieve, create, and explore as the highest values.[19]

This scheme is impressive, but the values it identifies will be variably ranked in particular instances. This is why I said earlier that I do not believe an analytically grounded hierarchical system of value-rules is achievable. That there may be field-invariant values does not alter this conclusion, because field-invariant values do not determine the reasons put forth or the conclusions offered in a communicative situation. They determine the qualitative viability of reasons and conclusions, and they imply the possibilities for further interactions. Field-invariant values stipulate the "givens" of give-and-take in reasoned interactions within a field. For example, in science *accuracy* is a field-invariant value. That value does not determine *what* reasons will be put forth for a claim; it constitutes a qualitative test that will be applied to *any* and *all* scientific reasoning.

Relative to human communication, the ranking of values suggested by Muller suffers from the inevitable problems of all such generalized orderings. First, how a value operates depends on time, place, topic, and culture. Second, the idea of a binding, general system of values disregards the fact that valuing is a *human action*. As Kenneth Burke said, "*Action* involves *character*, which involves *choice*. . . . Though the concept of sheer 'motion' is non-ethical, 'action' implies the ethical (the human personality)."[20] Humans are not identical with one another, nor are their valuings. Whether through perversity, divine inspiration, or genetic programming, people make their choices freely, and their choices will not be bound by ideal or "perfect" value systems—except of their own making.

At the risk of belaboring the point, let me examine one other potential source of an analytical hierarchy of values. Extending his study of early cognitive development, Jean Piaget investigated children's acquisition of moral character.[21] He and his followers eventually observed eleven different aspects in the child's learning of moral judgments. This led him to postulate a natural progression in the growth of humans from an authoritarian to a democratic ethic. Later investigations, however, do not support his conclusion.[22] The best that can be said of Piaget's work is that it suggests "the possibility of uncovering basic trends in the development of moral judgment."[23] We may hope that such trends are discovered, but we should not expect that discovery to result in a final ordering of values that will be a feature of all human reasoning and decision making.

114

RATIONALITY AND RHETORICAL COMPETENCE

If we cannot expect to find an invariant hierarchy of values that will reflect human choices in all communicative situations, must it follow that every communicative transaction will and must be governed by a unique, idiosyncratic set of values? I think not. In Western societies, at least, rationality is a transcendent value in any communication purporting to be or taken to be rhetorical. Accordingly, I maintain that *rationality is an essential property of rhetorical competence*. Rhetorical competence implies at the very least that one can invent content for communication, compose appropriate discourse for its communication, present a message in manners appropriate to the medium of communication, the audience, and the situation, and analyze and evaluate one's own and others' messages. To do these things with understanding of substance, method, and interactive relations, it is necessary to command what I have set forth as the logic of good reasons. One cannot be rhetorically competent without the ability to discern the presence, relevance, consequences, and consistency of values expressed or projected for expression within a specific rhetorical situation.

Being reasonable is more indicative of an attitude than an ability to participate effectively in communicative interactions. I do not mean to suggest that being reasonable is not a vital component of rhetorical transactions. I agree with Perelman's stand that reasonableness is prerequisite to a pluralistic view of the world, that it is the force that transforms rationality into a human exercise of the mind. The idea of a democratic person, which is a presumption of nonmonolithic societies, is consituted by the concepts of reasonableness and rationality. As Perelman notes, insofar as rationality is conceived as adherence to formal logic, where major premises are mandated by fixed concepts of government, the result is a monistic system—a closed society. Rationality becomes the handmaiden of conservatism. The concept of rationality that I propose makes it an instrument for reasoned change.[24]

Being reasonable is an aspect of rationality, not its substance. To say that someone is reasonable within a democratic system is to say that that person uses reasons and is appreciative of and tolerant toward others who use reasons to justify their views. Being rational, on the other hand, implies not only that one respects reasoning, it also indicates that one knows their nature of argumentative issues, the forms of arguments and their tests, and the rules that govern the particular kind of argumentative interaction in which one may be an actor, whether scientific, political,

115

legal, ethical, or other. One may be reasonable but not competent; one cannot be rational and incompetent.

To clarify this distinction further I want to consider a series of argumentative interactions. First, an instance in which *A* asserts: "Capital punishment is murder, clear and simple." *B* responds: "It's no such thing! Capital punishment is just retribution. Be reasonable." *A* reacts by declaring: "What do you mean, be reasonable? You're the one who is unreasonable." Here we can see a popular conception of argument at work—a verbal and emotional disagreement. No statements justify claims, and the issue between the disputants becomes personal rather than substantive. Indeed, the implicit message of a demand that one be reasonable is that the person proposing an argument either *(a)* is ignorant, he or she does not know the facts of the case; or *(b)* is stupid, he or she has the facts but does not know how to draw proper inferences from them; or *(c)* has the facts, reasons from them well but does not begin with the proper assumptions or premises. The situation I have described is clearly an unreasonable one. It is not self-perpetuating, it is manipulative, it is not bilateral in any meaningful way, and it is not deliberative, reflexive, or attentive to data.

Second, an interaction in which *A* says: "Capital punishment is immoral; it denies the injunction that thou shalt not kill." *B* replies: "That's a reasonable position, but I disagree. I think capital punishment is a civil act, not the action of an individual rejecting the laws of the state. It is justified morally by the precept of an 'eye for an eye.'" *A* responds: "I see what you are saying but I don't agree that there is a difference between the actions of the state and of an individual when it comes to putting a person to death." *B* counters: "Well, I guess we'll just have to agree to disagree. I see no way to resolve our differences."

This encounter exhibits reasonableness; that is, the disputants offer justifications for their claims, they respect each other's arguments, and they do not personalize the conflict. They part company on capital punishment, but do it amicably. The nature of their interaction implies a self-perpetuating rhetoric; that is, although they disagree, the manner of the disagreement invites deliberation on other topics. The interaction displays two important elements of rationality—the ability and willingness to support one's claims with evidence and regard for the other. It does not, however, reveal other significant components of rationality.

Modified by indications of special knowledge in rhetorical argument, the second interaction can be transformed into an adequate illustration of

116

rationality. The necessary features would include evidence that the arguers were aware of the historical positions that have been taken on the use of the biblical warrants of not killing and just retribution; recognition of other pertinent issues and arguments relative to capital punishment (such as the justice and equality of the law); and demonstration by the actors that they know and can apply the appropriate tests for each of the arguments they and their opponents put forth. (I do not mention here one further feature of rationality—the adherence to the rules of reasoning in a particular field. I shall have more to say of this feature later.) Rationality would be evident in the revised case by virtue of reasons and reasonableness and also by a rhetoric that is self-perpetuating, nonmanipulative, bilateral, deliberative, reflexive, and attentive to data. Such a rhetoric would reveal the logic of good reasons as it should be used in disputes.

A question that will inevitably arise when one considers rationality and reasonableness as superordinate values is: Can a person be rational without being reasonable? My answer is No, insofar as one is arguing with another; Yes, insofar as one is arguing, that is, reasoning within oneself. One cannot be rational and unreasonable in an interaction with another, as I have already implied. Being reasonable is an aspect of rationality, the social aspect. Being reasonable requires the presence of another. One offers reasons to persuade others and one can only be tolerant of someone other than oneself. Tolerance is a quality of interpersonal, not intrapersonal communication. One should not be considered fully rational in interpersonal interactions unless one is also reasonable.

If one accepts the view that being reasonable is a necessary constituent of rationality, where persons argue, one can develop a useful conception of what *manipulative* rhetoric is. All rhetorical interaction is manipulative in the sense that communicators intend messages, and all communicators are strategic in their chosen causes, selections of materials, designs of composition, and styles of presentation. Every communicator, in other words, seeks to make the best possible case for his or her position. "Manipulative rhetoric" is a term best reserved for use when there is evidence that the audience is being "played," "worked," or otherwise used for the communicator's ends rather than for their own ends. Among the evidences of this kind of "manipulation" are: (1) uses of technical knowledge of rhetorical strategies and tactics, of issues, argumentative forms, tests of arguments, and so on in a self-serving way; (2) indications that the communicator's aim is not to perpetuate dialogue, to encourage an authentic bilateral exchange, to further deliberation, to invite true criticism, or to advance the truth of the matter; and (3) clues that the function of the communication is to serve personal ambition rather than self-discovery or social knowledge or public action.

I do not mean to imply that these traits are always easy to identify, that one can quickly or surely claim that any given communicator at any given time is clearly manipulating the audience. I am arguing that there is a difference between adjusting ideas to people and people to ideas, and designing discourse to render people objects rather than rational persons.[25] It is a matter of fact that we do say, based on observing them over a period of time, that some communicators are manipulative. My point is that when we make such a claim, we should do so by virtue of evidence concerning the communicator's treatment of the audience as a means to his or her own selfish ends; the phrase "manipulative rhetoric" should be reserved to designate such cases.[26]

In maintaining that one can be rational by oneself, I take exception to the stand of John Hardwig that rationality can be demonstrated only by persons interacting in a dialogue. He insists that only in such encounters can one achieve the objectivity that rationality requires.[27] My response is twofold. First, his position assumes that inner dialogue does not involve another. Second, the position ignores the fact that inner dialogue and outer dialogue rely on the same body of knowledge when they are rational—the criterial considerations of the logic of good reasons. These are "objective" matters in that they are constituted and used intersubjectively; they are consistent and relevant elements whenever a rhetorical decision is at hand; and they provide a methodical way to identify issues, relevant data, and sound reasoning. As Perelman points out, the individual person can be considered a kind of particular audience, one that even has the capacity to incarnate the "universal audience." When this happens, the person "can enjoy the philosophic privilege conferred to reason."[28]

Hardwig confuses rationalization and rationality. Certainly all individuals rationalize from time to time, alone and in the presence of others, but it is also true that some, if not all of us, reason in such a way that our decision making can be called rational. To put the point concretely: Hardwig's essay, which is an example of monologic communication, exhibits rationality, and our exchange, which represents dialogic communication, also reflects rationality.

My claim is that when individuals, by themselves or in the presence of others, reason in such a way that their decision making can be called rationally competent, it can be shown that they will have used the elements of the logic of good reasons. By this I mean that they will have

118

employed special knowledge of the issues, both procedural and evaluative, that apply in the given case; they will have informed themselves of relevant data, assessed the arguments that can be made for and against the decision, weighed the values that impinge on the matter, and decided to adopt a position that satisfies the tests of coherence and fidelity. In advocating their position, they will exhibit reasonableness in monologic and dialogic interactions. Reasoning that can be characterized in this way is fully rational and reflects a significant degree of rhetorical competence regardless of the field of knowledge or action.

One familiar with Aristotle's *Nichomachean Ethics* may notice similarities between the logic of good reasons, including the concepts of rationality and reasonableness, and the Peripatetic's notion of "practical wisdom" *(phronesis)*.[29] There is a threefold parallel. First, in the kind of knowledge they presume. Unlike science, which investigates matters of necessity that can be demonstrated, and unlike art, which encompasses the realm of making and doing, Aristotle's practical wisdom "is a truthful rational characteristic of acting in matters involving what is good for man."[30] It is "concerned with human affairs and matters about which deliberation is possible. . . . The most characteristic function of a man of practical wisdom is to deliberate well; no one deliberates about things that cannot be other than they are, nor about things that are not directed to some end, an end attainable by action. . . . That man is good at deliberating who, by reasoning, can aim at and hit the best thing attainable to man by action."[31] In short, the logic of good reasons and practical wisdom share that kind of knowledge which is the province of rhetoric.

Second, the essence of the idea of reasonableness that I have presented is caught in Aristotle's statement that "to say that a person has good judgment in matters of practical wisdom implies that he is understanding and has good sense or that he has sympathetic understanding; for equitable acts are common to all good men in their relation with someone else."[32] Third, the logic of good reasons and "practical wisdom" are alike in the kind of end they manifest. Both treat the discovery and application of "right reason" as superordinately valuable. As Aristotle observed, "right reason is that which is determined by practical wisdom."[33] Possession of practical wisdom and use of the logic of good reasons yield intelligence in pursuit of proper and prudent conduct in those spheres of life that are not strictly matters of science or art. The specific sort of intelligence Aristotle marked as intrinsic to practical wisdom is that concerned with action where "truth" is "in harmony with correct desire." As he said, "reasoning must affirm what desire pursues."[34] The domain of practical wisdom and the logic of good reasons is, then, ethical and effective rhetorical perform-ance.

One establishes one's rationality in special fields by knowing and using the warrants indigenous to that field and adhering to the particular rules of advocacy followed in it. As Henry Johnstone, Jr., suggests, one may be considered competent in a school of philosophical thought if one exhibits its style, its style being fashioned by appropriate grounding of arguments on approved warrants and in respect to the accepted norms of argumen-tative interaction. In their book *An Introduction to Reasoning,* Toulmin, Rieke, and Janik demonstrated that the same general principle holds in regard to reasoning in such fields as law, science, art, ethics, and business management. They also point out that the variables of warrant and procedure will vary over time. They wrote:

> Indeed what makes it possible to speak of such enterprises as science and law and management as "rational" enterprises at all has as much to do with the ways in which they transform themselves in the course of their history as it does with the particular "rational standard" employed within them at any one time. It is not the truth or solidity of the positions adopted by scientists at any particular moment that makes the natural sciences "rational." It is, rather, the "adaptability" of scientific procedures and principles in the face of new experience and new conceptions. . . . It is the *openness of scientists to argu-ment*—their readiness if need be, to revise even their most fundamen-tal procedures of argument—that marks their activity off as an enterprise with some genuine claim to rationality.[35]

And the same may be said, I think, of any other field of endeavor that lives by reasoning.

CONCLUSION

In this chapter I have dealt with the problem of assessing fidelity in discourse that is about uncertain matters. I believe that this discussion, along with my earlier treatment of coherence and later chapters that will apply these principles, will show that there is a workable logic in narrative rationality. It goes beyond previous logics and provides a basis for consid-ering essential abilities in rhetorical competence—the capacity to make, use, and judge rhetorical discourse *with full understanding of its poten-tialities.* I grant that rhetorical competence in a specialized field of en-deavor entails awareness of that field's rhetorical presuppositions, pro-cedures, and practices, but the point I wish to stress is that being reasonable and rational are crucial dimensions of rhetorical competence in any specialty, any community, and any nation. These qualities, constituting narrative rationality, are particularly vital where equality of rights and freedom to decide exist as they do in any democratic, pluralistic setting. They are even more important in autocratic communities and societies, even though the nature and rules of "coherence" and the limits of "fidelity" are circumscribed.

NOTES

1. See Stephen Edelston Toulmin, *An Examination of the Place of Reason in Ethics* (Cambridge, England: Cambridge University Press, 1950); Chaïm Perelman, *Justice* (New York: Random House, 1967), and Chaïm Perelman and L. Olbrechts-Tyteca, *The New Rhetoric: A Treatise on Argumentation*, trans. John Wilkinson and Purcell Weaver (Notre Dame, Ind.: University of Notre Dame Press, 1969); Gidon Gottlieb, *The Logic of Choice: An Investigation of the Concepts of Rule and Rationality* (New York: Macmillan Co., 1968); Karl R. Wallace, "The Substance of Rhetoric: Good Reasons," *Quarterly Journal of Speech* 49 (1963): 239–49; Wayne C. Booth, *Modern Dogma and the Rhetoric of Assent* (Notre Dame, Ind.: University of Notre Dame Press, 1974). See also Ralph T. Eubanks and Virgil L. Baker, "Toward an Axiology of Rhetoric," *Quarterly Journal of Speech* 48 (1962): 157–68; Douglas Ehninger, "Validity as Moral Obligation," *Southern Speech Journal* 33 (1968): 215–22; Ray E. McKerrow, "Rhetorical Validity: An Analysis of Three Perspectives on the Justification of Rhetorical Argument," *Journal of the American Forensic Association* 13 (1977): 133–41; Joseph W. Wenzel, "Toward a Rationale for Value-Centered Argument," *Journal of the American Forensic Association* 13 (1977): 150–58; Thomas B. Farrell, "Validity and Rationality: The Rhetorical Constituents of Argumentative Form," *Journal of the American Forensic Association* 13 (1977): 142–49.

2. Gary L. Cronkhite, "Rhetoric, Communication, and Psychoepistemology," in Walter R. Fisher, ed., *Rhetoric: A Tradition in Transition* (East Lansing: Michigan State University Press, 1974), p. 262.

3. Stephen E. Toulmin, *The Uses of Argument* (Cambridge, England: Cambridge University Press, 1958), Introduction.

4. See, e.g., "The New Rhetoric," in Chaïm Perelman, *The Idea of Justice and the Problem of Argument*, trans. John Petrie (London: Routledge & Kegan Paul, 1963), pp. 134–42.

5. See Abraham Kaplan, *The Conduct of Inquiry: Methodology for Behavioral Science* (San Francisco, Calif.: Chandler, 1964) pp. 362–63.

6. Wallace, "The Substance of Rhetoric," p. 248.

7. Ibid., p. 247.

8. Booth, *Modern Dogma*, p. xiv.

9. Ibid., p. 143.

10. Stephen Toulmin, "Reasons and Causes," in Robert Borger and F. Cioffi, eds., *Explanation in the Behavioral Sciences* (Cambridge, England: Cambridge University Press, 1970), p. 4.

11. Ehninger, "Validity as Moral Obligation," pp. 215–22.

12. Virgil L. Baker and Ralph T. Eubanks, *Speech in Personal and Public Affairs* (New York: David McKay, 1955), pp. 89–108.

13. Karl Wallace, "An Ethical Basis of Communication," *Speech Teacher* 4 (1955): 1–9. See also Thomas R. Nilsen, "Free Speech, Persuasion, and the Democratic Process," *Quarterly Journal of Speech* 44 (1958): 235–43.

14. McKerrow, "Rhetorical Validity," pp. 139–41.

15. Booth, *Modern Dogma*, p. 121.

16. Perelman, *The Idea of Justice*, pp. 86–87, 169, 188–89, and Perelman and Olbrechts-Tyteca, *The New Rhetoric* pp. 30–35, 66–73 et passim.

17. To gain a knowledge about the nature and function of values, I would recommend the following: for a psychological perspective, Milton Rokeach, *The Nature of Human Values* (New York: Free Press, 1973); for a sociological perspective, Robin M. Williams, Jr., "Values in American Society," in *American Society: A Sociological Interpretation* (3rd ed.; New York: Alfred A. Knopf, 1970), pp. 438–504; for a historical perspective, Ralph H. Gabriel, *American Values: Continuity and Change* (Westport, Conn.: Greenwood Press, 1974).

18. The ideas of field-dependent and field-invariant elements in argument come from Toulmin, *The Uses of Argument*, pp. 14–15, 36–37.

19. H. J. Muller, *Man's Future Birthright: Essays on Science and Humanity*, ed. Elof Axel Carlson (Albany: State University of New York Press, 1973), pp. 110–11. For another important ranking of values, see Abraham H. Maslow, *Toward a Psychology of Being* (2nd ed.; New York: Van Nostrand, 1972), chaps. 11–12.

20. Kenneth Burke, *The Rhetoric of Religion: Studies in Logology* (1961; reprinted Berkeley: University of California Press, 1970), p. 41.

21. Jean Piaget, *The Moral Judgment of the Child*, trans. Marjorie Gabain (London: Kegan Paul, Trench Trubner, 1932).

22. Lawrence Kohlberg, "Development of Moral Character and Moral Ideology," In Martin L. Hoffman and Lois W. Hoffman, eds., *Review of Child Development Research* (New York: Russell Sage Foundation 1964), p. 399.

23. Ibid., p. 400.

24. Chaïm Perelman, "The Rational and the Reasonable." Lecture presented at the University of Southern California, December 1978. See also Mieczyslaw Maneli, "The New Theory of Argumentation and American Jurisprudence," *Logique et Analyse* 81 (1978): 30–37.

25. I have paraphrased Donald C. Bryant's classic statement that "the rhetorical function is the *function of adjusting ideas to people and of people to ideas*." See his essay "Rhetoric: Its Functions and Its Scope," *Quarterly Journal of Speech* 39 (1953): 413.

26. The possibility of ethical manipulation is posited usefully by Donald D. Darnell. He writes: "I would *define* an ethical controller as one who strives to make choices for others that they *would* make for themselves, given the knowledge, choice-making capacity, and opportunity to do so." See Donald K. Darnell and Wayne Brockriede, *Persons Communicating* (Englewood Cliffs, N.J.: Prentice-Hall, 1976), p. 62.

27. John Hardwig, "The Achievement of Moral Rationality," *Philosophy and Rhetoric* 6 (1973): 171–85.

28. Perelman and Olbrechts-Tyteca, *The New Rhetroic*, pp. 32–33. See also Ernest Cassirer, *The Logic of the Humanities,* trans. Clarence Smith Howe (New Haven, Conn.: Yale University Press, 1974), pp. 113–14.

29. I am grateful to Lloyd F. Bitzer for pointing out this connection between Aristotle's view of "practical wisdom" and the logic of good reasons.

30. Aristotle, *Nichomachean Ethics,* 6.7.11406 20, trans. Martin Ostwald (Indianapolis, Ind.: Bobbs-Merrill, 1978). For an analysis of the centrality of "practical wisdom" in Aristotle's conception of rhetoric, see Oscar Brownstein, "Aristotle and Rhetorical Process," in Walter R. Fisher, ed., *Rhetoric: A Tradition in Transition* (East Lansing: Michigan State University, 1974), pp. 19–32. See also Lois Self, "Rhetoric and *Phronesis:* The Aristotelian Ideal," *Philosophy and Rhetoric* 12 (1979): 130–36.

31. *Nichomachean Ethics,* 6.7.1141b 5–15.

32. *Nichomachean Ethics,* 6.11.25–35.

33. *Nichomachean Ethics,* 6.13.1144b 20–25.

34. *Nichomachean Ethics,* 6.2.1139a 20–30.

35. Stephen Toulmin, Richard Rieke, and Allan Janik, *An Introduction to Reasoning* (New York: Macmillan Co., 1979), p. 134.

6

NARRATIVE RATIONALITY AND THE QUALITIES OF AUDIENCES

Being reasonable and being rational are essential qualities signaling the presence of rhetorical competence, as we saw in Chapter 5. However, the issue of quality in rhetoric is inevitably influenced situationally. What is reasonable and rational in dealing with a child or someone else with minimal acquaintance with a subject cannot be thought of as reasonable and rational in discoursing with experts on the same subject. We must, therefore, judge the qualities of reasonableness and rationality in relation to the circumstances in which discourse occurs. A crucial question thus becomes: Is there any cross-situational principle according to which reasonableness and rationality in rhetoric can be judged? The modern scholar who made the most detailed effort to answer this question affirmatively was Chaïm Perelman, exponent of what he called the "new rhetoric." Because I wish to build further on a number of Perelman's conceptions of how reasonableness and rationality can be judged, I shall in this chapter make a detailed critique of his theory of how audiences relate to the qualities of rhetoric and I shall then suggest notions of my own that, I believe, make Perelman's theory more tenable.

The most crucial feature of Perelman's theory of rhetoric is his proposal of a system of logic and argumentation that denies the efficacy of formal rules of inference for assessing practical reasoning. "It can be shown," Perelman wrote, "that the practical reasoning involved in choice or decision making can always be expressed in the form of theoretical reasoning by introducing additional premises. But what is gained by such a move? The reasoning by which new premises are introduced is merely concealed, and resort to these premises appears entirely arbitrary, although in reality it too is the outcome of a decision that can be justified only in an argumentative, and not in a demonstrative, manner."[1] Carroll C. Arnold noted in his Introduction to Perelman's *The Realm of Rhetoric* that, once he has taken this position, Perelman "faces forthrightly the most serious and mooted question in theory of argument today: What gives an argument 'worth' or 'validity' if we grant that the supports of argumentation can never establish conclusions as *necessarily* true?" Perelman's answer, Arnold suggests, is "that our arguments are as worthy as our efforts to encourage reasonable people to follow the 'rule of justice.' "[2] A more accurate representation of Perelman's view, I shall argue, is that *arguments are as worthy as the audiences that would adhere to them.*

Arnold goes on to say that readers of *The Realm of Rhetoric* "are invited to participate in an ongoing debate over whether Perelman's test of the 'worth' of arguments is as firm as we can have."[3] I accept that invitation, but not initially as an advocate for or against the proposition. On the supposition that before one takes a stand in the debate, one should be sure of its terms, I wish to begin by explicating the full dimensions of Perelman's "test." What this means, in effect, is that my initial objective is to identify the characteristics that differentiate the qualities of audiences as Perelman apparently conceived them. I say *apparently* because, by and large, Perelman only suggested what they are. A better understanding of Perelman's project, its merit, and the man himself should also emerge from the analysis to follow. He once wrote: "To know a man it is important to know his model; to educate someone is for the most part to give him the desire to resemble a model."[4] This is the spirit of what I shall say in this chapter.

My earlier claim that Perelman's "test" should be stated as "arguments are as worthy as the audience that would adhere to them," rests on the assumption that "audience" is the decisive and most fundamental concept in Perelman's new rhetoric. That assumption rests on four aspects of his theory. First, *"it is in terms of an audience that an argumentation develops."*[5] The agreements on which an argument develops are facts, truths, presumptions and values, hierarchies, and lines of argument. They are those held in common by arguers and audiences, else there can be no argument. Second, the aim of all argumentation is an audience response: adherence. The "object of the theory of argumentation is the study of the discursive techniques allowing us *to induce or to increase the mind's adherence to the theses presented for its assent."*[6] Third, and most important in the context of my investigation, the audience "has the major role in determining the quality of argument and the behavior of orators."[7] The only other specific criterion of argumentative quality mentioned by Perelman is "efficacy." "An efficacious argument," he wrote, "is one which succeeds in increasing this intensity of adherence among those who hear it in such a way as to set in motion the intended action (a positive action or an abstention from action) or at least in creating in the hearers a willingness to act which will appear at the right moment."[8] In responding to Plato's charge that rhetoricians are more interested in success than truth, Perelman declared: "The techniques suited for persuading a crowd in a public place would not be convincing to a better educated and more critical audience, and . . . the worth of an argumentation is not measured solely by its efficacy but also by the quality of the audience at which it is aimed."[9] Perelman's avowed ultimate criterion of quality in argumentation was a "historically grounded conception of the universal audience."[10] And, fourth, audience is the basis of Perelman's key distinction between argumentation and demonstration. It is also the mark of difference between his theory of juridical reasoning and that of Stephen E. Toulmin. In the last year of his life, Perelman noted: "Not only does Toulmin in his book of 1958 [*The Uses of Argument*] ignore the role of audience, but his analysis concerns only the manner of establishing judgments of facts, while completely neglecting the reasoning about values, which are the center of juridical thought."[11]

What I propose is to establish that Perelman's concept of the quality of audiences, hence the quality of arguments, is complex, involving an inextricably intertwined set of requirements for rhetoric to reach its highest realization. Perelman's ideal audience for rhetoric would have these characteristics: commitment to pluralism, motivation toward justice, and competence in "critical rationalism." I want to examine these attributes and their implications in some detail. Then I shall relate these ideas to the concept of "narrative rationality" as I have developed it in earlier chapters.

PHILOSOPHICAL, POLITICAL, AND PERSONAL CHARACTERISTICS OF AUDIENCES

The first characteristic of audiences (and advocates) that Perelman's theory identifies as desirable is a commitment to pluralism that pervades one's view of reality, truth, the nature of society, and oneself. Advocates as well as audiences who subscribe to Perelman's new rhetoric will reject, along with Perelman, the perspective reflected in the metaphysics of Parmenides and Plato, the empiricism of Francis Bacon and John Locke, the rationalism of Descartes and Spinoza, and the logical positivism of the Vienna School. They will also dismiss the skepticism of Hume and many contemporary structuralists. They will join in Perelman's combat against "uncompromising and irreducible oppositions presented by all kinds of absolutisms: dualisms of reason and imagination, of knowledge and opinion, of irrefutable self-evidence and deceptive will, of a universally accepted objectivity and an incommunicable subjectivity, of a reality binding on everybody and values that are purely individual.[12] Adherents of the new rhetoric will hold that the world of human choice and action is open to reason and justice, that in this sphere of life, no one commands an indisputable position.

In regard to truth, persons acting in line with Perelman's new rhetoric will agree that "It is undeniable that in a great many areas of knowledge the ideal of truth must prevail over other considerations." On the other hand, they will also insist that "when we are concerned with action, knowing what is just or unjust, good or bad, what to encourage or forbid," it is argumentative, not demonstrative, reason that must rule.[13] "The idea of truth," Perelman maintained, "should serve as a criterion for opinions only to the extent that the techniques of control and verification allow it to be appropriately used without attempting to impose questionable ideologies in the name of truth."[14] The audience will thus recognize the existence and the role of truth as a decisive factor in some areas of knowledge and as a component in argument, but not as an ultimate determinant in reasonable choice of action.

Entailed in these views of reality and truth are certain political requirements implied by Perelman's new rhetoric. Chief among them is the presumption of a free and open society. "The democratic regime of free expression of opinions, of open discussion of all viewpoints," Perelman believed, "is the indispensable concomitant for the usage of the practical reason that is simply reasonable."[15] Perelman's rhetorical theory is incompatible with societies driven by monistic ideologies. In such systems, when the official agents of government fail in "persuading everybody of the truth of their point of view, they may justify coercion and the use of force against the recalcitrants in the name of God, of reason, of truth, or of the State's or party's interest."[16] A pluralistic state, on the other hand, fosters "respect for individuals and for the many groups which sometimes cooperate with each other and sometimes oppose one another." Pluralistic societies, therefore, support "freedom of belief, freedom of the press, and freedom of meeting and association."[17] Intrinsic to the vitality of pluralistic societies is practical philosophy—the new rhetoric. Without such a philosophy, "man becomes a plaything of his unconscious, or even a slave of cultural, political and religious traditions which . . . he can neither transcend nor adapt to new needs and situations."[18]

To avoid these failings and to be true to pluralism, one must be "reasonable," a person who in "judgments and conduct is influenced by *common sense*."[19] Being reasonable is thus a defining trait of advocates and audiences who employ the new rhetoric as Perelman conceived it. The reasonable person is tolerant of dissent, willing to listen to the other and perhaps "eventually to accept his point of view," concerned for others, modest, humble, prudent, responsible, honest, impartial, merciful, and generous.[20] Perelman's new rhetoric is therefore not a philosophy for fanatics or strict rationalists. It does not deny rationality but insists that "It is the dialectic of the rational and the reasonable, the confrontation of logical coherence with the unreasonable character of conclusions, which is the basis of the progress of thought."[21] The reasonable person is committed to justice and this commitment ensures that such progress will be humane, as I shall show shortly.

The import of Perelman's position in support of pluralism is given precise application in his view of the role of rhetoric in dealing with "confused notions." Confused notions include several of the notions I have already mentioned: reality, truth, freedom, reason, and justice. "It is the role of rhetoric . . . to arm us against the abusive use of confused notions. It is through the study of argumentational, rhetorical and dialectical procedures that we learn to distinguish acceptable reasoning from sophistical reasoning, to distinguish reasoning in which one seeks to persuade and to convince, from reasoning in which one seeks to deceive and to lead into error." Because he believed this, Perelman advocated teaching rhetoric "as a principal element of any liberal education."[22] Such teaching would promote pluralism in philosophy, politics, and one's personal outlook and behavior. It would be productive of advocates and audiences who characteristically exhibit the virtues of democratic regimes, especially reason and justice.

JUSTICE: THE MOTIVATIONAL CHARACTERISTIC

According to Perelman, pluralism sets the philosophical, political, and personal characteristics by which audiences (and advocates) may be assessed, but justice establishes the motivational characteristic against which they are to be evaluated. The emphasis on justice—as means and end—distinguishes Perelman's theory of rhetoric from other theories of human communication, which emphasize knowledge, truth, reason, ideology, action, or personal ambition. Perelman recognized the reality of those ends, but he used the concept of justice to contextualize and humanize them, to render them subject to rule and reasonable administration and realization. He made justice the overarching virtue in his theory of rhetoric because of his professional devotion to law and because

"All men—religious believers and non-believers, traditionalists and revolutionaries—invoke justice, and none dare disavow it." Justice, he held, is "a universal value."[23] It is, moreover, the specific value that informs Perelman's juridical model of reasoning.

Inspired by his early positivist orientation, Perelman first conceived justice as a formal rule: "beings of one and the same essential category must be treated in the same way."[24] As he worked further on the idea, however, he came to see it as a "confused notion." He saw, for instance, that the abstract rule had its counterpart in specific conceptions of justice:

1. To each the same thing.
2. To each according to his merits.
3. To each according to his works.
4. To each according to his needs.
5. To each according to his rank.
6. To each according to his legal entitlement.[25]

Entailed in these concrete conceptions were distinctive values and "a particular view of the universe."[26] He realized that application of the formal rule of justice required "criteria to indicate which categories are relevant and how their members should be treated, and such decisions involve a recourse to judgments of value." Given his aim—"to provide an ideal of practical reason, that is, to establish rules and models for reasonable action"—he had to give up the positivist notion that "There is no value which is not logically arbitrary."[27] Thus began the search that led Perelman to his new rhetoric.

After critical investigation of philosophical literature proved of no help, Perelman turned to the method of his mentor, Gottlob Frege, who had analyzed the reasoning used by mathematicians in order to cast new light on logic. With Mme L. Olbrechts-Tyteca, he embarked on a ten-year study of "the actual logic of value judgments" in the discourse of politicians, judges, moralists, informal discussants, philosophers, and so on. In the process of their research, the two authors rediscovered Aristotle's concept of dialectical reasoning in the *Rhetoric, Topics,* and *On Sophistical Refutations,* and the outcome was the new rhetoric. As I have indicated, the key distinction made in the new rhetoric was between demonstration, the logic that denies rationality to reasoning about values, and argumentation, which makes such reasoning reasonable. With this distinction, Perelman was able to transform his idea of justice into an open concept, subject to argument, a concept appropriate for a pluralistic world.

129

With this move, Perelman resolved the dilemma posed by the philosophies of Plato and Pascal. That dilemma was that if a rule of justice were to be formulated, it would have to be either a "realistic, objective, dogmatic conception" or a "nominalistic, subjective, arbitrary one."[28] By stipulating that the rule of justice is not absolute, that it is an argumentative construct that entails a concrete conception of justice in its application, Perelman was able to retain the original principle—that beings of one and the same essential category must be treated the same. But justice was now a dynamic, not a static, concept; it was a matter of commitment, ideology, and reason. Its function was to provide order and force for a pluralistic world and a way of acting with reason and humanity in all practical circumstances of decision and action.

Since Perelman's special interest was in juridical argument, it is natural that he repeatedly refers to *precedent* in statements that concern the application of the rule of justice. For instance, in his essay on "Legal Reasoning," he wrote:

> According to the values that prevail in society (respect for the divine word, or human law, the search for equity or the common good, the dignity of the individual and the veneration of certain individuals) such arguments give good reasons for the justification of a given decision. Such a precedent or law will have more or less authority for the judge, jurist and public according to the societal place and importance of the legislator and judge.[29]

The suggestion here and elsewhere is that *all forms of practical reasoning are marked by precedents*. But I shall claim more broadly that precedents must be a common feature of everyday reasoning if Perelman's juridical model is in fact a valid account of such reasoning. "Precedent," he maintained, "plays a quite primary role in argumentation, the rationality of which is linked with the observance of the *rule of justice*, which demands equal treatment for similar situations."[30] Acceptance of this view is essential if one is to adhere to Perelman's concept of "critical rationalism" and its attendant notions of rationality and reason, to which I now turn.

CRITICAL RATIONALISM: THE COMPETENCE CHARACTERISTIC

As pluralism provides the ideological ground and justice the motivation by which audiences (and advocates) can be assessed, critical rationalism sets the competence measure by which they can be evaluated.[31] Such competence is prerequisite to the enactment of pluralistic beliefs and behavior, and to the advancement of justice, whether advanced by audiences in criticism or by arguers in efforts to convince or to persuade. The competent audience and arguer, according to Perelman's theory, will know the distinctions between demonstration and argumentation, between the rational and the reasonable, the essential points of agreement between arguers and audiences, the structure and techniques of practical reasoning, and the legitimate means of audience adaptation. Once Perelman ties these notions to a conception of a "universal audience," competent knowledge and ability lead to decision and action that promote freedom, justice, and reason in the practical affairs of humankind.

"Unlike demonstrative reasoning," Perelman insisted, "arguments are never correct or incorrect; they are either strong or weak, relevant or irrelevant. The strength or weakness is judged according to the Rule of Justice, which requires that essentially similar situations be treated in the same manner. Relevance and irrelevance are to be examined by the various disciplines and their particular methodologies."[32] In Perelman's view, good audiences will not only adhere to arguments motivated by and productive of justice, they will also be persuaded by arguments informed by pluralism. And they will be competent critics of practical reasoning, making judgments based on knowledge of argumentation in general and its techniques in particular. Specialized audiences will, in addition, know the rules of advocacy and warranted reasoning peculiarly applicable within their fields of endeavor.

Perelman's distinction between the rational and the reasonable corresponds with his distinction between demonstration and argumentation. The rational is associated with demonstration in theoretical domains and with calculated, nonemotional action in human behavior.[33] Rationality, as commonly conceived, is the principal criterion fulfilled by those who pursue "truth" and the justificatory ground for those who promulgate "truths" in order to legislate the action of others. As such, strict rationality is devoid of passion, detached from considerations of circumstance, time, and place, and serves the interests of monolithic systems, whether philosophical or political.

The reasonable, in contrast, is associated with argumentation—as process and accomplishment. "To reason," Perelman maintained, "is not merely to verify and to demonstrate, but also to deliberate, to criticize, and to justify, to give reasons for and against—in a word, to argue."[34] The reasonable is not in opposition to the emotions, because even philosophical discourse, as Perelman conceived of it, "addresses itself to the whole

131

man, and not to an abstract faculty, 'the reason,' opposed to the will and to the emotions."[35] Hence, the reasonable is a more "flexible notion" than the rational. The reasonable is sensitive to the history, traditions, and culture of a community. What is reasonable in one society at one time may not be reasonable at another time or in a different society.[36] Perelman's concept of reason refers to "the capacity for argumentation, for furnishing and presenting objections."[37] The reasonable is indispensable for the existence and vitality of pluralistic thought and action, and for the realization of justice.

What ultimately distinguishes demonstration and argumentation in Perelman's theory is the dimension of audience. Argument involves human beings reasoning together to resolve their differences. In Perelman's view, the worthiness of reasoning is not determined by arbitrary rules, but by human judgment, which is fallible but can be governed by a commitment to pluralism, a motivation to advance justice, and competence in argumentation. His new rhetoric is saved from relativism by his elevated conception of audience, especially the "universal audience." The universal audience is not an actual audience but a construction in the mind of an arguer, whether an ordinary person or a philosopher. It is a conception of the most reasonable body of informed persons the arguer can conceive of. In lectures, Perelman sometimes translated "universal audience" into "an audience of the best body of critics you can imagine for your subject, given your situation." "To reason," Perelman wrote, "is to subject to the exacting demands that Kant imposed on moral action; that is to conform to the categorical imperative according to which only arguments which can be universally admitted shall be used." Regardless of who constructs the "universal audience," however, its validity would be subject "to the test of experiment, that is to say, dialogue."[38] A measure, then, of the worthiness of audiences and advocates is the worth of the conception of universal audience that they would endorse. "The appeal to reason is but an attempt to convince the members of this audience—whom common sense would define as well-informed and reasonable men—by addressing them."[39]

Competent audiences also have technical rhetorical knowledge. In general, this knowledge includes understanding (1) the points of agreement on which arguments must be founded: *facts*—"uncontroverted" statements; *truths*—"more complex systems relating to connections between facts"; *presumptions*—what is "normal or likely"; *values*—conceptions of the ideal; *hierarchies*—orderings of people, institutions, values, and so on; *loci*—"premises of a very general nature" such as quantity, quality, order, and so on; (2) the techniques of argumentation, which involve quasi-logical arguments, arguments of association that establish reality, and arguments of dissociation; (3) the ideas that concern argumentative composition, style, and audience adaptation.[40] All well-informed persons, Perelman held, are aware of these matters. A point that I would add, however, is that worthy audiences would also be fully knowledgeable and competent in using this knowledge. Hence worthy audiences would adhere to arguments that are in conformity with the best argumentative techniques that one might employ in the situation.

There is another trait of worthy audiences that emerges from careful consideration of Perelman's theory. The worthy audience has a special form of intelligence. The form of intelligence is implied, I think, by the claim broached earlier, that under Perelman's model of juridical reasoning, all forms of practical reasoning are marked by use of precedents. Several of Perelman's statements justify my interpretation: "The thesis which I have defended for thirty years is that *law plays a role in regard to argumentation analogous to that of mathematics in regard to formal logic.*"[41] And central to law is precedent. What is reasonable, Perelman wrote, "must be able to be a precedent which can inspire everyone in analogous circumstances, and from this comes the value of the generalization or the universalization which is characteristic of the reasonable."[42] He also insisted that "The mere fact of doing certain acts, whether they be appraisals or decisions, is regarded as an implicit consent to the use of these acts as precedents, as a sort of promise to behave in the same way in similar situations."[43] Implied by these statements is not only that precedent is fundamental in all practical reasoning, but also that *analogy* is a basic feature of such reasoning, despite the fact that Perelman treats analogy only as an "element of proof" in his work.[44] My interpretation derives additional support from the nature of Perelman's rule of justice. His application requires consideration of similarity and differences in people and situations, and the underlying structure of the techniques of argumentation. Quasi-logical arguments resemble formal arguments, and arguments by association and dissociation depend on comparison.

Two strong implications arise. First, worthy audiences will not only be knowledgeable, they will also be intelligent, that is, good in reasoning by analogy. This means that worthy audiences will be able to recognize the differences between monistic and pluralistic arguments, will be able to discern the just from the unjust, to distinguish between demonstration and argumentation, and will respect the reasonable in contrast with the rational when it reflects an absolutist position. Worthy audiences will agree with Perelman that "A rational decision is not simply a decision conforming to truth, but rather that decision which can be justified by the best reasons, at least inasmuch as justification is necessary."[45]

A second implication is that a useful project would be to investigate the nature and functions of precedent in nonlegal discourse. One approach to such inquiry would be to reformulate Perelman's rule of justice to say: What is given, granted, or legislated for one class of persons cannot be denied to another. One could seek to discover the recurrent cases used in arguments where this rule applies. Another line of research would focus on specialized audiences, for example, academic, economic, religious, political. One could identify examples that serve time and again to justify decision and action for each kind of audience. Such investigations would note values that provide rules for acceptance or rejection of new ideas, such as those mentioned earlier: "respect for the divine word, or human law, the search for equity or the common good, the dignity of the individual and veneration of certain institutions."[46] By locating precedents in everyday arguments, one could, in effect, discover what a given community regards as the foundation of good reasons, as Perelman conceived of them.

I have been arguing that Perelman's answer to the questions posed by Arnold concerning the worthiness of arguments would be that arguments are as worthy as the audiences that would adhere to them. This is neither a sophistic nor a solipsistic standard. It entails rigorous requirements and is fully informed by the highest values of the humanistic tradition: pluralism, justice, knowledge, intelligence, and reason. There is a temptation to claim that what I have summarized as the characteristics of worthy audiences should be viewed as the constituents of Perelman's own conception of the universal audience. I believe that they do provide a fair profile for his conception, but I do not make this claim unequivocally. I suspect that Perelman would have insisted, along with Plato, that the best rhetoric would please the god(s).

CONCEPTS OF AUDIENCES RECONSIDERED

To complete this consideration of Perelman's rhetoric in regard to narrative rationality, it is essential to reexamine his conceptions of audiences and the relationship between conviction and persuasion. Perelman's new rhetoric focuses on the acceptability of argumentative discourse as a whole. "Nonformal argument consists," said Perelman, "not of a chain of ideas of which some are derived from others according to accepted rules of inference, but rather of a web formed by all the arguments and all the reasons that combine to achieve the desired result."[47] In other words, audiences do not ordinarily assess isolated arguments but respond to them as an integrated message, a supported thesis submitted for their adherence. In Perelman's view, the decision to believe or not to believe, to act or not to act, depends on the quality of the audience that would adhere to it, and not on invariant criteria.

Perelman's conception of the universal audience is an ideal. Actual audiences will measure up to the ideal in varying degrees. An audience that fully satisfied Perelman's demands concerning pluralism, justice, and argumentative competence would be "universal" in its qualifications. This brings us to Perelman's distinctions between conviction and persuasion and between particular and universal audiences.

These two sets of distinctions are not always precise. One one page of *The New Rhetoric*, it is asserted that "We are going to apply the term *persuasive* to argumentation that only claims validity for a particular audience, and the term *convincing* to an argumentation that presumes to gain the adherence of every rational being."[48] But on the next page, it is maintained that the distinction is "always unprecise and in practice must remain so."[49]

The same ambiguity attends the distinction between particular and universal audiences. "There is," Perelman and Olbrechts-Tyteca declared, "no clear-cut dividing line between techniques of order designed for the universal audience and techniques that only have validity for some particular listener. For certain features of the universal audience will always coincide with the real concrete person: the universal audience will only differ from a particular audience in the measure that the conception held of the universal audience transcends given particular audiences."[50] The universal audience is of "primordial importance": it provides the norm by which all other audiences are to be assessed.[51]

To profit from Perelman's concept of the universal audience, one must recognize the difference between his personal construction of its composition and his formulation of the idea itself. As I suggested earlier, pluralism, justice, and argumentative competence constitute the norms of his view of worthy audiences. His own view, however, is but one: it is one that he proposes, but does not impose.[52] He holds that the universal audience is "an ideal audience, a mental construction of him who refers to it." Taken out of context, this is a misleading statement. It implies that conceptions of the universal audience are purely psychological and do not have material manifestation in the world. But such is not the case. Perelman invited misunderstanding by asserting that "the universal audience

135

never actually exists," because, while this is in one sense true, in another sense it denies what he goes on to say: "We could easily show that this so-called 'universal audience' varies with the epoch and with the person: each creates its own idea of the universal audience."[53] In his essay on "The New Rhetoric," he even specifies different groundings for the universal audience: "God, all reasonable and competent men, in man deliberating, and in an elite."[54] It cannot be that the universal audience is only an ideal figment of one's intelligence and imagination and that one can identify the constituents of the universal audience held by persons at different times and different cultures unless the nature of the universal audience becomes evident in some way or another.

Actually, there are two ways in which a person's construction of a universal audience can be discerned. One way is illustrated in this chapter: by observing what someone predicates in regard to ultimate questions of reality, truth, knowledge, and reason. The second way is by examining the implied, ideal audience in someone's discourse. My conclusion that Perelman's worthy audiences are to be known by their commitment to pluralism, motivation toward justice, and argumentative competence is substantiated, I think, by the fact that these are the characteristics of the implied ideal audience referred to in Perelman's writings and lectures. Nonetheless, it is equally clear that Perelman conceived of the universal audience as historically situated, evident in the world, and determinant for audiences that would qualify as the best that one could conceive.[55] I believe that Perelman revealed his own view and his own practice when he said in 1970: "Most important, the task is not, as often assumed, to address *either* a particular audience *or* a universal audience, but in the process of persuasion to adjust to and then to transform the particularities of an audience into universal dimensions."[56]

CONCLUSION

Perelman's aims and my objective are essentially the same: to formulate a theory of reason, value, and action that gives meaning and significance to everyday life and to human communication in particular. I agree with Perelman's view on the necessity of recognizing and accepting pluralism. However, I would place love as the highest virtue or motivation in life, displacing justice from the pinnacle in the hierarchy of values. Love provides the ground of being and is the motive that should inform all others in human decision making and action. Perelman may well have agreed with this idea, and he could have then argued, rightly I think, that justice is a form of love, that civic love is a way of honoring the dignity and worth of individuals and ensuring by rule their well-being in society.

Having said this much, I can now address the question suggested by Carroll Arnold: "Whether Perelman's test of the 'worth' of arguments is as firm a test as we have." I think not, for two fundamental reasons. First, while I agree that arguments can be usefully measured by the qualities of the audiences that would adhere to them, I think that the concept of argument implicit in that standard is both too broad and too narrow. It is too broad because argument is conceived of as a macrostructure, a "web," rather than as lines of inference. The focus of attention is on the force of argument-in-the-large and not on the merits of individual instances of good reasons. In fact, sophisticated audiences may be critical respecting *loci* and techniques of association and dissociation, whereas unsophisticated audiences are likely to respond only to *loci*. Put another way: When Perelman deals with responses of audiences and with evaluation of audiences, he does not treat arguments as the concrete inferential or implicative forms that he expertly displays in *The New Rhetoric*. To draw attention to argument-in-the-large, to concrete inferential and implicative forms, and to still other specific modes of reason in human communication, I have proposed that Perelman's favored term "argument" be replaced by the concept of "good reasons," which I have defined as *those elements that provide warrants for accepting or adhering to the advice fostered by any form of communication that can be considered rhetorical.* Within this view, individual units of all sorts of human communication can be isolated and assessed, and with the principle of coherence, macrostructures can be evaluated as well.

Proceeding as I have just suggested helps to solve the second problem I find in Perelman's new rhetoric. Perelman treats persons as arguers. I would replace this presumption with the presumption that they are storytellers and their mode of communication is asserting what are thought to be good reasons regardless of form, whether the communication be technical or public, literary or political, learned or social. To conceive of people as storytellers and assessors of stories allows one to include within one's account of human communication virtually all of Perelman's new rhetoric while at the same time generating more specific criterial tests and a broader view of informal logic than Perelman's account, by itself, contains. One no longer has to appeal to a privileged audience as the measure of rationality. Rationality is grounded in the narrative structure of life and the natural capacity people have to recognize coherence and fidelity in the stories they experience and tell one another. As I emphasized earlier, this

137

conception of narrative rationality still invites application of the tests of such lines of reasoning as cause, sign, analogy, classification, and example—all distinctive patterns well explained and illustrated by Perelman, and others. Also included in one's account will be the tests of values and valuation that I set forth in chapter 5 and that are in no way inconsistent with Perelman's emphasis on the role of values, even in forms of argumentation. I would, however, eschew Perelman's attempt to distinguish between conviction and persuasion. It is more accurate, I believe, to say that values determine the persuasive *force* of reasons, and that values may constitute reasons in and of themselves. My notion of narrative rationality thus becomes an elaboration of Perelman's concept of argumentative competence. It adds a set of logical principles—coherence and fidelity—and it adds precise criteria for assessing good reasons. These additions, however, are in no way incompatible with Perelman's broader but still useful view that an argument is as worthy as the audience that would adhere to it.

NOTES

The following abbreviations are used in the notes to this chapter.

IJ   Chaïm Perelman, *The Idea of Justice and the Problem of Argument,* trans. John Petrie (London: Routledge & Kegan Paul, 1963).
JLA   Chaïm Perelman, *Justice, Law, and Argument: Essays in Moral and Legal Reasoning* (Dordrecht, Holland: D. Reidel, 1980).
NR   Chaïm Perelman and L. Olbrechts-Tyteca, *The New Rhetoric: A Treatise on Argumentation,* trans. John Wilkinson and Purcell Weaver (Notre Dame, Ind.: University of Notre Dame Press, 1969).
NRH   Chaïm Perelman, *The New Rhetoric and the Humanities: Essays on Rhetoric and Its Application* (Dordrecht, Holland: D. Reidel, 1979).
REALM   Chaïm Perelman, *The Realm of Rhetoric,* trans. William Kluback (Notre Dame, Ind.: University of Notre Dame Press, 1982).

1. Chaïm Perelman, "The New Rhetoric: A Theory of Practical Reasoning," in *NRH,* p. 127.
2. Carroll C. Arnold, in Chaïm Perelman, *REALM,* pp. xix–xx.
3. *Realm,* p. xx. For attempts to enhance Perelman's theory of the worth of arguments, see Leo Apostel, "What Is the Force of an Argument?" pp. 99–109, and Sally Van Noorden, "Rhetorical Argument in Aristotle and Perelman," pp. 178–87, *Revue Internationale de Philosophie,* no. 127–28 (1979), an issue devoted to "Essais en hommage à Chaïm Perelman: ad *La Nouvelle Rhetorique.*"
4. *Chaïm Perelman, "The Role of the Model in Education," in NRH,* p. 136.
5. Chaïm Perelman and L. Olbrechts-Tyteca, NR, p. 5.
6. *NR,* p. 4.

7. Perelman, "The New Rhetoric, "in *NRH,*p. 14. See also: "Philosophy, Rhetoric, and Commonplaces," in *NRH,* pp. 57–58, and "Legal Reasoning," in *JLA,* p. 135.

8. *NR,* p. 45.

9. Perelman, "The New Rhetoric, "in *NRH,* p. 14. See also *Realm,* p. 140, where Perelman wrote: "Since the efficacy of an argument is relative to audience, it is impossible to evaluate it above and beyond references to the audience to which it is presented."

10. Perelman, "The New Rhetoric, "in *NRH,* p. 14.

11. Chaïm Perelman, "The New Rhetoric and the Rhetoricians: Remembrances and Comments," *Quarterly Journal of Speech* 70 (1984): 195.

12. *NR,* p. 510.

13. Chaïm, "Authority, Ideology, and Violence," in *NRH,* p. 142.

14. Chaïm Perelman, "The Philosophy of Pluralism, "in *NRH,* p. 70.

15. Chaïm Perelman, "Reflections on Practical Reasoning," in *NRH,* p. 132.

16. Perelman, "The Philosophy of Pluralism, "in *NRH,* p. 63.

17. Ibid., p. 67.

18. Chaïm Perelman, "Law, Philosophy, and Argumentation," in *JLA,* p. 149.

19. Chaïm Perelman, "The Rational and the Reasonable," in *NRH,* p. 118.

20. *NR,* p. 17.

21. Perelman, "The Rational and the Reasonable," in *NRH,* p. 120.

22. Chaïm Perelman, "The Use and Abuse of Confused Notions," in *JLA,* pp. 105–6.

23. Chaïm Perelman, "Justice and Its Problems," in *JLA,* p. 24.

24. Chaïm Perelman, "Concerning Justice," in *JLA,* p. 11.

25. Ibid., p. 2.

26. Ibid., p. 22.

27. Perelman, "The New Rhetoric, "in *NRH,* p. 8. See also Chaïm Perelman, "The Arbitrary in Justice," in *IJ,* pp. 56–57.

28. Perelman, "Justice and Its Problems, "in *JLA,* p. 25.

29. Perelman, "Legal Reasoning," in *JLA,* pp. 130–31.

30. Chaïm Perelman, "The Social Contexts of Argumentation," in *IJ,* p. 157.

31. *NR,* p. 514.

32. Chaïm Perelman, "Justice and Reason," in *Justice* (New York: Random House, 1967), p. 83 (p. 72 in *JLA*); see also "The New Rhetoric," in *NRH,* p. 25, and "Law, Philosophy, and Argumentation," in *JLA,* p. 150.

33. Perelman, "The Rational and the Reasonable," in *NRH,* pp. 117–18.

34. Chaïm Perelman, "Justice and Justification," in *JLA,* p. 59.

35. Perelman, "The New Rhetoric and the Rhetoricians," p. 195.

36. Perelman, "The Rational and the Reasonable," in *NRH,* p. 119.

37. Chaïm Perelman, "Dialectic and Dialogue," in *NRH,* pp. 78–79.

38. Perelman, "The Philosophy of Pluralism," in *NRH,* p. 70.

39. Chaïm Perelman, "Justice and Reason," in *Justice,* p. 82 (p. 72 in *JLA*).

40. This discussion reflects a reading of various of Perelman's work, especially *NR* and *Realm*.

41. Perelman, "The New Rhetoric and the Rhetoricians," p. 195.

42. Perelman, "The Rational and the Reasonable," in *NRH,* p. 119.

43. *NR,* pp. 108, 363; Chaïm Perelman, "Reflections on Practical Reasoning,"

in *NRH*, pp. 130–31; "Justice and Its Problems," in *JLA*, p. 27; and "Justice and Reasoning," in *JLA*, p. 77.

44. *NR*, p. 372. See also Chaïm Perelman, "Analogy and Metaphor in Science, Poetry, and Philosophy," in *NRH*, pp. 91–100.

45. Chaïm Perelman, "What the Philosopher May Learn from the Study of Law," in *Justice*, p. 108 (p. 172 in *JLA*).

46. Perelman, "Legal Reasoning," in *JLA*, p. 130.

47. Perelman, "The New Rhetoric," in *NRH*, p. 14.

48. *NR*, p. 28.

49. Ibid., p. 29.

50. Ibid., pp. 502.

51. Ibid., p. 31.

52. Perelman, "Justice and Reason," in *Justice*, p. 78 (p. 70 in *JLA*).

53. Chaïm Perelman and L. Olbrechts-Tyteca, "Act and Person in Argument," in Maurice Natanson and Henry W. Johnstone, Jr., eds., *Philosophy, Rhetoric, and Argumentation* (University Park: Pennsylvania State University Press, 1965), p. 103. See also "Dialectic and Dialogue," in *NRH*, p. 79.

54. "The New Rhetoric," in *NRH*, p. 14; see also "The New Rhetoric and the Rhetoricians," p. 191; *NR*, pp. 101, 110; "What the Philosopher May Learn from the Study of Law," in *JLA*, p. 173; "Philosophy, Rhetoric, and Commonplaces," in *NRH*, p. 58.

55. Perelman, "The New Rhetoric and the Rhetoricians," pp. 190–92. See also "Justice and Reason," in *Justice*, p. 77 (p. 69 in *JLA*).

56. Ibid., p. 192.

PART IV
APPLICATIONS

7

NARRATIVITY AND POLITICS:
The Case of Ronald Reagan

In Part IV of this book I propose to illustrate how the narrative paradigm helps a person to understand what goes on in human
communication. To this end I shall, in the next three chapters, use the
concept of the narrative paradigm and its logic—narrative rationality—as
a basis for interpreting three very different kinds of discourse. In this
chapter, I shall examine political discourse; in chapter 8, the critical
principles I have outlined will be applied to dramatic and literary texts,
and in chapter 9 I shall do the same with a text that is philosophical. If the
theory I have proposed in the preceding chapters is sound, it ought to
yield insights not otherwise easily derived when one looks across genres of
human discourse. In short, this and the two chapters to follow constitute
an empirical test of the usefulness of the theory I have offered.

When the narrative paradigm is used in exploring discourses, the texts
are viewed as verbal phenomena composed of good reasons (some reasons, of course, being better than others) as elements that function as
warrants for believing or acting in accord with the message of the text.
One must keep in mind that reasons may be expressed through a variety of
individuated forms of discourse and performance. Reasons can appear in
and through arguments, metaphors, myths, gestures, and other means of
creating communicative relationships. In sum, to view communication
through the perspective of narrativity is to focus on message, on the
individuated forms that constitute it, and on the reliability, trustworthiness, and desirability of what is said—evaluated by using the tests of
narrative rationality. Whatever the genre of the discourse, the narrative
paradigm allows one to view it as rhetoric. The criteria for assessing, say, a
scientific text, will differ from those one would use in assessing a popular
film, but the principles of coherence and fidelity apply no less to a
scientific treatise than to a filmic communication. Furthermore, as I have
said before, even technical discourse is imbued with myth, metaphor, and
strategy or design. I shall not press this particular point in this book,

although I believe it can be readily established. For the sake of conciseness, however, I shall restrict my illustrations to political, dramatic/literary, and philosophical texts.

I have proposed that one look at rhetorical communications as stories rather than as an "arguments" in the traditional sense. To do so allows one to make at least three kinds of important discriminations: (1) one will focus on the sequences of symbolic actions and their meaning, (2) one will recognize that no text is devoid of historical, situational, and biographical context, and (3) one will recognize that the meaning and value of any account are always influenced by how the account or story stands with or against other stories known to an audience or other observer.[1]

I have made the point that one may use the narrative paradigm and also acknowledge that a text belongs to one genre or another. Tennyson's *Maud* can be explored for narrativity and also as a lyric poem. Fitzgerald's *The Great Gatsby* can be examined as narrative in the sense that I use the term, and as a novel. I shall confine myself in what follows to exploration of what can be said of texts, whatever their genres, by treating them as rhetoric-through-narrativity. I believe that texts, whatever their subjects, times, places, or cultural contexts, can be characterized as expressing one or more of four, perhaps five, motives. By "motive" I mean what Kenneth Burke means by the term: it is a name that characterizes the nature of a symbolic action in a given situation.[2] On the (biological) assumption that symbolic actions affect the life of ideas/images in the minds of people, one may propose, as I have in "A Motive View of Communication," that texts function (1) to give birth to—to gain acceptance of—ideas/images, *affirmation;* (2) to revitalize or to reinforce ideas/images, *reaffirmation;* (3) to heal or to cleanse ideas/images, *purification;* and (4) to undermine or to discredit ideas/images, *subversion.*[3]

Since this generic scheme will be used in this and the next two chapters, I shall not provide specific examples of each of the categories here. In general, however, one will recognize rhetoric of affirmation in discourse designed to advance new theories, policies, programs, and so on; rhetoric of reaffirmation in discourse meant to resist such innovations or to celebrate prevailing beliefs, attitudes, and actions; rhetoric of purification in discourse that aims to correct false notions or to apologize for perceived misdeeds; and rhetoric of subversion in discourse that seeks, in Burke's terminology, symbolically to "kill" wrong or detrimental thoughts or practices. These categories overlap, of course. Affirmation implies subversion and vice versa. For example, any definition implies that other defini-

144

tions are inferior, and any refutation implies that something ought to displace that which is refuted. In any given situation and in any given moment of rhetorical experience, however, one motive will dominate in perception. Which motive dominates depends on the perception of the kind of symbolic action that is performed, how the discourse moves the mind toward assent, reassurance, corrected vision, or rejection. Whatever the motive of a message may be, its ultimate effect is to constitute or reconstitute listeners or readers as selves, to constitute or invoke the experience of community, and to shape the meaning of one's world.

I have suggested that there may be a fifth motive. It would name that kind of discourse that reflects nihilism. Perhaps it should be called *rhetoric of evisceration*. The other four motives all imply that there are true, healthy, sane ideas/images that should guide belief and action, but there is also discourse that implies or asserts the impossibility or absurdity of life. One could include in this genre *The Myth of Sisyphus* and *Waiting for Godot*. In this and the succeeding two chapters, I shall explore texts as rhetoric, using the paradigmatic concepts I have discussed earlier, and I shall try to be especially sensitive to the motives displayed in the texts. I begin with a specific question about Ronald Reagan's rhetoric: How is it that President Reagan enjoys a nearly unanimous evaluation as a "Great Communicator" despite the fact that he is also noted for making factual errors, making inconsistent statements, reasoning in only limited fashion, and frequently diverting attention from relevant issues?

REAGAN'S RHETORIC

It almost goes without saying that Reagan's presidential discourse fails the test of rhetoric if the rational-world paradigm is applied to it. Furthermore, it fails the tests of the narrative paradigm insofar as the tests of fidelity to fact, soundness of argumentative form, and relevance are applied. How, then, are we to account for President Reagan's equally uncontestable popularity and success in persuading?

If one heeds political commentators, the answer to this question is: Reagan's rhetorical achievement is aesthetic—a triumph of acting, telling stories, presence, and presentation. There is some truth in this view. But it also applies to other presidents, especially to John F. Kennedy and Franklin D. Roosevelt. They, too, were masters of the media; they, too, exuded confidence, competence, and comfort in the limelight. Superior performance is only a partial answer. One needs to consider Reagan's story and his character. These are matters neglected in the rational-world paradigm, but they are crucial to an understanding of Reagan's rhetoric and that of any other spokesperson.

The answer I propose is threefold. First, Reagan's story is grounded in American history and it is informed by central values of the American Dream. Second, his perceived character is constituted by this background and renders him virtually immune to "rational" criticism. Third, the implied audience of heroes in his rhetoric is as efficacious as just about any that one might conceive, given our troubled times. In pursuing these points, I shall compare and contrast Reagan's story and character with those of Jimmy Carter and Edward Kennedy.

REAGAN'S STORY

Reagan's story has its roots in nineteenth-century romantic democracy, the taproot of which was "the common glorification of the ideal of individualism."[4] This ideal was interpreted differently in different parts of the country, but it was at the heart of concepts fostered by the romantic Old South, the romantic East where the principles of capitalism were celebrated, and the romantic West where the frontier beckoned the pioneers and captured the imagination of all America in folktale and legend.

The ideal of individualism was, of course, significant in the American experience from the outset, and it remains significant today. Robert Bellah and his associates argue, in fact, that "it is individualism, not equality, as Tocqueville thought, that has marched inexorably through our experience."[5] It is not surprising, then, that Reagan's story, stressing individualism, should have appeal. His stances on various issues of foreign and domestic policy embody the ideal in action.

Bellah and his associates interviewed a large sample of middle-class Americans and concluded that individualism has two fundamental modes of expression: "a belief in the inherent dignity and, indeed, the sacredness of the human person" and "a belief that the individual has a primary reality whereas society is a second-order, derived or artificial construct, a view we call *ontological individualism*." This second view coincides with traditional heroism—"a man's got to be what a man's got to be"—and Reagan's notion that America and its people are essentially heroic.[6] Reagan's story consistently reinforces this belief: act according to our heroic nature and our destiny is assured. Reagan's popularity stems in no small part from the coherence and felt fidelity of this story.

The acceptance of Reagan's story, like any other story, derives from

146

timing and what stories it must compete with as well as from its coherence and fidelity. The stage was set in 1980 for the entrance of a heroic figure as president, a man on a white horse. A sense of impending disaster was present in the country and the performance of then President Carter was widely seen as weak. The inability of his administration to deal effectively with the eroding economy, the adventurousness of the Soviet Union, and the militancy of Iran in holding Americans as hostages led to a widespread impression that Carter was inept and America ineffectual.

The contrast between Carter's story, especially his references to "malaise," and Reagan's is telling. Carter envisioned a military comparable to Russia's; Reagan foresaw a military second to none. Carter promised an improved economy; Reagan pledged a perfected economy. Carter's vision of the future was fraught with curtailment, compromises, and circumscribed possibilities. He said, in effect, that America must forge into an uncertain future, that America could not go back to former strengths. Reagan's prophecy was sparkling with expansion, free rein, and restored glory. He foretold a future that was as certain as America's past; America could not only go back, but by making the past the future, America could solve all of its problems. Carter's rhetoric, in a sense, collaborated with Reagan's—making Carter the "anti-hero" and Reagan the hero.

Accenting these differences in stories were the actual modes of discourse employed by Carter and Reagan. Carter's rhetoric was conventional: argumentative, instrumental, and adapted to every segment of the citizenry. Reagan's rhetoric was that of the true storyteller: it was laced with narratives; it was not instrumental in the usual way for it invited participation in a story orally presented. It assumed an audience of poetic auditors rather than argumentative judges. In this sense the 1980 election was a contest between argument and narrative as individuated forms of address. The pragmatic ideas became overwhelmed by the romantic images. Epic (heroic) narrative marked by anecdotes overshadowed the homiletic and reasoned speech of Carter. Thus Reagan's style meshed with his story and added to its power to compel adherence.

REAGAN'S CHARACTER

Reagan's success also has to do with the coherence and fidelity of his character. As noted in chapter 2, character is an organized set of actional tendencies reflecting values. When one has determined that a person—ordinary or presidential—has a trustworthy and reliable character, that his or her heart is in the right place, one is willing to overlook or forgive many things: factual errors if not too dramatic, lapses in reasoning, and occasional actional discrepancies. These come to be seen as aberrations, probably induced by circumstances but not by incompetence. One can see this kind of judgment rendered in obvious forms where friends, loved ones, heroes, and saints are judged. In Reagan's case, commentators sum up this sort of popular response to him by saying that he has a "teflon personality." He seems somehow protected against the rational-world charges. In his case, as in other heroic cases, it takes an extraordinary series of words and deeds to undermine the perceived coherent qualities of trustworthiness and reliability. Reagan's critics, like those who would criticize any heroic figure, discover that *their* characters rather than his come under attack.

This view of character overlaps but is not exactly synonymous with the traditional concept of ethos or the contemporary notion of source credibility. Ethos, in Aristotle's theory of rhetoric, is a kind of proof that establishes a speaker's intelligence, integrity, and goodwill. Credibility, in recent communication research, is a function of an audience's attribution of such traits as expertise, trustworthiness, and dynamism to a source. Ethos-credibility has also been recognized as an aspect of one's reputation as a reliable, honest, and caring person. I have argued elsewhere that ethos-credibility also inheres in social-political roles, the presidency being an exemplar.[7] Character, as I have conceived of it in this book, is a generalized perception of a person's fundamental value orientation.[8] From this perception, one infers a person's probable decisions and actions, and determines the relationship of the person's orientation to one's own way of being in the world. This determination is key to whether or not one considers a person positively or negatively, as friend or foe. It is, in effect, a conclusion regarding the implied audience in a person's behavior. If one finds endorsement in a person's decisions and actions, one sees an extension of oneself in the community. When that person is a president, one becomes, moreover, a force in the state of the nation. Obviously Reagan enjoys a popular perception, and many citizens find comfort in identifying with him. He is perceived as a man of goodwill, and this perception overrides other features of traditional ideas of ethos-credibility, specifically, the "rational" components of intelligence and expertise.

I suggest that Reagan's seeming imperviousness to ordinary political attack is rooted also in the fact that it is easy to identify him with mythic qualities and forces that are often referred to collectively as "the American Dream." The American Dream is actually two myths shared in some degree by all Americans. There is the materialistic myth of individual success and the moralistic myth of brotherhood. It would be hard to find an American that has *no* allegiance to these two sets of ideals/aspirations. Each myth entails certain values. The materialistic myth espouses a work ethic and endorses such qualities as effort, persistence, "playing the game," initiative, self-reliance, achievement, and success. Competition is its presumed way of determining personal worth; hence the free-enterprise system, freedom from controls and regulations, and ascent in society's social-economic hierarchies are numbered among this myth's implied goods. The moralistic myth is, for example, well expressed in the Declaration of Independence: "all men are created equal" and "are endowed by their Creator with certain unalienable rights," among which are "life, liberty, and the pursuit of Happiness." Governments "are instituted to secure these rights," and governments derive "their just powers from the consent of the governed." One should observe also that the moralistic myth implies such goods as tolerance, charity, compassion, and true regard for the dignity and worth of each individual.

The materialistic myth fosters a concept of freedom *to do* as one pleases; the moralistic myth stresses freedom *to be* as one conceives oneself. Together these two myths or systems-of-ideas undergird culture in ways that seem uniquely American—as a good many historians, sociologists, and political scientists have pointed out. I have elsewhere discussed the rhetorical strengths and weaknesses that these two myths inject into public discourse, but my present concern is to explore Reagan's rhetoric in relation to these myths.[9] In the process it will be helpful to compare and contrast Reagan's rhetoric with that of Carter and Edward Kennedy, because Carter and Kennedy differ markedly from Reagan in character, and their stories contrast sharply with his.

It was documented at the end of the 1980 presidential campaign that voters perceived Reagan in "manly" terms and Carter in softer, more "feminine" terms.[10] Reagan's tough stands on America's military posture and his decisive views on domestic problems gave substance to the perception. But equally important, his manner was suggestive of manly values and virtues. He aroused a consciousness not of the stevedore, the athlete, or the truck driver, but of the quintessential hero of the West—the town marshal. Accenting this image were his origins, the West (California—the last frontier); his penchant for Western garb; his ranch; his pastime of riding horses; and several of his film and television roles. His physical appearance was reinforcing too: tall, lank, and rugged. Like the savior of the West, he exuded honesty and sincerity, innocence, optimism, and certainty. He announced in accepting his nomination that he would lead

149

the country in a "crusade to make America great again!"[11] The man and the mission were one. Here was tight coherence again. Like earlier presidential heroes, Reagan projected the image of one who loves "America more than selfish considerations."

Reagan rode the campaign trail reinforcing two intertwined myths: "hero of the West" and "the glory that was once America." The 1980 campaign would have been far different if Reagan's opponent had been Ted Kennedy rather than Carter. The election result may have been the same, Reagan winning, but the contest would have been fascinating to observe in that it would have pitted rival mythic figures and philosophies. The contrast between Kennedy and Reagan highlights the nature of romantic democracy in general and Reagan's rhetoric in particular.

Kennedy, the knight-errant of "New Freedom," "New Deal," and "New Frontier" politics, and heir-apparent to the Camelot dynasty, would have been a formidable foe for Reagan. In mythic terms, the campaign would have been a struggle, a combination of a "shoot-out" and "joust," between personifications of "liberalism" and "conservatism." It is likely that Kennedy would have been seen as a man on a black horse, because he would have had to spoil the Carter candidacy and because of the Chappaquidick chink in his armor; Reagan would have been viewed as the man on a white horse. That Kennedy and Reagan did not run against one another is perhaps fortunate in that the myths that Kennedy represents have been saved for a later contest, a time more propitious for their judicious consideration.

Whatever the rhetorical assets and liabilities of the "town marshal" and the "knight-errant" in American mythology, the principal source of Reagan's and Kennedy's persuasive appeals lies in their respective visions of the American Dream.

Reagan's solution to America's plight was to stress the materialistic myth of the American Dream. Salient features of this view of government are a belief in natural law, the Calvinist ethic, moral individualism, a "weak" state (the best government is one that governs least), and the efficacy of competition. Max Lerner summarized the view thus: "The idea and belief that the state must keep its hands off the economic life of the community and that only through this autonomy, sanctioned by positive and moral law, can economic activity flourish, society be healthy, and the individual reach his best effectiveness."[12] Reagan expressed these ideas and beliefs in this way: "The taxing power of Government must be used to provide revenues for legitimate Government purposes. It must not be used to regulate the economy or bring about social change. We've tried that and surely must be able to see it doesn't work."[13] The proper province of government, he seemed to say, is to allow economic forces to follow their natural and inevitable ends, and the people and the country will prosper.

The atavistic strain in Reagan's rhetoric and his vision of the American Dream are evident in the key verbs from his address accepting the nomination in 1980: *recapture, rebirth, renew, restore, reaffirm,* and *redeem.* It is not particularly surprising to find these words in an acceptance address, since such speeches belong to the genre of reaffirmation; but when they are tied to a conception of Americanism, it is clear that Reagan views America's destiny as a matter of returning to the conditions that defined America as it supposedly once was. America was a community of persons who shared consensus on the values of "family, work, neighborhood, peace and freedom."[14]

These are persuasive terms, even god-terms. They are also "code words." Deciphered, they read this way: "family" means the nuclear family—dad, mom, son, and daughter; "neighborhood" means no busing; "work" means no welfare but "work-fare"; "peace" means the United States must be the biggest, strongest country in the world in order that we preserve the peace and fulfill our manifest destiny to spread our way of life everywhere. "Freedom" means freedom from governmental interference in the "free-enterprise" system.

The values attendant on family, work, neighborhood, peace, and freedom are individualism, self-reliance, efficiency, practicality, and success. The enemy, the devil who denies these values and thwarts those who would live by them, is the government. As Reagan said in his Acceptance Address, the American system "will continue to serve us in the future if our government will stop ignoring the basic values on which it was built and stop betraying the American workers who keep it going."[15] Government, he declared in his 1980 Inaugural Address, "is not the solution to the problem, government is the problem."[16] The emphasis on the materialistic myth was made explicit in his State of the Economy speech (1981) in which he referred directly to the American Dream of owning a home and a car.[17]

It cannot be denied, of course, that Reagan's rhetoric has a strong moral appeal. There is no doubt of his belief in God.[18] It appears, however, that his religious beliefs are parochial, fundamentalist, and expansionist, if not evangelical. His congregation includes those who believe as he does in family, work, neighborhood, peace, and freedom—as he conceives them. His support by such groups as the Moral Majority gives credence to the fundamentalist interpretation of his moral pronouncements.

151

Lending substance to this interpretation is his political conservatism. Reagan's desire to extend his religious orientation is shown in his request in the Acceptance Address for a "moment of silent prayer,"[19] and in his Inaugural Address that "each Inaugural Day in future years . . . should be declared a day of prayer."[20] Whereas Reagan expresses compassion in his speech, he saves the sentiment for those who "fall," are "sick," or in need of help to become "self-sufficient." In short, Reagan's religious views combine piety with politics, making morality a means, not an end in itself; its significant expression is in "moral courage."[21]

Carter, of course, had considerable credentials as a religious man, but he was hindered, rather than helped, by their force in 1980. His stance differed from Reagan's in that it led to uncompromising stands on such issues as the human rights policy, the placement of nuclear weapons in Europe, and the development of the neutron bomb. It reflected a tragic view consistent with Carter's high regard for Reinhold Niebuhr. Carter presented himself as a moral man in an immoral world, an orientation that, for him, called for stoicism—suffering and ultimate sadness. Reagan's view, on the other hand, was optimistic—if we but will it, our righteousness will prevail.

Kennedy's America is very different from that of Reagan. First, although grounded on what America has been at its finest (any view must have historical context to be meaningful and persuasive), Kennedy's view is future-oriented. For Kennedy, the high points in our history are those moments when the "timeless truth" of the Democratic party has been the catalyst of thought and action. And those times have been when *new* visions were at work to improve the conditions of democracy: the New Freedom, the New Deal, and the New Frontier. His promise was new hope for the future, for the dignity of work, for the unemployed, for the environment, for a stable economy, and for "real tax reform."[22] In the conclusion of his 1980 Convention Address, he spoke not only of the present and the future, but also of the everlasting: "the work goes on, the cause endures, the hope still lives, and the dream shall never die."[23]

Kennedy's rhetoric differed from Reagan's further in its emphasis on the moralistic myth of the American Dream, on the values of cooperation and compassion for all Americans rather than on the materialistic values of individualism, competition, and self-reliance. Kennedy declared that the cause of the Democratic party "since the days of Thomas Jefferson" has been "the cause of the common man—and the common woman. Our commitment has been, since the days of Andrew Jackson, to all those he called the 'humble members of society—the farmer, mechanics, and laborers.' On this foundation, we have defined our values, refined our policies, and refreshed our faith."[24] He made it clear that, unlike Reagan, he was a friend of labor, New York and other "great urban centers across this nation," senior citizens, and the environment.

Whereas Reagan's rhetoric tends to be *re*actionary, implying an audience willing to revert in its thinking to get ahead or to recover things as they once were, Kennedy's discourse assumes an audience committed to the "revolutionary belief that all people are created equal," the "guiding star in the American firmament."[25] His dream for America was that of his martyred brothers:

> I am part of all that I have met . . .
> Tho much is taken, much abides . . .
> That which we are, we are . . .
> One equal temper of heroic hearts . . .
> To strive, to seek, to find and not to yield.[26]

The reference to "one equal temper of heroic hearts" is at least suggestive that Kennedy, too, many conceive of the American people and himself as heroic.

No contrast between Kennedy and Reagan so dramatically shows the difference between them as their views of government. As I have already indicated, Reagan argued that government is the source of America's problems. Kennedy took the position that "The demand of our people in 1980 is not for smaller government or bigger government, but for better government." Ted Kennedy's concept of government was that of his brother John, to make government do for others what they cannot do for themselves. From this view, all Americans at some time or another need governmental assistance, except for the rich and powerful. The Kennedys believed in a strong government. Reagan believes in a "weak" one, a limited one devoted primarily to providing incentives to feed individual initiative—whether of corporations or of particular persons. If he had been elected president, it is likely that Kennedy would have led the country as his brother did—as a champion of the "common man and woman."

Kennedy would have faced several problems in being elected, had he been nominated. Among them were difficulties with the Democratic party as an organization and remembrance of the Chappaquidick incident. Beyond these and Reagan's candidacy would be the problem of making popular a "champion of the people." This image seems not to have the persuasive power it once had. Poll after poll has shown that the great majority of voters identify themselves as "middle" or "upper-middle"

153

class. There are relatively few "forgotten men" and "common people" compared with the numbers who so identified themselves in the days of the New Deal. By and large, farmers, laborers, and mechanics are middle-class citizens. They may be economically depressed in some places, but they are not poorly fed, poorly housed, or poorly clad. There are poor people, of course, but they were not forgotten in 1980 or now. With women, militant minorities, and senior citizens, the poor were highly visible through the mass media and political disputes such as those about ERA, fair housing, and social security. Agitation over these questions even caused widespread fear of losing what one had, and resentment for what one had to contribute to the welfare of others. It is not clear where Kennedy would have found an active constituency that would rally to his moralistic stance and image. Reagan's essentially materialistic appeal urged voters to be *un*common and it had better prospects, in theory and in the event.

When the rival stories and characters of Carter and Kennedy are compared, it becomes even more clear why Reagan's story and character had such wide appeal. One must also note that Reagan's story and character have gained increased credibility during his second term. Many apparently feel that the country has seen "better times" during his tenure. In any case, the coherence and fidelity of stories and character depend on their confirmation by experience. Wish, desire, hope, and fantasy will not sustain them forever.

REAGAN'S IMPLIED AUDIENCE

Historical groundedness, timing, style, winning stories, and character all bear on the believability of public narratives. Equally important is the implied audience in a story. As noted in chapter 3: "Any story, any form of rhetorical communication, not only says something about the world, it also implies an audience, persons who conceive of themselves in very specific ways." I have also argued that *"The key to the ethos (character) of Presidents is their conception of the relationship to the people, for in this conception lies their image of themselves and the role of the Presidency."*[27]

Given statements from the first Inaugural Address, it is evident that Reagan conceived of "the people" in heroic terms. He said: "We are too great a nation to limit ourselves to small dreams"; "we have every right to dream heroic dreams"; "those who say that we're in a time when there are no heroes, they just don't know where to look. You can see heroes every

154

day"; and "I am addressing the heroes of whom I speak." Reminiscent of Carter's campaign rhetoric, he also said: "Your dreams, your hopes, your goals are going to be the dreams, the hopes and the goals of this administration, so help me God."[28] Different from Carter, Reagan's stress was on heroism rather than goodness. If the American people are heroes, it follows that Reagan as President and spokesperson is hero of heroes.

Whereas the image of "goodness" appeals to conscience, to one's sense of ethical being, the image of hero appeals to ego, to one's conviction that one can face hazards or hardships and prevail. The "ethical person" is; the "hero" does. Conscience is not always a source of joy or pride. At worst, ethical principles brought to consciousness make one feel guilty; at best, ethics creates self-examination and perhaps self-doubt. The "hero," on the other hand, is led to feel good about himself or herself no matter the adversity. In a time of distress and uncertainty, the hero image is as rhetorically efficacious as an image one might conceive, except a religious one that asserts that one's true being is not really of this world but of a "beyond." In a profane world, the hero is God.

Reagan's identification of and with heroes was reinforced in the conclusion of his first Inaugural Address in which he paid homage to the heroic presidents whose monuments he could see from the West Front of the Capitol: George Washington, Thomas Jefferson, Abraham Lincoln. He also offered tribute to those who gave their lives in war and who are buried in Arlington National Cemetery. His final celebration was of Martin Treptow, an unsung hero of World War I.[29]

The most dramatic demonstration of Reagan's heroic orientation was his behavior during and following the attempt on his life. As Thomas S. Szasz observed, "Mr. Reagan seemed to possess all the virtues of the Western hero he portrayed so often and so well on the screen."[30] His walking into the hospital with a bullet in his chest, his self-deprecations, and his humor bespoke fearlessness, courage, and what Ernest Hemingway would have called "grace." Here he did not play the hero; for that moment, at least, he was the hero.

CONCLUSION

The challenge of this chapter has been to resolve a paradox: How is it that Reagan succeeds when it is widely agreed that he fails the tests of the rational-world paradigm and the tests of narrative fidelity? The paradox is resolved if one accepts the analysis I have made of Reagan's rhetoric, for it shows that the paradox arises only if one insists that strict rational criteria are the only ones that are appropriate in the interpretation and assessment of discourse. The analysis demonstrates that for a full account of human communication one must consider the principle of coherence as well as that of fidelity. Reagan's appeal, as we have seen, derives not only from his superior performance, but also, and most important here, from the consistency of his story with the story of America, from the coherence of his character, and the compatibility of his image with that of his constituency. These are matters left unattended by the rational-world paradigm. I want to stress, however, that I do not mean to disparage the tests of the rational-world paradigm, for they are an integral part of narrative rationality. Indeed, their application to Reagan's rhetoric casts considerable doubt about Reagan's story, if not his character.

This analysis also suggests that Reagan's rhetoric, or any other political rhetoric, will remain viable as long as historical circumstances permit, as long as there is not an equally compelling story and character to confront it and to show its ultimate lack of coherence and fidelity. A persuasive story and character cannot be merely subversive, however; they must be true to the past, celebrate cultural values, provide a heightened perception of the people, and be presented with consummate skill.

NOTES

1. See Mary M. Gergen and Kenneth J. Gergen, "The Social Construction of Narrative Accounts," in K. J. Gergen and M. M. Gergen, eds., *Historical Social Psychology* (Hillsdale, N.J.: Lawrence Erlbaum Associates, 1984), pp. 173–89.

2. Kenneth Burke, *Permanence and Change* (Indianapolis, Ind.: Bobbs-Merrill, 1965), pp. 29ff.

3. Walter R. Fisher, "A Motive View of Communication," *Quarterly Journal of Speech* 56 (1970): 131-39.

4. Vernon L. Parrington, *The Romantic Revolution in America, 1800–1860,* vol. 2 of *Main Currents in American Thought* (New York: Harcourt, Brace & Co., 1927), p. vi.

5. Robert N. Bellah, Richard Madsen, William M. Sullivan, Ann Swidler, and Stephen M. Tipton, *Habits of the Heart: Individualism and Commitment in American Life* (Berkeley: University of California Press, 1985), p. viii.

6. Bellah, et al., "Mythic Individualism," pp. 144–47.

7. See Walter R. Fisher, "Rhetorical Fiction and the Presidency," *Quarterly Journal of Speech* 66 (1980): 119, 126.

8. For a related view, see James David Barber, *The Presidential Character: Predicting Performance in the White House* (Englewood Cliffs, N.J.: Prentice-Hall, 1972), pp. 8ff.

9. Walter R. Fisher, "Reaffirmation and Subversion of the American Dream," *Quarterly Journal of Speech* 59 (1973): 161–63.

156

10. See, e.g., *Time* 27, 1980, p. 25; and *New York Times,* Oct. 17, 1981, p. A22.

11. References to Reagan's "Acceptance Address" are found in the *Congressional Quarterly,* July 19, 1980, pp. 34–37.

12. Max Lerner, "The Triumph of Laissez-Faire," in Arthur M. Schlesinger, Jr., and Morton White, eds., *Paths of American Thought* (Boston: Houghton Mifflin, 1963), pp. 151–52.

13. Reagan, "Economic Address to Congress," *New York Times,* Feb. 19, 1981, p. 14.

14. Reagan, "Acceptance Address," p. 34.

15. Ibid., p. 36.

16. References to Reagan's first "Inaugural Address" are found in the *Los Angeles Times,* Jan. 21, 1981, pp. 16–17. The citation is from p. 16. See also the "State of the Economy Speech," *New York Times* Feb. 6, 1981, p. 8.

17. Reagan, "State of the Economy Speech," p. 8.

18. See, e.g., Reagan, "Acceptance Address," p. 37, and "Inaugural Address," p. 17.

19. Reagan, "Acceptance Address," p. 37.

20. Reagan, "Inaugural Address," p. 17.

21. Ibid., p. 16. For useful studies of discourse combining piety and politics, see Roderick P. Hart, *The Political Pulpit* (West Lafayette, Ind.: Purdue University Press, 1977); Sacvan Bercovitch, *The American Jeremiad* (Madison: University of Wisconsin Press, 1978). See also Max Weber, *The Protestant Ethic and the Spirit of Capitalism,* trans. Talcott Parsons (London: George Allen & Unwin, 1930).

22. References to Edward Kennedy's "Convention Address" are found in the *Congressional Quarterly,* Aug. 16, 1980, pp. 34–36.

23. Ibid., p. 36.

24. Ibid., p. 34.

25. Ibid., p. 35.

26. Ibid., p. 36. The lines are from Tennyson's "Ulysses."

27. Fisher, "Rhetorical Fiction," pp. 123–24.

28. Reagan, "Inaugural Address," p. 16.

29. Ibid., p. 17.

30. Thomas S. Szasz, *Washington Post,* May 6, 1981, p. A19.

8

ARGUMENT IN DRAMA
AND LITERATURE

> For although argument is a calculation and not a story, the plot or
> "myth" of a tragedy is its "argument."
>
> *Richard McKeon*

As has been said several times in this book, argument has been conceived traditionally in terms of clear-cut inferential structures. So viewed,
its essential constituents are *claims, reasons,* and *evidence* whether con-
ceptualized as logical product, rhetorical process, or dialectical procedure.[1] Thus, unless one deduces a conclusion from recognizable
premises or infers a claim from particulars, one presumably does not
argue.

Common experience tells us, however, that we do arrive at conclusions
based on "dwelling in" dramatic and literary works.[2] We come to new
beliefs, reaffirmations of old ones, reorient our values, and may even be led
to action. We know that fictive forms of communication can have rhetorical intentions and consequences. The consequences are results of inferential processes; some dramatic and literary works do, in fact, argue if that
term is given its conventional broad meaning: to show, prove, or imply.

To explore the modes of proof that operate in fictive discourse is the
objective of this chapter. For that purpose we shall consider the matter
generally and then explore the proofs of a famous American play and an
equally famous American novel. Were one to make a comparable analysis
of filmic communication, one's inquiry would generally parallel what we
offer in the case studies of a drama and a novel. At the level of general
theory, exploring the "arguments" of fiction lends special support to two
major claims made in this book: (1) argument operates on principles of
the logic of good reasons as outlined in chapter 5, and (2) people are as
much valuing as reasoning animals. The case studies will also demonstrate, we believe, that "aesthetic proof" can be more effectively and
systematically assessed using the specifications of the narrative paradigm
than is possible when one uses the rational-world paradigm.

RHETORIC, POETIC, AND AESTHETIC PROOF

"Rhetoric" and "poetic" are ambiguous terms. They concern theories, kinds of discourse, arts, intents, styles, and symbolic functions. This is not the place to review historical arguments designed to unravel their relationships. It is sufficient for present purposes to notice those uses of the terms that posit overlap: the appearance of the rhetorical in the poetic and of the poetic in the rhetorical. One traditional view is that poetic forms become rhetorical when they are didactic or convey a moral. Works as diverse as Aesop's fables, Hawthorne's *The Scarlet Letter,* and Frost's "Stopping by Woods on a Snowy Evening" can be seen as rhetorical on this principle. What distinguish such works in substance and form are generally their singularity of purpose and the explicitness of the claims they advance. These features, as qualities of argument, clearly point out the rhetorical nature of such didactic literature. The attentive audience is given little choice in understanding the aim of the work. Such works are explicitly assertive, but one can also show that works without such singularity and explicitness function rhetorically. The crucial difference is that with works of the latter type the auditor or reader must discover the works' claim through *the work.* How this discovery occurs and how it is verified are questions to be addressed later in this chapter.

Another familiar view follows Aristotle. Rhetoric and poetic, it is said, share stylistic features but differ fundamentally in form, function, or relationship to reality.[3] Aristotle clearly distinguishes the nature and functions of the rhetorical and poetic arts, but we should notice that he advises the student of rhetoric to go to the *Poetics* for "the poetical" matters of style, especially metaphor. And in regard to Thought—one of Aristotle's six essential elements of drama along with Plot, Characters, Diction, Melody, and Spectacle—he says, "We may assume what we said of it in our *Art of Rhetoric,* as it belongs more properly to that department of inquiry."[4] Perelman and Olbrechts-Tyteca develop this line of reasoning in their *New Rhetoric.* The principal connection between rhetoric and poetic is in their concept of "presence": the process by which a speaker makes "present, by verbal magic alone, what is actually absent but what he considers important to his argument, or, by making them more present, to enhance the value of some of the elements of which one has actually been made conscious."[5] Among the discursive, stylistic techniques used to achieve presence are: *hypotaxis* (or *demonstration*), *anaphora, conduplication, adjectio, amplification, sermocinatio, dialogism, onomatopoeia, personification, apostrophe,* and *prosopoeia.* "The effect of figures relating to presence," Perelman and Olbrechts-Tyteca wrote, "is to make the object of discourse present to the mind."[6]

Perhaps the most eloquent expression of the view that rhetoric and poetic overlap is that of Fénelon. W. S. Howell describes Fénelon's *Dialogues on Eloquence* as "indisputably the best statement we have of his rhetorical theory, and the earliest statement that we have of what may be said to have become the dominant modern attitude towards rhetoric."[7] Fénelon wrote: "Poetry differs from simple eloquence only in this: that she paints with ecstasy and with bolder strokes." Portraiture is a means common to both poet and rhetor, the duty of which is "carrying objects over into the imagination of men."[8] Poetry "is as it were the soul of eloquence." And poetry is "the lively portraiture of things."[9]

For eloquent modern statements of the view that "rhetoric and poetic are and must be closely and complementarily related," one should consult Donald Bryant's "Uses of Rhetoric in Criticism"[10] and "Rhetoric: Its Functions and Its Scope, *Redivivia*."[11]

Two perspectives provide innovations in the tradition just outlined here. They are the perspectives of Booth and Burke. Booth's position is clear from the first: "In writing about the rhetoric of fiction, I am not primarily interested in didactic fiction, fiction used for propaganda or instruction. My subject is the technique of non-didactic fiction, viewed as the art of communicating with readers—the rhetorical resources available to the writer of epic, novel, or short story as he tries, consciously or unconsciously, to impose his fictional world upon the reader."[12] Later he maintains "that the rhetorical dimension in literature is inescapable, evidence can be found in any successful scene, however pure, regardless of whether the author was thinking of his reader as he wrote."[13] Booth demonstrates the validity of this position with a masterful display of the ways authors control their readers. He concentrates especially on the rhetorical techniques of "telling" and "showing," manipulating styles of narration, and designing the characters of narrators.

No brief summary of Kenneth Burke's views on rhetoric and poetic could do justice to the subtlety of his thought. All that can be done is to provide a fair sense of his direction. His position is the most radical of those so far considered. He sees no philosophically defensible argument that can support an absolute distinction between rhetoric and poetic. Rhetoric is a symbolic function, the function of inducement.[14] Rhetoric arises whenever we attribute meanings to symbols, and where there is meaning, there is persuasion.[15] Rhetoric may be seen to operate in the experience of fictive forms of communication, not only in their inducement to feel or to believe or to act in given ways, but also in the appeal of the individuated forms that compose the work. "Form in literature," Burke wrote in *Counter-Statement,* "is an arousing and fulfillment of desires. A work has form in so far as one part of it leads a reader to anticipate another part, to be gratified by the sequence."[16]

If a distinction is to be made between rhetoric and poetic, it is to be caught in these ideas: "Where a rhetorician might conceivably argue the cause of Love rather than Duty, or the other way around, in Poetics a profound dramatizing of the conflict itself would be enough; for in this field the imitation of great practical or moral problems is itself a source of gratification."[17] Poetics is "the realm of symbolic action 'naturally' exercised for its own sake."[18] In other words, poetics concerns the aesthetic, consummatory function of symbols. In works such as *The Grapes of Wrath* and the "Gettysburg Address," both rhetorical and poetic functions occur. Such communications can be experienced as inducement *and* as pleasure in themselves.

What will be argued here is that a *rhetorical* interpretation of a work arises *whenever* the work is considered relative to an audience's response. Responses are the ways in which people are led to feel or to think or to act in reference to a symbolic experience. So to claim does not deny the notion that poetic discourse is rhetorical when it advances a lesson or a moral. Nor does it conflict with the claims that fictive and nonfictive genres share specific language forms, or that one can find rhetorical features in poetic discourse and poetic features in rhetorical discourse. The proposal offered in this chapter is that we focus not on authorial techniques or specific individuated forms but on audience response, the mental moves that will be made by auditors or readers in interpreting a work.

Let us consider how dramatic and literary works argue. The mode of their arguing is the process of suggestion. Through the revelations of characters and situations that represent different value orientations in conflict with each other and/or with the environment, the reader or auditor is induced to a felt-belief, a sense of the message that the work is advancing. This felt-belief of message is at first aesthetic.

An aesthetic belief is one based on an immediate, emotional, intuitive response to a representation of an enclosed fictive world. It is a response not based on deliberate thought or reasoned analysis. In *Death of a Salesman* and *The Great Gatsby* we know that the values of Willy Loman and Jay Gatsby are judged negatively. We know this less by reasoning about those values and the author's intentions than by our identifying

161

with the characters and experiencing their fates as our own. Fictive works that fail to evoke this kind of aesthetic response fail as aesthetic works. It does not follow, however, that they must fail as rhetorical works. *Uncle Tom's Cabin* is hardly an example of the art of novel writing, but it was an enormously powerful and artistically wrought piece of political and social rhetoric—partly because of telling arguments in the mouths of characters and the situations in which they were placed.

The felt-belief sense of a message can, as is obviously the case with *Uncle Tom's Cabin,* give rise to a reasoned belief and conviction—a clear and forceful rhetorical phenomenon. This happens, for example, when a reader or an auditor looks back to the elements of the work that led him or her to a given interpretation. The actions, the characters' words, and their results, which first provided an aesthetic sense of the work's message, now become the bases for a reasoned justification of a critical interpretation. The elements may be viewed now as "proof" invented by the author, experienced by the auditor or reader, and now used by the respondent to substantiate his or her judgment of the work's message. But these "proofs" had their origins in aesthetic response, so they may be called "aesthetic proofs" to distinguish them from experiences of direct assertions or formal argumentative structures.

Aesthetic proofs function outside the realm of regular argumentation in that they are neither general principles that become the bases for deductions nor real examples that are used as bases for induction. Aesthetic proofs are representations of reality that fall somewhere between analogies and examples. What is represented is not exactly our own world but something that bears a more essential relationship to it than analogy. By identifying ourselves and our worlds with the fictive world-representations, we experience the truthfulness of the work's message, the way the message impinges on our understanding of ourselves or some part of the world.

Aesthetic proof is constituted in verbal and nonverbal ways: by words and actions consistent or inconsistent with other words and actions (matters of the work's dramatic-literary probability); by considerations of whose words and actions dominate and survive or transcend the conflicts between or among characters and circumstances; and by consistency and validity when tested against one's own perceptions of "real" people and "real" events. Because dramatic and literary works move by suggestion rather than "logical" direction, different auditors or readers may arrive at different interpretations. Still, the range of possibilities is not infinite. Willy Loman cannot seem both a clear-sighted sage and a deluded fool.

And "legitimate" interpretations must be based on aesthetic experiences that are at least recognizable to others. They must permit an account of the work in a way that leaves the work recognizable to others. In other words, an acceptable interpretation must allow a reasoned account of how aesthetic proofs are organized to create meaning.

How these theoretical and critical possibilities serve interpretive purposes is illustrated in the remainder of this chapter.

ARGUMENT IN *DEATH OF A SALESMAN*

After Willy Loman is fired from his lifelong job, he visits his successful neighbor, Charley, to tell him the news and ask for a "loan" to pay his insurance premium. Charley, who has been the object of Willy's scorn for years, gives Willy his opinion of the business world and Willy counters with his own.

> CHARLEY: The only thing you got in this world is what you can sell. And the funny thing is that you're a salesman, and you don't know that.
> WILLY: I've always tried to think otherwise, I guess. I always felt that if a man was impressive, and well-liked, that nothing—
> CHARLEY: Why must everybody like you? Who liked J. P. Morgan? Was he impressive? In a Turkish bath he'd look like a butcher. But with his pockets on he was very well liked. . . .[19]

In the climactic scene at the end of the play, where Biff confronts his father and brother with the truth of their existence, the following revelation occurs:

> BIFF: We never told the truth for ten minutes in this house!
> BIFF: And I never got anywhere because you blew me so full of hot air I could never stand taking orders from anybody.
> BIFF: Pop! I'm a dime a dozen, and so are you!
> WILLY: I am not a dime a dozen! I am Willy Loman, and you are Biff Loman.
> BIFF: I am not a leader of men, Willy, and neither are you. You never were anything but a hard working drummer who landed in the ash can like all the rest of them! I'm one dollar an hour, Willy! I tried seven states and couldn't raise it. . . .
> WILLY: You vengeful, spiteful mutt!
> BIFF: Pop, I'm nothing! I'm nothing, Pop! Can't you understand that? There's no spite in it any more. I'm just what I am, that's all.
> WILLY: What're you doing? What're you doing? Why is he crying?

BIFF: Will you let me go, for Christ's sake? Will you take that phony dream and burn it before something happens? [p. 1052]

These two passages seem to embody two of the play's most important conclusions. In the first, Willy expresses his credo that appearance and reputation are the essential requirements for personal and material success. Charley, consistently a voice of harsh and even mocking realism, declares this belief to be false; and indeed, Willy's whole life, as revealed by the play, supports this inference. Willy's adherence to his illusion leads to embittered destitution. It is from this position that he must confront the more profound realization expressed in the second passage. Not only has he been wrong in his assumption about what being successful requires, he has deceived himself even about his reputation and character. Moreover, he has taught his sons, to their immense cost, the same tricks of self-deception. As a result, Willy does not—nor can he ever—understand what has happened to him and his sons. Thus Willy is portrayed as incapable of seeing that his misperception of the business world is a corollary of his inability (and final refusal) to confront himself realistically.

The two illusions that have guided Willy's life suggest a further conclusion. The price of self-deception is not merely inability to win in the business world, it is failure to realize that material success will not bring personal and family happiness. Willy's vision of the American Dream is material well-being; it is founded on "respectable" work, business, or the professions, but the manual labor he scorns (i.e., being a carpenter) seems to be his most genuine source of satisfaction. His self-deception has led him to desire and expect every material sign of status and success when self-knowledge might have led to happiness and a sense of well-being with more modest but real accomplishments. This side of Willy, and the general conclusion that underlies it, is expressed by Biff, who has been able to face his true self. He says, "He had the wrong dream. All, all wrong." (p. 1054)

These conclusions and interpolations are based on what is suggested. They cannot be shown to be absolutely or exclusively the meanings of the play. We can, however, identify the elements of the work on which we have relied and the processes of inference that led us to our interpretations. In doing so, we point to the modes of proof we identified in the preceding section of this chapter, and we illustrate the kinds of thinking that characterize inferences suggested in and inferences drawn from experience of fictive forms.

When we recount the ways in which a play argues for us, we shall be struck by the realization that many of our inferences about a play arise from actors' performance of it, not from the playwright's text. Tone, gesture, carriage, and other aspects of stagecraft can communicate persuasively in ways that words alone cannot. Performers create much of the meaning of a play, and the immediacy of identification with the performers makes performer-derived meanings especially important to playgoers. To be sure, the playwright included stage directions to guide the actors and director: but in actual performance actors and director may seek to interpret the play as the author seems to have intended, or they may try to alter meanings through performance. Meaning in drama is thus the product of collaboration between author and performers; and if auditors are to account for the result, they must explain the collaborative maneuvers. This is why a critique of any play without reference to a specific performance is never entirely satisfactory, for then the commentator must rely on the stage directions and use imagination to do the rest. In any case, the performance aspects of any drama are crucial parts of the play's mode of argument.

For instance, our first impression (felt-beliefs) about the Lomans is based largely on their physical appearance. We must be able to see at Willy's first entrance that he is a beaten man. The directions describe his exhaustion, the "soreness of his palms," and his sigh. The ensuing despondent conversation with Linda confirms his sense of defeat about his own life and Biff's. These images provide the background for our conclusion that he has an abiding faith in appearances and reputation.

Almost immediately afterward we see Willy transported back to more hopeful times. Willy instructs his sons on polishing the car and explains his belief:

And they know me, boys, they know me up and down New England. The finest people. And when I bring you fellas up, there'll be open season for all of us, 'cause one thing boys: I have friends. . . .
    That's why I thank Almighty God you're both built like Adonises. Because the man who makes an appearance in the business world, the man who creates personal interest, is the man who gets ahead. Be liked and you will never want. . . . [p. 1026].

Auditors are likely to contrast this brave statement with what they have just seen, and they will arrive at a different conclusion. Even in this scene, however, there are intimations of the falseness of Willy's belief in the efficacy of a good appearance. Bernard comes to warn Biff that he cannot succeed on appearance alone, "Just because he printed University of Virginia on his sneakers doesn't mean they've got to graduate him, Uncle

165

Willy!" (p. 1026). Again, in actual presentation the visual contrast will be additionally important. Biff's appearance and self-confidence overwhelm Bernard, who is small, worried, and unathletic, but when the play reveals Biff as a confused failure and Bernard as a confident young lawyer, the play gives further evidence of the falseness of Willy's belief.

Other incidents in the play confirm this conclusion in similar ways and reinforce the coherence of the characters. Willy assures Biff that Bill Oliver will lend him money if he has the correct appearance and manner because "personality always wins the day" (p. 1035). But auditors soon learn that Biff had no real chance of getting a loan. Remembering Biff's high school days, again Willy assures himself of Biff's promise with the words "A star like that, magnificent, can never really fade away" (p. 1036). When Charley finally tells Willy the truth about appearance and personality, there can be little doubt that the play has been designed to support the charge of delusion. The Lomans are physically attractive, yet the plot of the play brings them to failure. The dramatic action "argues" in this way that faith in the appearance is delusion. But we must see that Willy's actions and delusions are—or can be—true to life. Dependence on charm and self-confidence *does* exist, and this fact gives the play its realism and generalizability.

Others of Willy's illusions reveal why he cannot understand his life. On his return home at the play's beginning he says:

> If old man Wagner was alive I'd a been in charge of New York by now! That man was a prince, he was a masterful man. But that boy of his, that Howard, he don't appreciate. When I went north the first time, the Wagner Company didn't know where New England was! [p. 1021].

Early in the second act he says of Howard, "I'll put it to him straight and simple. He'll just have to take me off the road" (p. 1036). But when the actual interview comes, Willy's real position is revealed as he is shown pleading pathetically for any job at all. When he is fired he is shocked, but the auditor has been prepared for the conclusion that this shock is mostly the product of Willy's exaggerated sense of his own value. Indeed, all of Willy's talk about his success as a salesman is undercut early in the play when he is made to report to Linda his sales for one trip. He begins by reporting 1,200 gross and retreats gradually to 200, and then makes excuses for his performance, ending with:

166

Oh, I'll knock 'em dead next week. I'll go to Hartford. I'm very well-liked in Hartford. [Pause] You know, the trouble is, Linda, people don't seem to take to me [p. 1027].

Collectively these scenes have subtle but important rhetorical functions. If an audience sees Willy as simply foolish or deceitful, the author's apparent point cannot be made. The play needs to be performed in ways that make it clear that Willy is genuinely confused, and that this confusion is the result of his long habit of self-deception. Here the importance of presentation (Perelman's *presence*) to inference drawing cannot be mistaken. Willy played as buffoon or mere braggart could not undergird the play's conclusion; Willy played as a potentially likable man lost in his delusions, can.

In a parallel way, Willy is shown as failing to understand Biff's problems because he has refused to admit they exist. He says of Biff's aimless life: "Certain men just don't get started till later in life. Like Thomas Edison, I think. Or B. F. Goodrich. One of them was deaf. I'll put my money on Biff." Yet only moments earlier he has said "Biff is a lazy bum" (p. 1022). He really believes neither statement, but they are what, momentarily, he acts upon. Thus he avoids real understanding.

Willy consistently refuses to acknowledge the part he played in shaping Biff's character. He says of Biff at one point:

He's got spirit, personality. . . . Loaded with it. Loaded! What is he stealing? He's giving it back, isn't he? Why is he stealing? What did I tell him? I never in my life told him anything but decent things [p. 1028].

Yet the audience has already seen Willy laugh at Biff's theft of a football, and later seen him encouraging the boys to steal from a building site. Willy tells Bernard that he is mystified by Biff's loss of initiative after high school. Willy is eager to deny any responsibility, but we later learn that Biff found Willy in Boston with another woman and was crushed by the discovery. The playwright gives us instance after instance of Willy's blind evasions of reality and responsibility. They are not as much examples leading to generalizations as they are cohering instances that interplay with other clusters of incidents to build up a story and a picture of a self-deluding man.

Biff and Happy themselves are clearly portrayed as products of Willy's mentality. This is nowhere clearer than in the scene where they plan Biff's new business venture. Biff is reluctant to believe in the plan, but his father and brother encourage him until all three are caught up in the idea. Here the stage directions are basic to interpreting the meaning. Both Biff and Happy are "lost," but in different ways. Biff, who has escaped much of his father's self-deception, has a "worn air and seems less self-assured"; it is Happy who clings to the self-deception and who is "thus more confused . . . although seemingly more content" (1022–23). If actors realize this description, the scene will make an additional statement about the connection between self-deception and personal confusion.

Willy's tragic death shows the ultimate loss of self that lack of self-knowledge can bring. Happy is a less extreme but equally clear example. Happy's compulsive womanizing and his pursuit of the symbols of success have no real meaning for him, and he does not understand why he pursues them. As he tells Biff near the play's beginning:

> I get that any time I want, Biff. Whenever I feel disgusted. The only trouble is, it gets like bowling or something, I just keep knockin' them over and it doesn't mean anything. . . . I don't know what gets into me, maybe I just have an overdeveloped sense of competition or something, but I went and ruined her, and furthermore I can't get rid of her. . . . I hate myself for it. Because I don't want the girl, and, still, I take it and—I love it [p. 1024].

Surely the playwright is arguing for self-discipline and self-knowledge as virtues. Even after Willy's death, Happy clings to his illusions, endorsing Willy's dream to be "number-one man" and vowing to "win it for him" (p. 1054). Audiences cannot project happiness for him.

Only Biff, who has had the painful realization that he is "a dime a dozen," can face his future with some peace. He will not be important or rich, but he can have "the things I love in this world. The work and the food and the time to sit and smoke." For Willy and Happy those things can never be enough. They must pursue ideals they can never achieve because they cannot see themselves as they are. The suggestion of this conclusion is built into the words and actions of the Lomans and further reinforced by the author's directions for performance.

The play "argues" for a thesis: mistaken, unrealistic values yield unhappiness. The methods of "arguing" are not those traditionally associated with the term "argumentation." The play argues narratively, piling up incidents and bits of discourse that coherently, through narrative time, suggest the thesis over and over in different terms and in relation to different characters. This disciplined coherence does not leave an audience free to read, see, and hear just any thesis or to interpret the author's thesis in just any way. With varying strategies but with affirmation of a theme, the playwright has built a story with an unmistakable moral; but the moral is never directly asserted *on the author's own authority.* The moral is suggested through stories of several lives, different yet morally alike.

Without being explicitly didactic or moralistic, *Salesman* argues for a conclusion that has relevance beyond its own characters and their actions. It meets the tests of narrative fidelity. It suggests that the set of illusions with which Willy Loman destroys himself are built deeply into many versions of the American Dream and that the dreamers are more often like Willy than like Ben. It is hardly possible that members of an audience will not have known someone with illusions comparable to Willy's. The fictional world of the play represents aspects of reality, and this gives the story "realism" or fidelity to the worlds and lives of the playgoers. According to *Death of a Salesman,* even those who succeed in acquiring the outward signs of success are rarely as sure of their destinies as Willy's idealized Ben. They are all too often like Happy's boss, who "builds an estate and hasn't the peace of mind to live in it" (p. 1024). Such self-deluded but "successful" people are only incidental in *Salesman,* but they form the main subject of *The Great Gatsby.*

ARGUMENT IN *THE GREAT GATSBY*

Near the end of *Gatsby,* the narrator, Nick Carraway, meets Tom Buchanan, the man who was in many ways Gatsby's opposite and who was to a large extent responsible for Gatsby's death. Carraway, in recording the meeting, observes:

> I couldn't forgive him or like him, but I saw that what he had done was, to him, entirely justified. It was all very careless and confused. They were careless people, Tom and Daisy—they smashed up things and creatures and then retreated back into their money or their vast carelessness, or whatever it was that kept them together, and let other people clean up the mess they had made. . . .
> I shook hands with him; it seemed silly not to, for I suddenly felt as though I were talking to a child. Then he went into the jewelry store to buy a pearl necklace—or perhaps only a pair of cuff buttons—rid of my provincial squeamishness forever.[20]

At the novel's conclusion, only a few hundred words later, Carraway reflects on Gatsby,

> I thought of Gatsby's wonder when he first picked out the green light
> at the end of Daisy's dock. He had come a long way to this blue lawn,
> and his dream must have seemed so close that he could hardly fail to
> grasp it. He did not know that it was already behind him, somewhere
> back in that vast obscurity beyond the city, where the dark fields of the
> republic rolled on under the night.
>
> Gatsby believed in the green light, the orgiastic future that year by
> year recedes before us. It eludes us then, but that's no matter—
> tomorrow we will run faster, stretch out our arms farther. . . . And
> one fine morning—
>
> So we beat on, boats against the current, borne back ceaselessly
> into the past [p. 182].

These observations summarize a conclusion, or a set of related inferences,
suggested by the novel as a whole.

The first quotation suggests the vast privilege of the rich, a privilege that
is portrayed as unhealthy in its disregard for the dignity and worth of
others. This conclusion leads in an important way to the second quotation. Here the narrator points to the futility of clinging to a static dream
and how, in such cases, the dream bewitches and perhaps destroys the
dreamer. What links these two ideas is Gatsby as the book's central
character. His idealized, romantic dream, the undivided love of a pure
Daisy, is confused with the acquisition of the privileges of the world of
wealth in which she lives. His huge house and wealthy guests demonstrate
to him that he has overcome the important obstacles to Daisy's love. The
novel's revelation of the falseness of this belief leads us to the third and
main conclusion: even the privileges of wealth cannot transform the ideal
into the real. Gatsby's acquisition of every symbol of material success
cannot make him a member of Daisy's world, the secure and settled world
of the *old* rich. Nor can it turn back the clock and bring him Daisy, his
dream's palpable symbol, as she was before her marriage. The American
Dream, as Gatsby has (and presumably others have) dreamed it, is hollow
and deceptive. The false dream implies that if one achieves the rewards of
material success—wealth, power, and status—this will also provide the
rest of what one wants, including happiness and spiritual well-being.
Gatsby is destroyed by his relentless pursuit of this false dream, and he is
caught by the self-centered compassionless indifference of those he would
emulate.

This is the general story and implicit argument of *The Great Gatsby*.
Details of the novel cohere to stress these major argumentative themes.
The "argument" is, of course, largely suggested rather than asserted. To

170

trace it out, as my theory of the narrative paradigm directs, we must isolate the details that contribute to the major theme, discover how well they cohere, using the several tests of coherence. Once we have completed that survey, we can ask ourselves whether or not the overall argument and its elements satisfy the tests of fidelity, whether or not they are faithful to readers' realities.

Respecting fictive literature generally, the first inference a reader must make is one regarding the narrator's reliability. In *Gatsby,* if we accept Nick's judgments, we will be convinced that the author intends us to view him as a competent observer, a fair judge, and a reasonable representative of our own perception of characters and events in the story. Apparently to direct the reader's attitude toward Nick, the novel opens with a discussion of his carefulness and reserve in making judgments. This trait has "opened up many curious natures" to him and it promises the audience an unusually able observer of human affairs. He is modest in establishing his credentials as an observer, asserting that "most of the confidences were unsought" (p. 1). We are assured of Nick's ethical normality as he confesses that his tolerance has limits and that he wishes for a world in which morality is a stabilizing force. He relates to us a set of biographical circumstances that mark him as both thoroughly trustworthy and completely stable in his values. He comes from solid stock, "prominent, well-to-do people in this Middle Western city" (p. 2), but he is not unusually wealthy. He has been conventionally but well educated; he has served his country in war; and he has now, after his youthful wanderings in the East, settled in his hometown.

He stands in an ideal position for the narrator of a story about unusual people. He is not himself unusual, but circumstances have given him unusual opportunity to observe a special, privileged world. He has the personality to take full advantage of that opportunity while remaining essentially like his audience in values.

Having been introduced in this way, Nick must be made to conduct himself in accordance with these characteristics throughout the novel. In the novel's many unusual situations we learn not only of the occurrences but also of Nick's feelings about them. Attending Gatsby's extravagant parties, meeting Tom Buchanan's mistress Myrtle, seeing Meyer Wolfsheim, and arranging Gatsby's funeral are all situations in which Nick participates while assuring us of his reluctance, discomfort, and even disapproval. Yet in each case he conducts himself with that cautious reserve that allows him to continue as a reliable observer. In his relations with Jordan Baker he is, by his own admission, excessively punctilious;

but, as he says, "I wanted to leave things in order and not just trust that obliging and indifferent sea to sweep my refuse away" (p. 178).

Readers who wish reasons for considering Gatsby's narrator a reliable guide to the story's action and meaning are given both a general claim and particulars to support it. As audience, they may then feel secure in looking to the next question. By what means, other than the sort of overt commentary cited above, does the narrator convey his conclusions and his reasons for them? If we make a rough division between those things the narrator reports and the way in which he reports them, we can begin to see what the audience's answer to the question is likely to be.

Much of the book's argument is clearly derived from the reported actions and words of the characters. For instance, the view that the privilege of the rich is unhealthy is supported by a number of narrated events. The behavior of the guests at Gatsby's parties is dramatized as boorishness. The lack of a true regard for others is finally verified by the failure of any of them to attend his funeral. Similarly, Tom Buchanan's cavalier mistreatment of his own mistress and his wife is highlighted in our final view of him unconcernedly buying jewels. Even Daisy is willing to have Gatsby take the blame for her having run over Myrtle. Numerous other examples are given. Tom's smug and foolish racial views, Daisy's bored thrill-seeking, and Jordan's avowed carelessness are all alike in this regard. In all these cases the characters, through their own actions and words, portray themselves; the narrator merely selects and reports. However, this "showing" of support for a general belief about privilege is consistently and coherently supported by the narrator's "telling" of events.

In recording the actions of Gatsby's guests, Nick tells us that their laughter is "vacuous" (p. 47), that their conversation is characterized by "causal innuendo and introductions forgotten on the spot" (p. 40), and that they "had found little that it was necessary to whisper about in the world" (p. 44). These and other descriptive remarks give a tonal coloration that corroborates the apparent meaning of the overt events themselves. Once we have accepted Nick as a trustworthy observer, such coloration becomes evidence supporting the conclusions toward which the novel as a whole seems to move. Indeed, much characterization is accomplished by commentary rather than by direct speech or action. Before we hear him speak, we learn that Tom Buchanan was "one of those men who reach such an acute and limited excellence at twenty-one that everything afterwards savors of anticlimax," that he had "a rather hard mouth and supercilious manner" and "a cruel body," and that he had an air of "paternal contempt" (p. 7). When we also learn that he is "enormously wealthy" (p. 6) and that "Something was making him nibble at the edge of stale ideas as if his sturdy physical egotism no longer nourished his peremptory heart" (p. 21), additional support is added to our conclusion about the rich. By the same process, we are prepared to interpret "correctly" Tom's subsequent treatment of Daisy and Myrtle. In a similar way we learn that Daisy has an "absurd, charming little laugh," and that her looking "promising that there was no one in the world she so much wanted to see" is in fact mannerism (p. 9). In Daisy's flightiness we see another feature of unhealthy privilege, and her ultimate irresponsibility toward Gatsby is foreshadowed. Again, Nick's description of Jordan as "incurably dishonest" (p. 58) and "this clean, hard, limited person who dealt in universal skepticism" (p. 81), shows another example of the danger of privilege, and we are given a critical cue by which to understand Jordan's pose of carelessness. Each element of proof strengthens others in an essentially argumentative fashion. It is their consistency and coherence that persuades us. Nick's authoritative judgments are also rendered surer by the same consistency of the examples that support them, and the examples are clarified and given force and meaning by his judgments.

Similar elements of proof are presented in support of the notion that pursuit of a static ideal is futile, but the elements are rather differently arranged. There is only one significant event that supports this conclusion, Gatsby's pursuit of Daisy. But this pursuit forms the main action of the book. As such it carries great weight. The futility of Gatsby's quest is made clear in the climactic scene in the hotel where Daisy tells him that he wants too much and that she cannot deny that she has loved Tom. Thereafter Gatsby's world disintegrates. Still clinging to the dream, he assumes the blame for Myrtle's death and attempts to protect Daisy from Tom. Daisy, however, uses the opportunity not to elope with Gatsby but to be reconciled with Tom and leave town. By the time Tom betrays him to Wilson, Gatsby's death seems inevitable. Obviously, Daisy is no longer (if she ever was) the woman Gatsby had cherished in his dream. This chain of events culminating in Gatsby's death is not all that the author of *Gatsby* gives to readers to help them to appreciate the futility of pursuing unchanging dreams.

Our first intimations of Gatsby's dream come in a conversation in which his obvious posing tempts Nick to "incredulous laughter" (p. 66) and leaves him "more annoyed than interested" (p. 62). As we gradually discover the precise nature of the dream we are frequently reminded of its fantasy and hopelessness. Of the first afternoon that Daisy and Gatsby meet, Nick comments "there must have been moments even that afternoon when Daisy tumbled short of his dreams—not through her own fault, but because of the colossal vitality of his illusion" (p. 97). Later, as Nick realizes the extent of Gatsby's illusion, he attempts to warn Gatsby and again reminds the audience of the realism that dreamers must eventually confront:

> "I wouldn't ask too much of her," I ventured. "You can't repeat the past."
> "Can't repeat the past?" he cried incredulously. "Why of course you can."
> He looked around him wildly, as if the past were lurking here in the shadow of his house, just out of his reach in his hand [p. 111].

During the climactic confrontation in the hotel room, we are told that Gatsby's "dead dream fought on . . . trying to touch what was no longer tangible" (p. 135). In the same scene, Nick contrasts Jordan to Daisy by saying, "Jordan . . . was too wise ever to carry well-forgotten dreams from age to age" (p. 136). And finally, when Gatsby reveals his true past to Nick, it is "because 'Jay Gatsby' had broken up like glass against Tom's hard malice, and the long secret extravaganza was played out" (p. 148). Even Tom, hard as he is, is judged to be driven by a comparable illusion, for we are told, "I felt that Tom would drift on forever seeking, a little wistfully, for the dramatic turbulence of some irrecoverable football game" (p. 6). Both Nick's overt commentary and the tonal coloration of his reports of actions reinforce the novel's general claim about the pursuit of dreams; any reader impelled to grasp this claim can find a convincing, justifying combination of precept and example in support.

A reader's impulse to discover the relationships, if any, between the themes we have so far traced is assisted by the narrator's commentary and interpretation. The events already mentioned reflect at one level a confusion of the privileges of wealth with the realization of a romantic dream. The two can seem only parallel sources of error. We are given direct evidence of the confusion when Gatsby says of Daisy, "Her voice is full of money" (p. 120). It is not until the narrator expands on this theme that we grasp the full import of the remark and begin to see the two sources of error as related.

> That it was. I'd never understood before. It was full of money—that was the inexhaustible charm that rose and fell in it, the jingle of it, the cymbals' song of it. . . . High in a white palace the king's daughter, the golden girl . . . [p. 120].

174

The combination is explored in other places. In discussing Gatsby's origins, Nick explains that Gatsby's view of wealth is almost reverential. "Jay Gatsby . . . sprang from his Platonic conception of himself. He was a son of God—a phrase for which, if it means anything, means just that—and he must be about his father's business, the service of a vast, vulgar, and meretricious beauty" (p. 99). Daisy, young, healthy, and "the first 'nice' girl he had ever known" (p. 148) becomes the embodiment of that beauty. "Gatsby was overwhelmingly aware of the youth and mystery that wealth imprisons and preserves, of the freshness of many clothes, and of Daisy, gleaming like silver, safe and proud above the hot struggles of the poor" (p. 150). Thus he is trapped. He has "wed his unutterable visions to her perishable breath" (p. 112), and it only remains for him to act out the consequences of his tragic delusion.

The conclusion comes clear. One may obtain the symbol of achievement and satisfaction, but these are not the means to the ends they symbolize. By themselves they are hollow, and the very hollowness of the symbols becomes a cause of depravity and desperation.

CONCLUSION

The steps by which one can test one's interpretation of a dramatic or literary work were suggested in earlier remarks about aesthetic experience. The procedure entails four considerations. First is determining the message, the overall conclusions fostered by the work. Second is deciding whether one's determination of message is justified by *(a)* the reliability of the narrator(s); *(b)* the words or actions of other characters; and *(c)* the descriptions of characters, scenes, and events—which are verbal in literature and both verbal and nonverbal in drama. Third is noting the outcomes of the various conflicts that make up the story, observing whose values seem most powerful and/or worthy, whether events are controlled by characters or by forces outside them. Up to this point, one's primary concern is whether or not the story rings true as a story in itself and what "truth" it makes known. Fourth is weighing this "truth," the set of conclusions advanced by the story, against one's own perceptions of the world to determine their fidelity. The questions are: *(a)* Does the message accurately portray the world we live in? and *(b)* Does it provide a reliable guide to *our* beliefs, attitudes, values, actions?

A parallel may be drawn between these four considerations involved in testing one's interpretation of a dramatic or literary work and the criterial questions that identify and test good reasons. As was pointed out earlier, dramatic and literary works display value-laden conflicts between or among characters, events, and, external forces. It follows that dramatic and literary "messages" are value-laden. In this chapter, we have seen in *Salesman* and *Gatsby* that the materialistic myth of the American Dream can be a tragic delusion, capable of leading not to happiness or well-being but to self-destruction. Both works reaffirm the values of self-knowledge, of self-acceptance over conformity and false dreams.

The first three considerations in testing one's interpretation of a dramatic or literary work are parallel with the criterial questions of the logic of good reasons—*fact* and *relevance*. The fourth consideration, concerning the accuracy of dramatic and literary portrayal and the value of the message, coincides with the criterial questions of *consequence, consistency,* and *transcendent issue*. We, the authors of the earlier version of this study, are convinced that *Salesman* and *Gatsby* satisfy the aesthetic requirements detailed in the first three considerations. The works are aesthetically sound, as our preceding analyses argue.

Questions now arise about the accuracy of the portrayals of life in the two works and whether their conclusions are worthy of adherence. We begin with our own experiences. Based on our experiences, we judge the characters of *Salesman* and *Gatsby* to be true to life—in principle. We have not known a "Willy Loman," a "Gatsby," or people like the Buchanans, but we have "dwelled in" their characters and their relationships and found their experiences similar to our own or to other persons we have known. As Bronowski observes, "The most moving experience of literature makes us aware that we too are swept by the waves of lust and destruction that overwhelm other men. We too taste in inner agony the salt tang of cruelty that we call inhuman, and learn that it is most human. We have it in us to be murderers and con-men and perverts and the scum of the earth."[21] *Salesman* and *Gatsby* portray such experience, and they ring true to the human condition as we know it generally. The works seem "true" in principle, though we cannot testify to all details portrayed.

To the question, Are the central conclusions of these works reliable/desirable guides for one's own life? we would say Yes. We are reassured in this judgment because we believe that construction of a positive self-image, improvement in one's behavior toward others and society, and enhancement of the process of rhetorical transaction are all fostered by the recognition that the materialistic myth of the American Dream can be a tragic delusion and that self-knowledge and acceptance are higher values

176

than conformity to unexamined standards. This message is confirmed in our own experiences, the experiences of others, and in the pronouncements of spiritual leaders from all segments of society. Finally, we are confident in our judgment that self-knowledge and self-acceptance are prerequisites to happiness and well-being, and that these values are transcendent. The fact that the conclusions are familiar, even though the works in which they appear are fresh and compelling, indicates both the transcendence and the immediate worth of the values.

Saul Bellow's words summarize what has been said in this book about argument in dramatic and literary works: "The artist, as R. G. Collingwood tells us, must be a prophet, 'not in the sense that he foretells things to come, but that he tells the audience, at risk of their displeasure, the secrets of their own hearts.' That is why he exists. He is a spokesman of his community. . . . Art is the community's medicine for the worst disease of mind, the corruption of consciousness."[22] Such is the medicine offered by *Death of a Salesman* and *The Great Gatsby*.

It is not original to say that literary and dramatic works "argue." Readers of nineteenth-century introductions to great poems and, sometimes, novels and plays will recall that the plot was often called the "argument." The major points we have tried to illustrate in considering *Death of a Salesman* and *The Great Gatsby* are that such works "argue" in identifiable ways and that one can test the rhetorical worth of fictive argumentation by raising a relatively few questions about coherence and fidelity. *Salesman* and *Gatsby* argue coherently and with fidelity for significant theses. They do so by "piling up" incidents and bits of discourse that directly and indirectly suggest dominant themes—the theses. Strictly "logical" questions about entailment and sufficiency of direct evidence cannot possibly get at these narrative processes of arguing. Questions suggested by the concept of narrative rationality, however, *do* expose the rhetorical structures and strengths of at least some literary and dramatic works, as our illustrations show. If we had chosen less well-made works, would the principles of the narrative paradigm have identified and exposed rhetorical weaknesses? Yes, at least some kinds of weaknesses would assuredly come to notice: the presence of irrelevant and digressive incidents and discourse; incidents and discourse that cohere or cluster to support conflicting themes; representations of seldom-experienced or fantastic situations; inconsistencies in character portrayal. Of course, it can be argued that if the narrative paradigm works anywhere for purposes of rhetorical analysis, it should work on plays and novels. This is true, but we emphasize that the lines of critical inquiry used in this chapter were the *same* as those used successfully in analyzing Reagan's political rhetoric. It seems to us that a major value of the narrative paradigm is that it yields useful critical insights to *both* typical persuasive prose *and* discourse that is obviously narrative in structure. The task of the next chapter is to test the narrative paradigm against still another sort of discourse—philosophical dialectical discourse.

NOTES

1. Joseph W. Wenzel, "Perspectives on Argument," in Jack Rhodes and S. Newell, eds., *Proceeding of the Summer Conference on Argumentation* (Annandale, Va: Speech Communication Association, 1980), pp. 112–33.

2. See J. Bronowski, *The Identity of Man* (rev. ed.; New York: Natural History Press, 1971), pp. 77ff., 118–40; M. Polanyi, *Personal Knowledge* (New York: Harper Torchbooks, 1962), pp. 17ff.; M. Polayni and H. Prosch, *Meaning* (Chicago: University of Chicago Press, 1975), pp. 41ff.; Wayne Booth, *The Rhetoric of Fiction* (Chicago: University of Chicago Press, 1961), p. 169.

3. Wilbur Samuel Howell, "Rhetoric and Poetics: A Plea for the Two Literatures," in L. Wallach, ed., *The Classical Tradition* (Ithaca, N.Y.: Cornell University Press), pp. 374–90.

4. Aristotle, *Poetics,* 19.1456b. Trans. Ingram Bywater (New York: Modern Library, 1954).

5. Chaïm Perelman and L. Olbrechts-Tyteca, *The New Rhetoric: A Treatise on Argumentation,* trans. John Wilkinson and Purcell Weaver (Notre Dame, Ind.: University of Notre Dame Press, 1969), p. 117.

6. Ibid., p. 174.

7. Wilbur Samuel Howell, *Fénelon's Dialogues on Eloquence* (Princeton, N.J.: Princeton University Press, 1951), p. 46.

8. Ibid., p. 93.

9. Ibid., p. 94.

10. Donald C. Bryant, "Uses of Rhetoric in Criticism," in *Papers in Rhetoric and Poetic* (Iowa City: University of Iowa Press, 1965), pp. 1–14.

11. Donald C. Bryant, "Rhetoric: Its Function and Scope, *Rediviva,*" in *Rhetorical Dimensions of Criticism* (Baton Rouge: Louisiana State University, 1973), pp. 3–23.

12. Booth, *Rhetoric of Fiction,* Preface.

13. Ibid.

14. Kenneth Burke, *A Rhetoric of Motives* (Englewood Cliffs, N.J.: Prentice-Hall, 1950), pp. 19–46.

15. Ibid., p. 172.

16. Kenneth Burke, *Counter-Statement* (rev. ed.; Berkeley: University of California Press, 1968), p. 124.

17. Kenneth Burke, "Rhetoric and Poetics," in *Language as Symbolic Action: Essays on Life, Literature, and Method* (Berkeley: University of California Press, 1968), p. 296.

18. Kenneth Burke, "Poetics and Communication," in H. E. Kieffer and M. K.

Munitz, eds., *Perspectives in Education, Religion, and the Arts* (Albany: State University of New York, 1970), p. 409. See also Kenneth Burke, "Rhetoric, Poetics, and Philosophy," in D. Burks, ed., *Rhetoric, Philosophy, and Literature: An Exploration* (West Lafayette, Ind.: Purdue University Press, 1978), pp. 15–33.

19. Arthur Miller, *Death of a Salesman,* in H. M. Block and R. G. Shedd, eds., *Masters of Modern Drama* (New York: Random House, 1962), p. 1043. All further references to the play will be cited by page from this text.

20. F. Scott Fitzgerald, *The Great Gatsby* (New York: Charles Scribner's Sons, 1925), pp. 180–81. All further references to the book will be cited by page from this text.

21. Bronowski, *Identity of Man,* p. 75.

22. Saul Bellow, "Culture Now," in A. M. Eastman, et al., eds., *The Norton Reader: An Anthology of Expository Prose* (3rd. ed.; New York: W. W. Norton, 1973), p. 423.

CHOOSING BETWEEN SOCRATES AND CALLICLES:
An Assessment of Philosophical Discourse

As the analyses of Reagan's rhetoric and the rhetoric of *Death of a Salesman* and *The Great Gatsby* illustrate, diverse forms of discourse make claims of presenting knowledge, truth, and specifications of reality. In fact, no serious discourse fails to make such claims. However, some forms of communication explicitly purport to present truth claims and to defend them systematically. This is the case with philosophical and scientific discourse. Having tested the usefulness of the narrative paradigm for understanding political rhetoric, drama, and prose fiction, I want now to apply the paradigm to an example of philosophical discourse. The example I shall use is the dialogic exchange between Socrates and Callicles in Plato's *Gorgias*. The episode is justly famous, is universally accepted as philosophical, and is in dialogue form that renders it somewhat dramatic as well as philosophical. An analytical system that will work with political rhetoric should also apply to straightforward philosophical argumentation. But the Socrates-Callicles exchange is more complex than straightforward philosophical argumentation. As dialectical dialogue, it comes close to representing the informal rhetoric that might occur almost anywhere between persons of high intellect and passionate commitment to rival conceptions of the good life. It is also philosophical inquiry of the highest sort—an expression of wonderment designed to elevate the quality of human existence through deep reflection and understanding.

As I said in chapter 7, no story stands alone. A story is always embedded in other stories. The story told by Socrates in the *Gorgias* reappears in several of Plato's dialogues, especially in the *Protagoras,* the *Apology,* and the *Republic.* It can be found in the *Phaedrus,* where Plato elaborates the story further in direct connection with rhetoric. While the story concerns choosing the life of philosophy, as exemplified in the life of Socrates, over a life of political hedonism, as represented by Callicles, it would be a mistake to see this choice as a purely philosophical one. It involves an eminently and fundamentally practical issue, a decision that affects the mode of a person's personal and public behavior and the way education, politics, and communication are conceived and practiced. As it appears in the *Gorgias*, the story is, as E. R. Dodds observes, "more than an *apologia* for Socrates; it is at the same time Plato's *apologia pro vita sua*."[1] A basic theme of the story and of Socrates' life is that "the man and woman who are noble and good" are "happy, but the 'evil and base' are wretched."[2] There was but one way that the good life could be achieved—living by Socrates' idealism.

A rival of this form of life was and is the life represented by Callicles, a political hedonist. The key theme of this life was and is that the powerful person determines what is happy and just and that happiness and justice are realized by the exercises of one's own proclivities.

The conflict between Socrates and Callicles begins when Callicles enters an ongoing conversation about the nature and functions of rhetoric, at the point at which he asks, "Tell me, Chaerephon, is Socrates in earnest or joking?" (481b). That Socrates is serious is demonstrated by several statements: philosophy is his "love" (his life); it is never capricious. He would rather that "the majority of mankind should disagree with and oppose me" than that he "should be out of tune with and contradict" himself (482b, c). Later: "and do not take what I say as if I were merely playing, for you see the subject of our discussion—and on what subject should even a man of slight intelligence be more serious?—namely, what kind of life one should live, the life to which you invite me, that of a 'real man,' speaking in the assembly and practicing rhetoric and playing the politician according to your present fashion, or the life spent in philosophy, and how one differs from the other" (500c). Plato's seriousness is also evident in his tone and his willingness to forgo the elenchus, his customary method of cross-examination, in order to persuade Callicles (507ff.). That Callicles is equally serious may be seen in his willingness to enter the conversation, from his fervent manner, and from his persistent questioning of Socrates' seriousness.

SOCRATES' STORY

The themes of Socrates' story are these: "every man is his own master" (491d); pleasure is not synonymous with the good; pain is not synonymous with evil; "all our actions should be done for the sake of the good" (499e); a true art must be grounded on a conception of the good (as medicine is founded on the conception of health); rhetoric is not an art, it is an irrational knack tied to an irrational conception of politics (justice); true virtue is marked by harmony and order; a true rhetorician should be occupied with "how justice may be implanted in the souls of the citizens and injustice banished, how temperance may be implanted and indiscipline banished, and how goodness in general may be engendered and wickedness depart" (504e); such a rhetorician has never existed; a happy life is a temperate life; an unhappy life is an intemperate life; "if justice is the greatest of evils to the wrongdoer . . ., it is an even greater evil, if that be possible, to escape punishment when one does wrong" (599b): "For to arrive in the other world with a soul surcharged with many wicked deeds is the worst of all evils" (522d).

These statements are offered in sequence but are not formally tied together to render to a formal argumentative conclusion. The logic through which they work is narrative rationality. The various statements *suggest* a common theme; they *cohere* to form consistent support for *a* message. The message of the dialogue is that one should chose to live as Socrates lived or at least by the values he celebrated. He is the "enactment," the living proof, of his philosophy.[3] Perhaps the capstone of Plato's view is this: "I renounce the honors sought by most men, and pursuing the truth I shall endeavor both to live and, when death comes, to die, as good a man as I possibly can" (526e). He also has Socrates assert: "I think that I am one of the very few Athenians, not to say the only one, engaged in the true political art, and that of the men today I alone practice statesmanship" (521d).

The following points deserve notice here. These summing-up statements are not clear-cut inferences from the more specific, earlier statements. Rational-world tests would not reveal how it is that they "sum up." The principles of narrative analysis will do so. The general statements are highly personal in form: "*I* renounce . . .," "*I* think that I am. . . ." These "conclusions" *represent* Plato's views. Socrates' life illustrates these views in life, much as Reagan's heroes illustrated his political-social theses and as Willy and Gatsby illustrated outlooks to be disvalued. It is also treating Socrates' observations as a "story" that allows us to see these narrative characteristics of Plato's "argument."

Socrates' story is informed by the values of truth, the good, beauty, health, wisdom, courage, temperance, justice, harmony, order, communion, friendship, and a oneness with the Cosmos. These are the values that humankind has historically professed and aspired to. They are compatible, for instance, with the values of the moralistic myth of the American Dream: tolerance, charity, compassion, and true regard for the dignity and worth of each and every individual.

182

The appeal of Socrates' story resides in his character, in his commitment to his philosophy to the point of martyrdom, and in the coherence of all of his positions. There can be no question of the coherence of Socrates' story. One can, of course, show that Socrates is a "logic-chopper," but that misses the point. Logic, as we know it, was not in existence until Aristotle "invented" it. Plato's dialectic is based on ontology and is structured by definitional moves, not formal logic. The only recourse in opposing his philosophy is to propose an alternative philosophy or story about how to live. Callicles offers an alternative philosophy: political hedonism; but, at least as presented, it is an easy mark for an idealist, especially since it is grounded in relativism. There is no philosophical way to reconcile the views of Socrates and Callicles. Hedonism is, of course, not the only alternative one could propose to Socrates' idealism. Plato's pupil, Aristotle, offered another alternative. Of him the Aristotelian scholar John Herman Randall, Jr., wrote: "There are for Aristotle no general rules, no universal moral laws, no 'principles' in ethics save the one single *arche,* always to act intelligently in any individual situation, and thus to realize human welfare."[4] Plato, however, chooses to set hedonism against Socrates' idealism.

The good reasons that constitute Socrates' story are arguments and myths centered on the meanings and implications of his values, particularly the good, the true, and the just. To the question of why Socrates should resort to myths, one can suggest several answers. Frustration is one. His move to myth is not, however, as some have argued because his dialectical argument has failed.[5] There is no approach to persuasion that will not fail if an audience refuses to attend to a message. A historical answer is that in Plato's time myths were still a generally accepted mode of communication; technical logos had not yet supplanted mythos, so Socrates was trying to speak in a form that was appropriate for his audience. A third answer is that myths are the most efficacious means of communicating a sense of transcendental truth, in this case, of the afterlife. As Dodds notes, "the *Gorgias* myth (the one at the end of the dialogue) is called *Xoyos* because it expresses in imaginative terms a 'truth of religion.' "[6] In other words, Plato's conception of mind *(nous)* is of "the imaginative vision of truth."[7] Myth, at least Plato's version of it, not only offers support for his dialectical argument, it is also a mode of discourse in which a *vision* of truth is made manifest.

The problem that arises with Socrates' story concerns its fidelity to the world, the world we know from ordinary experience. No matter how deeply one may want to emulate the life of Socrates, to adhere to his ideals, one knows that frustrations and possible martyrdom can result from doing so. One may admire Socrates, but one is also likely to recognize the "ring of truth" in Callicles' representation of the way people and things actually are. As Randall observes, "Man cannot live without ideals, but equally man cannot live by ideals alone."[8] I shall return to this matter later in discussing the appeal of Callicles' story.

It is important to recognize that the values espoused by Socrates can be used to justify (or mystify) elitist systems of governance. Indeed, they are the grounds of Plato's *Republic,* which is structured as an aristocracy of talent. The same values are also celebrated by the USSR. The differences between the two systems are in where "truth" is to be found—in the noumenal or phenomenal world—and in their "religious" orientations: Plato would please the "gods." In the USSR, there is no "god," only Marxist doctrine and the Presidium. In both systems, public and social knowledge are denied authority and rhetoric is relegated to a purely instrumental role. There is another difference worthy of note: Plato was not a friend of democracy.[9] On the other hand, we should recognize that in the *Gorgias* he was not proposing a political system, and in the *Republic* he was offering an imagined utopia meant to contrast with the society in which he lived. In neither case should he be held to espouse the Soviet system or any other for a modern nation-state. His mind was on the Greek system he knew. It is the fact that all stories occur *in context* that should caution us against extrapolating from Socrates' ideal to twentieth-century political life.

CALLICLES' STORY

The themes of Callicles' story are these: nature rather than convention is the guide to life (484c); philosophy is a study for youth; when a man who is "growing older still studies philosophy, the situation becomes ridiculous" (485b); philosophy leaves a person defenseless in the political arena (486b); natural justice is realized in the principle that "the better and wiser should rule over and have more than the inferior" (490a); "anyone who is to live right should suffer his appetites to grow to the greatest extent and not to check them, and through courage and intelligence should be competent to minister to them at their greatest and to satisfy every appetite with what it craves" (492a); the truth is: "Luxury and intemperance and license, when they have sufficient backing, are virtue and happiness and all the rest is tinsel, the unnatural catchwords of mankind, mere nonsense and of no account" (492c); conventional justice and equality are values fostered by the weak to control the strong; there are some rhetoricians who were good men—Themistocles, Cimon, Miltiades, and Pericles (503c); and one should live "to serve and minister" to the polis (521b). In sum, Callicles' story celebrates hedonism, relativism, and power politics—the "survival of the fittest." The story is justified on the basis that this is the way nature itself dictates that things should be. Callicles' story is not incoherent, but the themes do not "argue" as coherently as Socrates' themes do. That is partly, of course, because, as Callicles is allowed to present it, hedonism is less a system than an attitude.

Callicles' position is informed by the values of pleasure, expediency, self-aggrandizement, courage, strength, political acumen, material success, and the will to power. As Socrates' values correspond with the values of the moralistic myth of the American Dream, Callicles' values accord with the values of the materialistic myth: effort, persistence, "playing the game," initiative, self-reliance, achievement, and success.

It would be a mistake, however, to see the materialistic myth of Callicles without a moral dimension. Callicles' materialistic myth is tied to what would later be called the Calvinist ethos. Callicles obviously was not a Calvinist; he "does not deny the significance of ethical-judgments, but like Nietzsche he 'transvalues' them." Callicles is portrayed as believing that "might really is *right*."[10] Friedlander characterizes Callicles' ethics in this way: "There is a morality by nature, genuine, original, and founded upon true being—a morality of powerful men to whom suffering wrong is not only worse, but more disgraceful than doing wrong."[11] If Callicles had not held a position with philosophical grounding, he would not have been such an attractive opponent for Socrates. His orientation to the "good life" made him an ideal foil for Plato, who as a youth had shared many of the inclinations of Callicles. In the *Seventh Letter,* Plato wrote, "Once upon a time in my youth I cherished like many another the hope of entering upon a political career as soon as I came of age."[12] Dodds notes, "We may even conjecture, with Festigiere (387) and Jaeger (*Paideia,* ii, 138), that 'in his character Plato had so much of that unruly will to power to find, and fight, part of himself in Callicles'; or with Alain (*Idées,* 17) that 'Plato paints *himself* here as he might have been, as he feared to be.' "[13]

The appeal of Callicles' story derives from its narrative probability and its fidelity to the way politics is often practiced—whether democratic, republican, feudal, fascist, or socialist. The good reasons that constitute his story are inevitably circular; they are expressed in the idea that "might

185

makes right" (right is might). Callicles' overall philosophy is coherent (tautological), but Socrates shows, on many counts, that elements of his story are inconsistent. On a central theme of their dispute—whether it is better to suffer wrong than to do it—Socrates demonstrates that Callicles' position, that it is better to do wrong than to suffer it, is incompatible with his admission that the good is not the same as pleasure (500a). Socrates' own position, for which he was ready to die, was that "we should be more on guard against doing than suffering wrong" (527b). Callicles may have died because of his beliefs, or actions based on them, but he does not express in this dialogue a willingness to do so, as Socrates does. Callicles' "God" was the polis and his commandments were the standards by which one could serve as its leader.

The problems in Callicles' story arise from evasion of such values as truth, universal good, equality, harmony, order, communion, friendship, and a oneness with the Cosmos. It also poses difficulties if we consider what life would be like if everyone believed and behaved as Callicles advises. This criticism is appropriate because any ethical stipulation about how one ought to live must be subject to generalization. One cannot argue that one can live one way and claim that others cannot. "To the extent that the seeking of pleasure and the avoidance of suffering and death could be made the basis of ethics," said Perelman, "there would be no further need for rhetoric. One needs rhetoric only to overcome fear or suffering, in order not to give in to temptation."[14] Neither Callicles nor Nietzsche should be held accountable for the tyrannies the world has suffered throughout history, but the motive they espoused—the will to power—must be seen as the source of much of humankind's material progress, and also of many social and political ills.

Callicles' refusal to continue the conversation at 505c merits second thoughts before I conclude this section. Several interpretations of this feature of the story are possible: (1) Callicles willfully refuses to pursue a truth other than his own; (2) Plato has made Callicles refuse to continue in order to portray him and his position as inferior to Socrates'; (3) Plato himself was unwilling to continue the exploration; (4) Callicles' refusal is Plato's way of saying that the two positions are irreconcilable; and (5) this is Plato's way of saying Socrates has obviously bested Callicles in the exchange. Each of these interpretations is supportable by reference to the text and by what we know of Plato as author and thinker. One interpretation that cannot be supported, however, is that Callicles has defeated Socrates.

No matter which interpretation one supports, certain critical conclusions are justified. First, the meaning of this moment in the story is ambiguous. Second, as Hans-Georg Gadamer has put it, "there is no means of compelling someone to see the truth who does not want to see it."[15] A general truth is illustrated: the power of human communication to enlighten is ended when an interlocuter withdraws from the transaction. Whether Plato intended it or not, his story dramatizes that universal fact. Third, and less obviously, the abrupt ending of the interaction can, if we choose to so read it, be a statement to the effect that anyone who denies the *possibility* of truth and goodness as having reference to the real world also denies a rational basis on which to judge the evil or the good as a way of life. Callicles' refusal may or may not signal this truth, but that "message" is at least potentially there.

CHOOSING BETWEEN SOCRATES AND CALLICLES

That the Western world has celebrated the values that mark the story of Socrates is, I believe, beyond question. Along with other martyrs to truth—Jesus, Gandhi, and Lincoln—Socrates' story is preferred to that of Callicles in principle, if not always in practice. In the same way, Milton's *Areopagitica* is preferred to Machiavelli's *The Prince,* and John Stuart Mill's *On Liberty* to Nietzsche's *The Will to Power.* The ideal is often preferred over the pragmatic.

Though many people seem to prefer idealistic stories, a modern reader of *Gorgias,* Randall believes, "is apt to sympathize with the Romantic ideal of Callicles. There is much in the modern temper that wants to live to the full, to get a thrill out of it, rather than live with Socrates' wisdom."[16] I think this is a correct judgment if one considers how people *live* rather than how they may *celebrate* virtue. I suggest that *all good stories function in two ways: to justify (or mystify) decisions or actions already made or performed and to determine future decisions or actions.* This is true of *both* Socrates' and Callicles' stories. The narrative perspective leads to the further conclusion that idealistic stories, Socrates' story being an example, generate adherence because they are coherent and "ring true" to life *as we would like to live it.* Such stories tend to put before us characters in competition with other characters, leading us to choose our "heroes" and our "villains." The choice is a statement about our own existence.

The appeal of idealistic stories resides in their evoking the best in people and activating it. As I said in chapter 3, "Any story, any form of rhetorical communication, not only says something about the world, it also implies an audience, persons who conceive of themselves in very specific ways." It appears that there is a permanent public, an actual community existing over time, that believes in the values of truth, the good, beauty, health, wisdom, courage, temperance, justice, harmony, order, communion, friendship, and a oneness with the Cosmos—as variously as these values may be defined or practiced in "real" life. In terms of the logic of good reasons, people have found these values *relevant* to the good life; *consequential* in advancing moral obligation and civilized relations; *consistent* with their highest experiences, with the testimony of leaders in thought and action, and with the demands of the best audience one might conceive; and satisfying in regard to the *transcendental issue:* the ideal basis for human conduct.

On the other hand, there is another public, an actual community existing over time, that practices even if it does not celebrate, the values of pleasure, expediency, self-aggrandizement, courage, strength, political acumen, material success, and the will to power. This is a public ranging in commitment from authoritarianism to pragmatism. Persons have found these values *relevant* to their material lives, *consequential* in determining their survival and well-being, *consistent* with statements made by those who subscribe to the myth that humans are masters of their fates and with examples of those who succeeded by following it. In some instances, these values are satisfying as ideal standards for human conduct. I suspect, however, that if confronted by Socrates, or the better part of themselves, even these persons would admit that while Callicles' philosophy has some fidelity with the way they *must* live their lives, it is not entirely coherent or true to their whole lives, or to the life that they would most like to live.

Earlier I said that there is no way to reconcile the philosophies of Socrates and Callicles. This is not quite true, for the values they espouse can and do inform one another in practice. For instance, they do so in the lived experience of the American Dream. Trying to live according to both the moralistic and the materialistic myths of the American experiment can lead to a kind of "schizophrenia." When one of the myths tends to dominate, whether in the culture or in an individual, the other myth is always haunting there in the background. The point to be seen is that there is some truth in both Socrates' and Callicles' stories. Yet, in life, there is tension between choosing to live for the moment or for "eternity." Whether Plato meant this or not, it is a message that emerges from the exchange, a truth pertinent to this time as well as his.

This interpretation and assessment of the exchange between Socrates and Callicles should resolve the problem posed at the beginning of the chapter regarding the applicability of narrative to philosophical discourse.

188

It complements the earlier analyses of Reagan's rhetoric, *Death of a Salesman, The Great Gatsby,* the nuclear controversy, and *The Epic of Gilgamesh.* My reading contrasts with other readings of Plato's *Gorgias* in several ways. It is not analytical, philological, historical, or aesthetic—except tangentially. It does not privilege "argument" over myth, or myth over "argument." It considers not the truth of the stories per se, but the consequences of accepting them after determining their truth qualities as assessed by the tests of narrative rationality.

CONCLUSION

Beyond its adequacy in demonstrating the narrative paradigm in use and how it differs from other interpretive schemes, one may consider the importance of my interpretations relative to Plato's stance toward rhetoric. Whether rhetoric is the "real theme" of the *Gorgias* or not, the life represented by Callicles requires rhetoric for its being, and the life urged by Socrates necessitates dialectic and Plato's metaphysical position. There can be no doubt that Plato's concern about rhetoric was pervasive: it distorted education, corrupted politics, and failed as philosophy and a way of life. The interpretation presented here supports the conclusion that Plato did not relent in the *Phaedrus* from the view of rhetoric he took in the *Gorgias.* It is not the case that "Plato opposed only a particular view of rhetoric unsuccessfully defended in the dialogue by Gorgias, Polus, and Callicles, and probably defended by leading Sophists and rhetoricians of Plato's time."[17] Plato's position, as brought to life in the character of Socrates, is an ontological one. It is not a view he could have changed without rejecting his metaphysical beliefs.

It is fair to ask if a reading of narrativity such as I have presented in this chapter yields more than ad-hoc statements about *parts* of an author's conceptual system. To determine whether or not this is so, one may check a conclusion from analysis of one story with another by the same author. In the present case this can be done by taking a look at what Plato said about rhetoric in the *Phaedrus.* The "art" of discourse outlined at the end of the *Phaedrus* is not an art concerned with contingent matters; it is a "science" parallel with medicine. It would make a rhetorician a physician to the soul of the body politic. "Those who see in the *Phaedrus* a 'correction' of the uncompromising views of the *Gorgias* (Pohlenz, p. 343)," Dodds writes, "or a 'new stage in Plato's developing attitudes towards rhetoric' (Jaeger, *Paideia,* iii, p. 185) seem to overlook the present passage (503a). The two dialogues differ widely in emotional tone . . . ,

189

but the implication of both is that the only true ῥήτωρ is Socrates himself."[18] At 503a, Socrate says of rhetoric:

> . . . for even if there are two sides to this, yet one part of it, I suppose, would be flattery and shameful mob appeal, while the other is something fine—the effort to perfect as far as possible the souls of the citizens and the struggle to say always what is best, whether it be welcome or unwelcome to the hearers. But you yourself have never seen rhetoric of this kind, or if you can mention any such orator, why do you not tell me his name at once?

In the *Gorgias,* Socrates plainly rejects Callicles' story of life. In the *Phaedrus,* he rejects a central tool of that life: rhetoric. There is consistency and coherence is taking these views of the good life. Plato's version of the good life, personal and public, could not endorse rhetoric as long as it was an art of probable, practical discourse.

NOTES

1. E. R. Dodds, *Gorgias* (London: Oxford University Press, 1959), p. 31.

2. Plato, *Gorgias,* trans. W. D. Woodward, in Edith Hamilton and H. Cairns, *Plato: The Collected Dialogues, Including the Letters* (Princeton, N.J.: Bollingen Series LXXI, Princeton University Press, 1973), 470c. All further citations from Plato's *Gorgias* will be from this text.

3. See Charles Kaufman, "Enactment as Argument in the *Gorgias,*" *Philosophy and Rhetoric* 12 (1979): 114–29; Karlyn K. Campbell and Kathleen Jamieson, "Form and Genre in Rhetorical Criticism: An Introduction," in *Form and Genre: Shaping Rhetorical Action* (Falls Church, Va.: Speech Communication Association, n.d.), pp. 9–12; Steven Rendell, "Dialogue, Philosophy, and Rhetoric: The Example of Plato's *Gorgias,*" *Philosophy and Rhetoric* 10 (1977): 165–79; Adele Spitzer, "The Self-Reference of the *Gorgias,*" *Philosophy and Rhetoric* 8 (1975): 1–22.

4. John H. Randall, Jr., *Aristotle* (New York: Columbia University Press, 1960), p. 268.

5. See Kaufman, "Enactment as Argument."

6. See Dodds, *Gorgias,* p. 377. See also E. R. Dodds, *The Greeks and the Irrational* (Berkeley: University of California Press, 1951); Paul Friedlander, *Plato: The Dialogues, First Period,* trans, H. Myerhoff (New York: Bollingen Series LIX, Pantheon Books, 1928).

7. John H. Randall, Jr., *Plato: Dramatist of the Life of Reason* (New York: Columbia University Press, 1970).

8. Randall, *Plato,* p. 149.

9. Karl R. Popper, *The Open Society and Its Enemies: The Spell of Plato* (Princeton, N.J.: Princeton University Press, 1971). See vol. 1.

10. Dodds, *Gorgias,* pp. 15, 314. See also Friedlander, *Plato,* p. 261.

11. Friedlander, *Plato,* p. 260.

12. Plato, *Letters,* trans. L. A. Post, in Hamilton and Cairns, *Plato: The Collected Dialogues,* p. 1562.

13. Dodds, *Gorgias,* p. 267.

14. Chaïm Perelman, "The Rhetorical Point of View in Ethics: A Program," trans. D. R. Tourrille, *Communication* 6 (1981); 319. M. G. Singer, *Generalization in Ethics: An Essay in the Logic of Ethics, with the Rudiments of a System of Moral Philosophy* (New York: Atheneum, 1971).

15. Hans-George Gadamer, *Dialogue and Dialectic: Eight Hermeneutic Studies on Plato,* trans. P. C. Smith (New Haven, Conn.: Yale University Press, 1980), p. 116.

16. Randall, *Plato,* p. 91.

17. Edwin Black, "Plato's View of Rhetoric," *Quarterly Journal of Speech* 44 (1958): 367.

18. Dodds, *Gorgias,* p. 330. See also Thomas Conley, "Phaedrus 259ff.," *Rhetoric Society Quarterly* 11 (1981): 11–15.

IN RETROSPECT

Before the advent of philosophy in ancient Greece, all modes of human communication were regarded as *mythos/logos, form/content,* and *feeling/reason.* No instance of human communication was privileged over another as having a special capacity to convey knowledge, truth, or reality. The pre-Socratics began the "technologizing" of discourse, but it was Plato and especially Aristotle who set the foundations for the view that only philosophical, later technical, discourse could provide wisdom and certainty in the world. Their successors fought intellectual battles over which genre of discourse—philosophy, science, rhetoric, or poetic—had the right to preside over and generate and evaluate ideas, and which genre should be assigned the lesser tasks of supervising the communication of ideas created elsewhere.

Through stages that have been traced in Part I of this book, we have arrived at a point where a host of scholars from diverse disciplines find this situation *(a)* inaccurate in regard to the data before them, *(b)* inadequate in explaining or assessing the totality of human discourse, and *(c)* inadequate in accounting for the mental processes by which discourse is created, perceived, and evaluated. There is a widespread exigence for an improved, more comprehensive understanding of discourse. Structuralists have offered *form* as the seminal phenomenon from which comprehensive meaning flows. Logical positivists proposed *verifiable content* as the heart of meaning. In literary theory and criticism and some of the social sciences, the concept of *text,* variously defined, is offered as the comprehensive concept by means of which the depths of human meaning (or nonmeaning) can be plumbed. In modern philosophy multiple *logics,* including logics of informal reasoning, have been proposed. And, of course, there have been those who have proposed that since no overarching concept will be comprehensively revealing and since meaning is in the eye of the beholder, the search for unifying notions about communicative meaning is a useless enterprise and there is no escape from utter relativism or even from communicative anarchy.

This book has been an attempt to do several things in response to these intellectual challenges. First, I have proposed that there is merit in recalling and making use of the original meanings attached to the ancient term "logos." To adopt this view at least escapes the notion of a single mode of human communication that has exclusive jurisdiction over knowledge, truth, and reality; it perhaps provides a fresh start for looking at human communication. Second, I have proposed that narration is the foundational, conceptual configuration of ideas for our species. This does not imply that narrated ideas and feelings are better than those conveyed through other modes of discourse. I simply take the position that narration is the context for interpreting and assessing all communication—not a mode of discourse laid on by a creator's deliberate choice but the shape of knowledge as we first apprehend it. We interpret our lives and our literature as stories that emerge within other stories of history, culture, and character—within all of which struggles and conflicts inhere. Third, I have contended that narration is omnipresent in human discourse and that we innately respond to that aspect of meaning *rationally*. It is at this point that I have begun to diverge from rhetorical and logical traditions. I have not denied that those traditions offer conceptions that are true to at least some human communication. There *are* deliberately conceived structures that can be and are imposed on ideas and feelings. They include introductions, climaxes, sonnet form, epic form, types of formal argumentation, and other structurations of communication. I have diverged from rhetorical, logical, and poetic traditions, however, by claiming that *behind* any structure that is *given to* human communication, the perceptual framework of narration will always also be constraining and projecting meaning. Ideas and feelings will always be sensed *in* and *through* time. Because I hold this basic view, I have undertaken in this book to conceptualize and illustrate how we discriminate good from less good accounts. I have argued that there is, for our species, such a thing as "narrative rationality" and that we all understand and test for this rationality whenever we create or experience communication.

The rhetorical tradition has given us some concepts of rationality that apply where there is dispute. Those concepts provide clear and systematic tests of rationality. "Lines of argument" should be tested to discover whether or not they are *relevant* to the *issues* in dispute and whether or not, of all the topics that might be discussed, those chosen by competing arguers were the most pertinent and the strongest the arguers could select in the immediate case. Classical tradition in rhetoric provides assistance in making this judgment by stressing that, in controversies, arguments and counterarguments come to "stands" or *stases*—points of impasse that must be resolved before argumentation can continue toward decision. This is the essence of "rhetorical logic" as we have inherited it. My concern in this book has not been to deny the usefulness of this logic but to discover and illustrate a logic that governs discourse whether it is transparently argumentative or not. The two major principles of such logic are, I believe, *coherence* and *fidelity*. We naturally and without formal instruction ask about any account of any sort whatever whether or not it "holds together" and adds up to a reliable claim to reality. We ask whether or not an account is faithful to related accounts we already know and believe. On these terms we *identify* with an account (and its author) or we treat it as mistaken. We identify with stories or accounts when we find that they offer "good reasons" for being accepted. Good reasons are elements in human discourse or performance that we take as warrants for belief or action. Reasons are good when they are perceived as (1) true to and consistent with what we think we know and what we value, (2) appropriate to whatever decision is pending, (3) promising in effects for ourselves and others, and (4) consistent with what we believe is an ideal basis for conduct.

This is the logic that I believe comes into play when anyone experiences an account that implies claims about knowledge, truth, or reality. Beyond it, other logics, such as the rhetorical logics we have inherited from tradition, come into play if they are appropriate to the special forms we sometimes give to ideas. The logic I have outlined and critically applied in interpreting and assessing political, aesthetic, and philosophical discourse is, I believe, a universal logic. As such, it is paradigmatic of human discourse. The narrative paradigm is the foundation on which a complete theory of rhetoric needs to be built. To do so would not displace subordinate logics. It would incorporate them within a comprehensive explanation of the creation, composition, adaptation, presentation, and reception of symbolic messages.

AUTHOR INDEX

Adamson, Robert, 27, 36, 50, 52
Alter, Robert, 79
Andrews, J. D., 99
Apel, Karl-Otto, 81, 100
Apostal, Leo, 138
Aristophanes, 10
Aristotle, 7, 26–30, 50, 67, 71, 83, 119–120, 123, 178
Arnauld, Antoine, 33–34, 51
Arnold, Carroll C., 124–125, 138
Austin, J. L., 53
Ayer, A. J., 51

Bacon, Francis, 8, 31–32, 51
Bain, Alexander, 21
Baker, Virgil L., 109, 121–122
Bantz, Charles R., 82
Barber, James David, 99, 156
Barrett, William, 51, 80
Barthes, Roland, 82, 90, 99
Bateson, Gregory, 65, 83
Baumer, Franklin L., 51
Beach, Wayne A., 98
Bellah, Robert N., 146, 156
Bellow, Saul, 177, 179
Benjamin, Walter, 73, 83, 84
Bennett, W. Lance, 59, 68, 79, 83
Bercovitch, Sacvan, 157
Bernstein, Richard, 21, 86, 93–94, 98, 100
Bird, Otto, 52
Bitzer, Lloyd F., 16, 23, 80, 123
Black, Edwin, 191
Blair, Hugh, 21, 42–43, 53
Blair, J. Anthony, 53
Blumer, H., 99
Boccaccio, Giovanni, 11, 21
Bochenski, I. M., 51
Booth, Wayne, 66, 80, 83, 99, 107, 109, 110–111, 121, 122, 160, 178
Bormann, Ernest G., 63–64, 82
Brinton, Alan, 23
Brockriede, Wayne, 46–47, 53, 54, 81, 98, 122

Bronowski, J., 176, 178, 179
Brownstein, Oscar, 123
Bryant, Donald C., 122, 160, 178
Buber, Martin, 25, 50, 101
Burke, Kenneth, 18–19, 23, 26–27, 50, 63, 65, 82, 83, 99, 114, 122, 156, 160–161, 178
Burleson, Brant, 81

Campbell, George, 21, 42, 52
Campbell, Joseph, 84
Campbell, Karlyn K., 17, 23, 190
Capra, Fritjof, 21
Carlton, Walter M., 23
Carnap, Rudolf, 34, 51
Cassirer, Ernst, 82, 123
Cherwitz, Richard A., 23
Cicero, 14–15, 22, 36–38, 52
Comte, Auguste, 34
Conley, Thomas, 191
Copleston, Frederick, S. J., 50
Cornford, Francis M., 50
Croce, Benedetto, 12, 22
Cronkhite, Gary, 106, 121

D'Angelo, Gary, 101
Daniels, Thomas D., 98
Danto, Arthur, 79
Darnell, Donald K., 122
Delia, Jesse G., 99
Derrida, Jacques, 79, 91, 100
Descartes, René, 8–9, 21, 33, 51
Dewey, John, 61, 80
Dieter, Otto Alvin Loeb, 40, 52
Dodds, E. R., 181, 183, 185, 190, 191
Duncan, M. B., 82

Ehninger, Douglas, 23, 46–47, 53, 54, 81, 109, 121, 122
Eliade, Mircea, 84
Emerson, Ralph Waldo, 15, 22

Enriques, Federico, 50, 51
Eubanks, Ralph T., 109, 121, 122

Farrell, Thomas B., 16–17, 20, 23, 64, 79, 80, 81, 82, 83, 121
Feldman, Marsha S., 68, 79, 83
Fitzgerald, F. Scott, 179
Foucault, Michel, 97, 101
Frandsen, Kenneth D., 98
Frentz, Thomas S., 64, 82
Friedlander, Paul, 185, 190

Gabriel, Ralph, 122
Gadamer, Hans-Georg, 75, 80, 82, 83, 84, 94–95, 98, 100, 101, 187, 191
Gallie, W. B., 79
Gardner, John, 76, 84
Genette, Gérard, 99
Gergen, Kenneth J., 83, 156
Gergen, Mary M., 83, 156
Gillan, Garth, 101, 156
Gödel, Kurt, 35, 51
Goffman, Erving, 87, 99
Goldberg, M., 79
Gombrich, E. H., 99
Goodnight, G. Thomas, 83
Goody, J., 82
Gottlieb, Gidon, 53, 81, 121
Graff, Gerald, 22, 57, 78
Grassi, Ernesto, 15–16, 22
Gregg, Richard B., 23
Gusfield, Joseph R., 72, 83

Habermas, Jürgen, 21, 61, 80, 91–92, 100
Hardwig, John, 118–119, 122
Hart, Roderick P., 157
Hauerwas, Stanley, 79
Hausknecht, S., 70, 83
Havelock, Eric, 20
Hawes, Leonard C., 79
Hegel, 26
Heidegger, Martin, 20, 63, 80, 82, 83, 84, 94, 100
Heider, Fritz, 98, 99
Heisenberg, Werner, 35, 51
Hermagoras, 40–41
Hermogenes, 40–41
Hikens, James W., 23

Hill, Adams Sherman, 21
Hollis, M., 80
Holton, G., 73–74, 83, 84
Hovland, Carl I., 99
Howell, Wilbur Samuel, 52, 178
Huizinger, John, 22
Hultzén, Lee S., 52
Hyde, Michael, 100
Hymes, Dell, 65, 82

Ijsseling, Samuel, 6, 20
Isocrates, 13–14, 22

Jackson, Sally A., 81
Jacobs, Scott, 81
Jacobsen, Thorkild, 84
Jamieson, Kathleen, 190
Janik, Allan, 53, 81, 120, 123
Janis, Irving, 99
Jardine, Lisa, 51
Johannesen, Richard L., 50
Johnson, Ralph H., 53
Johnstone, Henry W., Jr., 81, 120

Kant, 26
Kaplan, Abraham, 121
Kaufman, Charles, 190
Kelly, Harold H., 98, 99
Kermode, Frank, 79
Key, V. O., 67–68, 83
Kidd, Virginia, 82
Kneale, William and Martha, 29, 50
Kohlberg, Lawrence, 122
Krashen, Stephen D., 82
Krieger, Murray, 99
Kuhn, Thomas, 79

Langer, Susanne, 82
Leff, Michael, 52
Lemert, Charles C., 101
Lerner, Max, 150, 157
Locke, John, 9, 21, 32–33, 51
Lonergan, Bernard J. F., 80, 84
Longinus, 10–11, 21
Lyne, John, 80

MacIntyre, Alasdair, 53, 58, 61, 65, 66, 74, 78, 79, 80, 82, 83, 84, 93, 99, 100

Madsen, Richard, 156
Marshak, Alexander, 48, 54
Martin, Martha Ann, 23
Marx, 26
Matson, Floyd W., 50
Maslow, Abraham H., 122
Masterman, Margaret, 59, 79
McCracken, S., 70, 83
McGee, Michael Calvin, 23
McGuire, Michael, 76, 84
McKeon, Richard P., 49, 52, 158
McKerrow, Ray E., 80, 81, 109, 121, 122
Mead, George Herbert, 99
Meador, Prentice, Jr., 52
Medina, Angel, 69, 83
Megill, Allan, 49
Miller, Arthur, 179
Mink, Leon O., 79
Montagu, Ashley, 50
Muller, H. J., 114, 122

Nadeau, Ray, 52
Nelson, John S., 79
Newcomb, T. M., 99
Newman, John Henry Cardinal, 53
Nilsen, Thomas R., 122
Nofsinger, Robert E., 98
Noorden, Sally Van, 138

Ogden, C. K., 35, 51
Ogden, S. M., 84
O'Keefe, Daniel J., 81
Olbrechts-Tyteca, L., 23, 51, 81, 121, 122, 123, 159–160, 178
Ong, Walter, S. J., 6, 20, 41, 52, 82

Parrington, Vernon L., 156
Perelman, Chaïm, 17–18, 23, 34, 44–45, 51, 53, 81, 83, 97–98, 109, 115, 121, 122, 123, 124–138, 159–160, 178, 191
Piaget, Jean, 114, 122
Pierre, A. J., 70–71, 83
Plato, 7, 26, 180–184, 190, 191
Polanyi, Michael, 80, 178
Popper, Karl R., 190
Porter, L. W., 82
Price, Robert, 21
Prosch, H., 178

Ramsey, Ian T., 83
Randall, John Herman, Jr., 60–61, 80, 183, 184, 187, 190, 191
Rarick, David L., 82
Rendell, Stephen, 190
Richards, I. A., 12, 22, 35, 51
Ricouer, Paul, 79, 82, 96, 99, 101
Rieke, Richard, 53, 81, 120, 123
Rokeach, Milton, 122
Rorty, Richard, 21, 53, 80, 82, 93, 100
Ross, W. D., 50
Russell, Bertrand, 35

Sandars, N. K., 84
Schell, Jonathan, 69, 83
Schiller, Friedrich von, 11–12, 22
Schrag, Calvin O., 21, 51, 68–69, 79, 80, 83, 101
Scott, Robert L., 22, 79
Searle, John R., 53
Self, Lois, 123
Sennett, Richard, 80
Sidney, Sir Philip, 11, 21
Simons, Herbert W., 79
Singer, M. G., 191
Spitzer, Adele, 190
Sprat, Thomas, 9, 21
Stewart, John, 50, 101
Sullivan, William K., 156
Swidler, Ann, 156
Szasz, Thomas S., 157

Tate, Allen, 12–13, 22
Teller, Edward, 72
Tennyson, Alfred, 58, 78
Thompson, J. B., 99
Thibaut, J. W., 99
Todorov, Tzvetan, 79, 99
Toulmin, Stephen, 21, 27, 44–45, 50, 51, 53, 73, 78, 79, 80, 82, 83, 84, 120, 121, 123
Turner, Victor, 65, 79, 82

Valesio, Paolo, 90, 99
Verene, Donald Phillip, 42, 52
Versenyi, Laszlo, 6, 20

197

Vico, Giambattista, 15, 22, 24–25, 41–42, 49, 52
Vogelin, Eric, 80

Wallace, Karl, 78, 84, 107, 109, 110–111, 121, 122
Watt, I., 82
Weber, Max, 157
Wenzel, Joseph W., 81, 82, 121, 178

Whately, Richard, 21, 43, 53
White, Hayden, 65, 68, 80, 82, 83, 99
Willard, Charles A., 81
Williams, Robin M., Jr., 122
Windelband, Wilhelm, 50
Wittgenstein, Ludwig, 35, 53

Zeno, 26
Ziman, J., 80

SUBJECT INDEX

Aestheticism, 49. *See also* Proofs, aesthetic
After Virtue, 69, 74, 93
Aletheia, 6
American Dream, 148–149; Callicles'
accord with, 185, 188; Gatsby's view of,
170, 176; in Kennedy's rhetoric, 152; in
Reagan's rhetoric, 150; Socrates'
compatibility with, 182, 188; Willy
Loman's vision of, 164, 176
Analogy, 37, 133
Analytic/post-analytic philosophy, 44, 92–
93. *See also* Philosophy, analytic/post-
analytic
Argument, 26–28, 31–33, 36–38, 43–48,
59, 61, 111, 116–117, 158 (*see also*
Argumentation); bureaucratic, 70;
classification of, 29, 37–38; ideological,
70; in drama and literature, 161–178;
public moral, 71–72; technical, 70
Argumentation (*see also* Argument):
Ehninger and Brockreide's view of, 46–
47; narrative rationality's difference from,
48–49; Perelman's view of, 17–18, 45,
124–138; viewed by critical theorists,
91–92
Attribution theory, 86. *See also*
Communication, social scientific theories
Audience, 118, 134–136; implied, 75, 136;
Reagan's implied, 154–155; universal,
45, 109, 126, 135–136

Balance theory, 86. *See also*
Communication, social scientific theories
Burden of proof, 43

Cartesianism, 86–87
Character, 47; Reagan's, 147–148
Communication: social scientific theories,
86–88 (*see also* Attribution theory;
Balance theory; Constructivism;
Reinforcement theory; Social-
convergence theory; Social-exchange

theory; Symbolic interactionism);
humanistic theories, 89–98 (*see also*
Analytic/post-analytic philosophy;
Critical theory; Hermeneutics;
Structuralism/post-structuralism)
Confused notions, 34, 128
Constructivism, 86. *See also*
Communication, social scientific theories
Conviction and persuasion, Perelman's
distinction between, 135, 138
Credibility, 148
Critical rationalism, 130–133
Critical theory, 91–92. *See also*
Communication: humanistic theories

Death of a Salesman, 163–169, 176–177
Demonstration as distinguished from
argumentation, 127, 129, 131–132
Dialectic, 7, 25–26, 29
Dialogue, 15–16, 25, 95; between Socrates
and Callicles, 180–190
Discourse: poetic, 5–7, 10–13, 24–25, 85–
86, 159–161, 192; rhetorical, 5–7, 13–
19, 24–25, 85–86, 159–161, 192;
technical, 5–7, 8–10, 24–25, 85–86, 192
Dramatism, 18–19, 63. *See* Narrative
paradigm, differences from Burke's
dramatism; Symbolic interactionism. *See
also* Burke, Kenneth, in Author Index.

Empiricism, 8–10, 30–36, 60–66
Enthymeme, 28–29, 36–37
Epicheireme, 36–37
Epic of Gilgamesh, The, 77–78
Ethos, 148, 154
Experts, 7, 9, 19, 67–68, 72–73

Fantasy theme analysis, 63–64
Fate of the Earth, The, 69–71, 74
Foucault's theories, 97
Foundationalism, 93

Genre, 58, 62–63, 90, 143–145, 192; of
persuasive discourse (Aristotle), 30;
motive view, 144–145
Good reasons, 48, 75, 94, 107, 137, 143,
194 (*see also* Logic; Reasoning); Booth,
106–107, 110–111; defined, 48, 106–
108; logic of, 47–48, 88–89, 108–113;
relation to phronesis, 119–120, 123;
Wallace, 106–107, 110–111
Gorgias, 180–190
Great Gatsby, The, 169–175, 176–177

Hermeneutics, 13, 94–97
Hierarchy in relation to the narrative
paradigm, 66–67; of values, 113–114
Homo narrans, 62–63
Humanistic theories, 89–98. *See*
Communication, humanistic theories

Ideal speech situation, 92
Identification: as operative principle of
narrative rationality, 66; Burke's view of,
18–19, 87, 94; with stories of accounts,
194
Incommensurability, 74–75
Individualism, 146
Induction, 8, 31–32, 46
Ingenium, 15–16, 42
Invention: Bacon's concept of, 8, 32, 51;
Blair's view of, 42–43; Romans' use of,
30, 36, 38–41

Jurisprudential, model of, 44–46;
reasoning, 126, 130–134
Justice, 128–130; formal, 129–130; rule
of, 129–130, 133

Knowledge, 13, 25, 26; of agents
(Toulmin), 78, 85; of objects (Toulmin),
78, 85; poetic (Croce), 8–10, 12; public,
7, 16–18, 60; scientific (Croce), 8–10,
12; social, 16–18, 60

Language action paradigm, 4, 63–64
Logic, 24–49, 88–89, 106 (*see also*
Deduction; Induction; Narrative
rationality; Rationality; Reasoning); of
good reasons, 47–48, 88–89, 108–113,

118–120; Perelman's, 125, 130–134;
rhetorical, 27–30, 36–49, 193–194;
technical, 27–28, 30–36, 48
Logical positivism, 8–9, 27, 34–36, 192
Logos, 5–7, 9, 13, 16, 24, 68–69, 76, 85–
86, 183, 193
Logos/mythos, 6–7, 49
Love, 136–137

Modernism, 60–61
Monologue, 15–16, 25, 117–119
Mythos, 5–7, 19–20, 85, 183

Narrative, 17, 58, 75, 89–90, 193;
universal features, 65–66, 75
Narrative logic. *See* Logic; Narrative
rationality
Narrative paradigm, 5, 35, 47–49, 58, 62–
69, 85–86, 143–144, 189–190, 195;
differences from Burke's dramatism, 18–
19; postulates of, 5, 64–65; relation to
humanistic theories, 89–98; relation to
social scientific theories, 86–89, 98
Narrative rationality, 19–20, 25, 47–49,
66–68, 75–76, 87–89, 90, 94–98, 137–
138, 182, 193–194 (*see also* Rationality;
Narrative paradigm); as rhetorical logic,
47–49; coherence (probability), 5, 47–
49, 64–65, 75, 78, 155–156, 170–171,
183–186, 194; fidelity, 5, 47–49, 64–65,
75, 78, 105–121, 155–156, 169, 170–
171, 185–186, 194
Narratology, 90
Naturalism, 60–61
Nuclear controversy, 69–73

Ontology, as philosophical ground of
narrative paradigm, 65–93; of rhetoric,
17–18

Paradigm (*see also* Narrative paradigm):
defined, 58–59
Philosophy, 35–36, 44 (*see also* Discourse,
technical); analytic/post-analytic, 44,
92–94; in relation to technical discourse,
8–9, 16; practical (the new rhetoric), 127
Phronesis, 89, 94–95, 119–120
Pluralism, 115, 126–128, 136–137

Poetic (*see also* Discourse, poetic): cognitive significance, 13; relation to rhetoric, 159–161; voices on behalf of, 10–13

Portraiture, 160

Precedent, 130, 133–134

Presumption, 43

Proof, 36–37, 46; aesthetic, 161–163, 173, 175–177; apodictic, 27–28, 42; argumentative, 49; inartistic, 38

Rationality, 45, 57, 60, 64, 131–132 (*see also* Narrative rationality); relation to narrative rationality, 66–68; relation to rhetorical competence, 115–120

Rational-world paradigm, 46–47, 59–62, 66–69, 71, 145–146, 155–156, 182; philosophical ground of, 60

Reagan's rhetoric, 145–155

Reasonableness, 41, 107–108, 124, 127–128, 131–132

Reasoning, 48–49, 57, 68–69 (*see also* Deduction; Induction; Logic; Narrative rationality); dialectical, 25–27, 29, 129; natural (Vico), 41–42; practical, 17–18, 26, 45, 124–125, 129–134

Reinforcement theory, 86. *See also* Communication, social scientific theories

Rhetoric, 13–19, 26, 36, 95, 189–190; as epistemic, 16–17; instrumental, 31–32, 184; managerial, 8, 42–43; manipulative, 117–118; relation to logic, 27–29, 44; relation to poetic, 159–163

Rhetorical competence, 105, 115–120

Social convergence theory, 86. *See also* Communication, social scientific theories

Social exchange theory, 86. *See also* Communication, social scientific theories

Social science, 20 (*see also* Communication, social scientific theories); theories and the narrative paradigm, 86–89

Speech-act theory, 44, 92

Stasis, 28–30, 38–41, 194

Story, 5, 18–19, 24, 49, 58, 65, 73, 78, 180, 187; as rhetorical communication, 49, 62–63, 143; Callicles', 184–187; Reagan's, 146–147: Socrates', 181–184

Storytellers: humans as, 5, 18, 24, 62–65, 137–138. *See also* Homo narrans; Narrative paradigm; Story

Structuralism/post-structuralism, 89–90, 192

Syllogism: Aristotle's view of, 28, 30; Bacon's view of, 31–32; Campbell's view of, 42; Cicero's view of, 36–37; Ehninger's view of, 46; Ehninger and Brockriede's view of 46–47; English philosophers' view of, 33; Locke's view of, 9, 32–33

Symbolic interactionism, 86–87. *See also* Burke, Kenneth, in Author Index

Test of interpretation of dramatic or literary work, 175–177

Text, 96, 192

Topics, 28–30; Bacon's view of, 32; Cicero's view of, 38; Descartes' view of, 33; Locke's view of, 9, 33; McKeon's view of, 41; Romans' formalization of, 38–41; Vico's view of, 42

Toulmin model, 44–45, 111–113

Uncle Tom's Cabin, 162

Validity claims, 91

Values, 18, 34–35, 48, 60–61, 76–78, 87–89, 105–106, 110–114, 115, 122, 126, 129, 151, 161, 175–176, 182, 185; context-specific, 113; field dependent, 113; field invariant, 113–114; hierarchy of, 113–114; tests, 109, 137–138; transcendent, 109, 114, 177

Verifiability principle, 34–35, 192

CPSIA information can be obtained
at www.ICGtesting.com
Printed in the USA
BVHW032211150821
614456BV00001B/3